THUNDER IN AMERICA

THUNDER IN AMERICA

BY BOB FAW & NANCY SKELTON

FOREWORD BY DAN RATHER

TexasMonthlyPress

Texas Monthly Press, Inc.
P.O. Box 1569
Austin, Texas 78767

A B C D E F G H

Library of Congress Cataloging-in-Publication Data

Faw, Bob, 1944–
Thunder in America.

1. Presidents—United States—Election—1984.
2. Jackson, Jesse, 1941– . 3. United States—
Politics and government—1981– . I. Skelton,
Nancy, 1940– . II. Title.
E879.F38 1986 973.927'092'4 86-6030
ISBN 0-87719-052-6

To those who watched and tried to understand.
Especially A. B.

CONTENTS

FOREWORD

Jesse Jackson is an American enigma and a difficult man for a reporter to cover.

Friendly, complicated, unpredictable. He has been that way since he joined Martin Luther King, Jr., in the 1960's, all fresh and eager and filled with guile and gusto. The Reverend King once said to me, "Jesse is nothing if not enthusiastic."

Jackson was never as close to nor admired by Dr. King as was, say, Andrew Young. But with the possible exception of Young, Jackson studied King as closely as anyone—especially King, the orator.

No wonder that when we hear Jackson speak there are echoes of the Martin Luther King past. Jackson, besides his oratorical skills, learned from King a sense of dramatic timing and a sense of how to seize the historical moment.

When Jackson flew to Syria in December 1983 to rescue a downed U. S. Navy pilot imprisoned by the Syrians, he was already a candidate for President of the United States. He brought Lieutenant Robert Goodman home, and we knew then that Jackson wasn't going to be just another also-ran in the 1984 presidential campaign.

Truth to remember, Jesse Jackson already had made many of us uncomfortable. He does that often, sometimes intentionally, sometimes not.

I have covered Jackson for more than twenty years. That I may agree or disagree with him at any given time or on any particular issue is not important. Experience has taught me that many people (at times including myself) make the mistake of underestimating Jackson, underestimating his potential for good. That he knows who he is and what he believes, that he is eager to be heard, has a nostril for publicity, is willing to fight for what he believes, and is willing to be unpopular makes him what we reporters call "good copy." Jesse Jackson is what is known as news. I recognize that is not a basis for judging a human being, and yet, when one is consistently newsworthy, one is out there for all the world to judge, and judgments become inevitable.

In 1984 we saw the best and the worst of Jesse Jackson. His references that February to Jews as "Hymies" and to New York as "Hymietown" were repugnant to every decent intending American. The remarks, compounded by his unwillingness to admit them or apologize for them provided an unflattering insight into his character, to say the least.

His subsequent refusal to condemn the worst rhetoric of Louis Farrakhan demonstrated that Jackson, so devoted to human freedom, could walk perilously close to black racism as offensive as its white equivalent. Yet in the same campaign, we saw a Jesse Jackson rise above partisan squabbling to speak passionately about a human's most basic rights and responsibilities. He told blacks, young and old, that their time had come. He preached a gospel of opportunity and told people they could be better, they could have more—provided they studied and worked.

Jackson was, and is, at his most effective best addressing the hopes and fears, the dreams and despair, of blacks at the lowest end of the economic spectrum. For whatever harm he is blamed, he must be given credit for at least preaching the politics of hope and the pursuit of hope within the American constitutional framework.

As the 1984 campaign rolled on, we came to understand better that Jackson is a gifted, complicated person with great strengths and major flaws.

Two of the pieces of which I am most proud from that election year ran on the CBS Evening News the week before the Democratic party's nominating convention in San Francisco in July 1984. The stories were on the lessons of the Jackson campaign. Those lessons, we discovered, had little to do with politics and had to do with more than Jesse Jackson. The real lessons of that effort told us more than we had previously known about ourselves. As people, as a society. We had learned about hate and about love. We were to realize how far we had come as brothers and sisters, and how much farther we needed to travel. It was both reassuring and painful. And it was fascinating.

Bob Faw and Nancy Skelton covered Jesse Jackson for the better part of a year. The facts were always right. Their observations were acute, their insights sharp and clear. That's what separates reporters from stenographers and what makes reading this book worthwhile.

Dan Rather
River Camp, New York
June 7, 1986

INTRODUCTION

This book is an attempt by two reporters to come to terms with Jesse Louis Jackson. "Thunder," to the United States Secret Service detail which guarded him; "Reverend," to his staff; "one hundred and ninety pounds of intellectual dynamite . . . a bad black dude . . . our Savior," to adoring congregations. And a conniving, grandstanding Elmer Gantry to his detractors. We found him playing all those roles—and more. Across America we watched him, publicly and privately, in good times and bad, at his best and worst.

When his crusade began, we felt it would be a charade. Jackson might be a symbol, we reasoned, but few would take him seriously. We also heard the conventional political wisdom—"oh Jesse, he's just promoting himself again . . . " And as white reporters, we were hamstrung: many in Jackson's entourage distrusted the media and kept us at a distance

Not Jackson. He was always accessible, often too much so. The more we saw and listened, the more we came to respect—and to distrust him. His words could hypnotize but we learned that very little he said could be taken at face value. One minute he could be childish; the next, profound. He could infuriate and inspire, could savage egos or make the downtrodden feel more important than ever before; he was as exasperating as he was endearing. Sometimes we applauded, and other times we cursed. Still, his instinct for survival, his showmanship, his quick wit and lightning reflexes were like no other public figure's we'd ever met. Even when repulsed, we were always fascinated. Whatever we might think, we would always marvel at him. Finally we realized that our reactions were ambivalent, even contradictory, because there is no *one* Jesse Jackson. That his quicksilver personality constantly adapts, forges ahead; that he operates on different levels at different times. And that each is an authentic Jesse Jackson.

One of the reporters had known him years earlier in Chicago when Jackson was struggling for recognition, and the reporter had written off the young minister as little more than a loudmouth. Since those days the reporter and Jackson rarely saw each other, but the past remained a bond. In late 1983, the two were walking through the *souk* (public market) in Damascus, Syria, the candidate trailed by U.S. security agents as curious Syrians looked on.

"Can you believe this?" Jackson asked, his eyes sparkling as the reporter shook his head.

"Wouldn't it be something," Jackson continued, "if the folks back home could see us now."

The other reporter sat down with Jackson the first time in January, 1984. Thirty thousand feet over Florida, she tried to break the ice by asking him which minority candidate would make it to the White House first. A woman? Or a black?

The candidate glowered. "White women," he said, with undisguised anger, "already have access to power. Those who don't, inherit it from their husbands when they die, or from their fathers. Blacks don't have those channels open to them." Blacks first, he said, women later.

The reporter was struck by Jackson's bitterness. What's with this man? she wondered. He was running for president, with all the Secret Service trappings, the screaming sirens, the enchanted throngs. He was getting his message out, was being heard. Why the anger?

During the campaign he would come to call her "Miz Nancy," Often it was with a friendly smile. Yet other times the words were laced with sarcasm, like a servant feigning politeness for the lady of the house. She was never sure which was the more sincere.

February 28, 1984. Washington, D.C. As the Iowa caucus vote

dribbled in, Jackson was pacing nervously in a nearly empty hotel banquet room, snapping at aides, picking up finger food from a refreshment table, inspecting it, slapping it back down. He was getting only 3 percent of the vote, while Senator Gary Hart, the hero of the new left that Jackson himself wanted to be, had broken out of the pack of eight candidates to gain second place behind Walter Mondale.

Only a few reporters showed up to hear Jackson's assessment of the vote. His press secretary scurried around trying to find stray reporters to fill the room. Jackson was waiting to go live with CBS News anchorman Dan Rather at 11:30, skulking about the room in his best navy blue pin-stripe suit, when a TV technician hollered at a colleague: "Wait a goddamn minute, would ya!" Jackson stiffened: "That's what's wrong with the world. People using that kind of language."

A few minutes later the word came that Rather would be switching to Hart and not to Jackson. The candidate did not react immediately. Instead, he drifted into the hallway and began kibbitzing with reporters. Someone said the night was at least a partial success in that some of Jackson's issues had won. Jackson sneered. "Success, shit," he said, loud enough for anyone in the lobby to hear, ignoring his admonition of a few minutes earlier. "Success, shit," he repeated. "We blacks have learned to measure success in all kinda ways."

April 28, 1984. Ville Platte, Louisiana. Seldon Ardoin, Jr., 28, had positioned himself behind a clump of berry bushes alongside the Ninth Baptist Church.[1] Only his black patent leather shoes showed, and now and then his head, as he'd poke it through the leaves to see if Jesse Jackson was coming. Ardoin was four feet two inches tall. "They call me Shorty," he said, his eyes cast downward. Being black and a midget in Ville Platte, Ardoin said, had left him with few options but to grow his own vegetables and to rely on relatives. "Nobody has no work around here . . . me, I've been unemployed all my life. I'm just a little farmer in Ville Platte," he joked halfheartedly. Jackson might talk jobs—that's what Ardoin had heard, anyway, so he had come down to the church. Jobs meant hope, and "it's about time for some hope around here," he said, absentmindedly edging out of the bushes.

Jackson arrived late and was making his way quickly through

the crowd when his attention was drawn to Ardoin. "Hey, buddy, walk along with me," the candidate yelled.

"Sure," Ardoin replied, hurrying to catch up.

The political underdog, looking for votes. And the physical underdog, looking for hope—a mismatched set, sauntering down a dusty Louisiana road, fulfilling each other's needs. When Jackson went off to make some phone calls, Ardoin strutted up to a group of men on the church lawn and began to chat enthusiastically, thirty or forty feet away from the bushes.

May 24, 1984. Passaic, New Jersey. "Damn right, I'm excitable—but not about politicians," said Doris Gilchrist, a black secretary. She was standing on a street corner, crying. For the last thirty minutes she had been listening to Jesse Jackson. "What it does for me, it takes me on a high. This is better than drugs. It's better than a joint for me. It's a message of hope. It's so positive. I've got my fix for the day, I'm so high."

She insisted that her color—and Jackson's—didn't matter. "It's a matter of hope. It's not a matter of color. The man is a winner in my heart because of the message. It's so positive, it's the truth. You can't argue with the truth."

April 28, 1984. Tanjapahoa Parish, Louisiana. The white woman stared hard at Jackson and listened to every word he said. Then she turned away, shaking her head. "I'm afraid to see a black man with that kind of power. He's with the Black Muslims, right? Black Muslims do not recognize God. They recognize black power. That bothers me a lot. They believe if it's weak, get rid of it."

The Tanjapahoa woman was 45, divorced, the mother of two, a Pentecostalist, living on Social Security, nothing else. Her house had no lights, no heat, no phone, no running water. "We tote water from another neighbor next door. I don't ask nobody for nothing." She had walked more than two miles to see Jackson because that day she had nothing else to do. He seemed OK, she concluded. But "they" didn't.

"My fear is having a black man in power and turning the tables on white people. Black people will be able to commit crimes and get by with it freely. They're just evening the score for what our ancestors did to them. . . . I fear for my children. If a black person raped my child, I'd have to kill him. That's what's on my mind.

That's what I fear."

May 27, 1984. Hackensack, New Jersey. A black couple was walking away from the Thomas L. Della Torre Athletic Field, where Jackson had addressed three thousand people.

"That man got a lot of nerve," the man said to the woman.

"If he don't be a winner, he sure give them a fright," she replied with a smile.

June 1, 1984. Suisan, California. At Solano College, dapper Levi Bolton listened to Jackson and slammed down his walking stick in approval. "Like a dose of castor oil in the springtime! Yes sir," said Bolton, a black retired military officer. He eyed the reporter for a long moment, watched him write down quotes. "You took note of the gold piece around my neck," he said finally, "but did you take note of what's in my heart?"

The country had never seen anything quite like what Jesse Jackson did.

Almost one hundred years earlier, at the Republican National Convention in Chicago in 1888, abolitionist Frederick Douglass of Rochester, New York, was the first black man to be nominated for president by a major political party. In 1972, Shirley Chisholm, a black Democratic congresswoman from Brooklyn, New York, ran a largely symbolic campaign for the presidency in fourteen primaries and received 151.25 delegates at the party's national convention in Miami. Jackson's effort in 1984, given his proven ability to attract the media, promised to be the first serious presidential bid by a black.

"This ain't no ordinary campaign. It's about finding the light," he thundered to one audience; along the way, his whirlwind dash generated hope—and hate. Gyrating wildly between the needs of a black revival and the demands of a national campaign, it attracted those who needed to believe and repelled those who couldn't, or wouldn't, understand the new symbols, who feared change, who disliked, even detested him.

Guaranteed one constituency, largely black, he was deprived of another, largely white. Trying to do too much, and too little, his effort ultimately collapsed under its own weight, falling far short of its stated goal; the notion that it could succeed was only an illusion. In the process the campaign exposed—and rubbed raw—

the nerve of racism in America. White racism. And black racism. In the end, he was one measure of how far the country had come—and how far it had to go.

It was a remarkable experiment: a black man running for an office he knew he couldn't win—running, to reach out to thousands who'd never been part of the political process before—running, he said, because this time their presence, and his, should be felt. This book is not an insider's account of that campaign. Instead it is an attempt—hard-nosed, we hope, but sometimes affectionate—to understand the effort that brought joy to many, disappointment to others, and in the process became a special—sometimes magical, sometimes perverse—moment in American political history.

This is the story of a political transition—and the tension that resulted. "You know, twenty years ago, if he'd come here, they'd probably have hung him," said a deputy sheriff who listened to Jackson in Evangeline Parish, Louisiana. "Now people accept them more; they can go to white restaurants, stay in white motels; it's not like it once was," the officer continued.

Many who saw the change didn't like it. In Fayetteville, North Carolina, white landscape architect Jimmy Jones heard Jackson and then complained to a reporter: "in the South, to be a Negro was to be a white man. I grew up with them, played, ate, and worked with 'em. A Negro wouldn't have anything to do with white trash. I wouldn't have anything to do with a nigger. Nowadays, it's hard to tell the difference."

Jackson and others felt that the change had been long arriving, that the progress had to be pushed along, shoved even. "Some people spend all their time going around putting bandages on the lions' victims, afraid to take on the lion," he once said. "Spend all week putting thousands of bandages on the lions' claws. That's fine too. It's gotta be done. But somebody got to take on the lion."

Since that's what Jackson tried to do, this is largely a book about his "taking on the lion": about one force—largely black, untapped, and disorganized—colliding with another force, largely white, more mainstream, more interested in winning elections than in fulfilling dreams. A new form of power confronted an older one. Neither fully understood the other or knew quite how to proceed. In each the values and aspirations differed. Power was changing. But which way? How far? How fast?

This is a book about that contest. But the subject is more than Jesse Jackson. It is also about the people who encountered him along the way—their hopes, their fears, their biases. It is about dancing eyes in project windows and the cold sweat of fear in a Jewish synagogue—about hope he breathed into those who had never believed, and about hopelessness.

When we revisited campaign stops months after his caravan had gone through, people were still talking about his visit; they were still anxious to share their impressions. In many he struck the deepest chords; some embraced him, others spit at the mention of his name, but few were neutral.

So this book is their story too, the story not of one America, but of the many Americas that sometimes knew very little about each other and often preferred to keep things that way. This helps explain not just the joy and the bitterness surrounding the Jackson candidacy—but also why his was an improbable, perhaps even impossible campaign.

1. GETTING READY

October 21, 1979. Halloween in Chicago. At 10:30 P.M., the brown Honda raced down Lake Shore Drive, then skidded along the rain-slicked streets on the city's south side. On Constance Avenue, orange hobgoblins and fairies in rubber masks still darted from house to house looking for candy.

The car's two passengers didn't pay much attention to the revelers. Frank Watkins and Bernard Layfayette, co-workers at Operation PUSH, had been talking for several hours, and the plan they'd hit upon wouldn't wait, not even until morning. Without knocking, they barged into the big white stucco house. "He's already gone to bed," a startled Jacqueline Jackson told the visitors.

Bounding up the stairs, Watkins and Lafayette entered the large bedroom. "Reverend, sorry to interrupt you, but we've been giving it lots of thought—and we've decided that you ought to run for president."

The large man under the sheets wiped his eyes and propped himself up on one elbow. After listening a few seconds, he interrupted the visitors. "You guys been out trick or treating too long," he said, dismissing them with a wave and pulling up the covers. "Either that or you're crazy. Now get the hell out of here and let me get some sleep," Jesse Jackson added.

Jesse Jackson's campaign for the presidency began taking shape in Chicago, mid-winter, 1983. In the cold fury of his anger. For years he had curbed his resentment of the white political establishment, but this was the breaking point. This was one insult too many. All Senator Edward M. Kennedy and former vice-president Walter F. Mondale had done was play by time-honored political rules; each was merely repaying an earlier political debt. But by endorsing someone other than the black candidate for mayor of Chicago the two politicians were, Jackson argued, thumbing their noses at blacks throughout the city. "We don't have to take this any more," he argued.

Chicago's political scene was crowded then—but not confusing. After months of wrangling, most of the city's black community had united behind congressman Harold Washington's bid to unseat incumbent mayor Jane Byrne, who was also being challenged in the city's Democratic party primary by Richard M. Daley, eldest son of former Chicago Mayor Richard J. Daley. Kennedy endorsed Byrne: after all, she had supported Kennedy's ill-fated 1980 presidential bid against Jimmy Carter. And Mondale made good on a pledge he'd given Daley two years earlier when Daley had supported the Carter-Mondale ticket.

Jackson was appalled. Washington's liberal voting record, he argued, should have earned him the support of white liberals in the party. That was only consistent. Besides, he told Mondale, supporting a black candidate in a city that is nearly 40 percent black simply makes good political sense. Furthermore, he continued, you owe us: blacks helped deliver Chicago for Carter-Mondale in the 1980 Reagan landslide. Nor was Jackson bashful about his own involvement, reminding Mondale that Jackson had stumped for the Democratic ticket in twenty-nine states and seventy-two cities.

Mondale saw the logic but was trapped. He had given his word to Daley well before Washington had even considered entering the race, and he felt he couldn't renege now. With a few complimentary words about the black congressional challenger, Mondale stayed committed to Daley. Jackson could understand Kennedy's action: he understood Kennedy's sense of loyalty; besides he felt that Kennedy probably wouldn't be a presidential candidate in 1984. But Mondale's decision was at best, Jackson argued, a bad miscalculation. At worst, he considered it insulting.

For Jackson, the proposition was simple. Were white leaders in the party ready to accept, even make room for blacks? Or did they wish that blacks would continue to play what he called the "Harlem Globetrotter role" in the party: "to give it its soul, its excitement, its rhythm, its margin of victory, and yet not be allowed to set any policy"?[2] Blacks are tired of "being the party concubines," he said. "They get the fun with us, then they marry other people. We want to be full-partners."

We've been loyal in the past, and this is how we're treated, he grumbled openly. No other group would tolerate this kind of treatment. And blacks shouldn't either. Maybe, he began suggesting, it's time for us to run our own candidate for the presidency. Maybe that's what it takes for them to take us seriously: for us to take ourselves more seriously.

Frank Watkins, Jackson's loyal aide, had reached that conclusion Halloween night, 1979. Ever since he had been kicking the idea around with friends: why not a black candidate? And why not Jackson? In June, 1982, Watkins drafted a 10-page memo for Gary (Indiana) mayor Richard Hatcher that spelled out what Jackson should do. "Jackson should not run as a 'realistic candidate' with a chance to win," but rather as an independent Democrat in 1984 "to solidify primarily a black political power base." Watkins' objective was clear: "blacks must deal from a position of political power or they will simply be negotiating for the crumbs as in the past."[3]

Jackson didn't need any memo. He could look around—and he could count. The potential of the black vote was becoming apparent. In 1982, a PUSH voter registration drive in Chicago had been so successful that Democratic gubernatorial candidate Adlai Stevenson IV came within five thousand votes of toppling Republican governor James Thompson. That wouldn't have happened without an aroused black electorate, political observers in Chicago agreed. And Jackson knew that Chicago wasn't unique: in the same year in Texas, black voters helped Democrat Mark White upset incumbent governor Bill Clements, and in several southern congressional races a greater than expected black turnout had contributed to Republican defeats.

In 1983, the pattern was being repeated. On February 22, with overwhelming black support, Harold Washington won the Democratic mayoral primary in Chicago. Gleefully, Jackson grabbed the microphone at Washington's victory headquarters and led the crowd in chants of "We Want It All" until embarrassed—and worried—Washington aides hustled Jackson off to the side.

The celebration would have to wait. Ordinarily in Chicago the winner in the Democratic primary would be considered a shoo-in for the general election, but no black candidate had ever gotten this far before, and Chicago's white-dominated political establishment began trying to make sure this one wouldn't get any further. Within hours of the Washington victory, many Democratic leaders began throwing their support to the other candidate, Bernard Epton, a relatively obscure, white Republican attorney.

With the battle lines sharply drawn between black and white, the contest soon became the ugliest in the city's political history; Washington's campaign slogan—"It's Our Turn"—was matched by Epton's equally inflammatory "Before It's Too Late." In the end, black prevailed over white. Washington was elected mayor with a massive turnout in the black community—but he won less than one out of every five white votes cast.

To Jackson, the message was clear. Given a choice, most whites would not support a black candidate. And in a crunch, white politicians would turn to their own. It was time, Jackson argued, to face facts. Blacks had to help themselves because no one else would. "Plantation politics must make way for peer politics," he preached.

Others were thinking along the same lines. Fifty or so elected black officials banded together as the Coalition for 1984 Election Strategy and later became known as the "black leadership family." They debated for hours in several cities—New York, New Orleans, Washington, and Atlanta—over how blacks might achieve maximum influence with the other candidates, within the Democratic party, and after the election. Should they proceed the old way, positioning black advisors in each campaign, the way most ethnic groups worked? Or should they try a new approach?

A handful of black leaders wanted more than an agenda. They wanted their own flesh-and-blood candidate—and they wanted Jesse Jackson. Mostly they were young, somewhat impatient, and relatively inexperienced in national politics. Many came from nearly all-black constituencies. There was Richard Hatcher, mayor of Gary, Indiana. And Marion Barry, mayor of Washington, D.C. From New York City came Basil Patterson and former Manhattan borough president Percy Sutton, both savvy and experienced. From Alabama, Southern Christian Leadership Conference state director John Nettles and state senator Michael Figures; from Georgia, state representative Tyrone Brooks. And from Los Angeles, African Methodist Episcopal Bishop H. H. Brookins.

Their feelings were strong but far from unanimous. Many other black officials, who'd spent years carefully putting together coalitions with white liberals, did not want a black candidacy, especially not Jesse Jackson's. The time just isn't right, they concluded. And Jesse Jackson isn't right for the times: too young, too inexperienced, too flamboyant, too likely to do what he wants rather than listen to us. Over the years Jackson had alienated many with what they regarded as his egotistical, freewheeling ways. These nay-sayers were strong, practical men—Detroit mayor Coleman Young, Birmingham (Alabama) mayor Richard Arrington, Los Angeles mayor Tom Bradley—and they made strong, practical arguments: where would the money come from?—if the black candidate takes black votes away from Walter Mondale, won't he really be helping Ohio senator John Glenn, and ultimately Ronald Reagan?—and would Jackson's personal life withstand scrutiny?

The black elected officials weren't the only ones who felt that way. "I don't think a black candidate has a ghost of a chance," said the NAACP's executive director, Benjamin Hooks. For some, Jackson was anathema. "He suffers from a lack of follow-through," said the head of the black congressional caucus, Julian Dixon. California assembly speaker Willie Brown had the same kind of criticism: too much noise, too little action. "You can't teach Jesse anything," Brown complained. "He never has been disciplined." And the people around him aren't very skillful, Brown added.

The signals Jackson was getting were mixed. A few white liberals urged him to run—"let them polish up their credentials," he once cracked—but the black community was divided, and some of the opposition to any black running—in particular, to Jesse Jackson's running—was intense.

Other men might have paused. Not Jackson. No one, he argued, knew black America as he did—its hopes, its dreams. No one, he insisted, had traveled through that land more often or had gone so far, had talked to as many of its people. No one, he could argue, was as highly esteemed.[4] At last, Jackson figured, here was a cause to match his ambition, his talents, and his energy. It was the next logical step, he believed. And he knew there were people in the country, black and white, waiting for a black political hero; some had been waiting for generations. Avery Alexander was one. And there were others, thousands of others.

Autumn, 1923. A late afternoon sun set over Ashland, a large farm near Houma, Louisiana. In a cotton field, a 9-year-old boy looked off in the distance and saw a group of children his own age. They were white and were returning from school. He was black, and his day was spent in the fields; his workday started at sunrise and stretched until dusk. For several minutes, Avery Alexander stared at the passing students. "All I remember is feeling trapped," he recalled many years later. "I was full of hatred, and all I could dream of was running away."

Growing up in the South then taught Avery Alexander lessons he never would forget. Like the day the young white overseer Mr. Greenwich rode up on his horse and talked to Avery Alexander's elderly grandfather. The young boy who listened couldn't understand why the old man kept calling the overseer "Mr. Greenwich" while the overseer referred to the old man as "Arthur." "You see, I had been hearing my parents say to us that you're supposed to answer your elders 'yes sir' and 'no sir.' So when Mr. Greenwich left, I said to my grandfather, 'Why do you say "Mr. Greenwich"—and he calls you "Arthur"?' And my grandfather, he never did answer. But years later I discovered why. If he didn't say 'Mr. Greenwich,' he would have been in trouble. And in fact, some of the blacks used to tip their hats when, you know, when whites would pass. And I'm not speaking about tipping your hat to a lady."

August, 1983. Gil Kulick—white, liberal, and Jewish—was pretty sure that Jesse Jackson was a flimflam man. But when the huge crowd that had gathered at Washington's Lincoln Memorial to celebrate the twentieth anniversary of Dr. Martin Luther King, Jr.'s March on Washington began to chant "run, Jesse, run . . . run, Jesse, run," Gil Kulick joined in. "Avidly," he recalled, with a smile.

Then 42, the State Department political officer had never met Jackson. Kulick remembered watching on Israeli television as Jackson spoke to Arabs in the West Bank town of Nablus in 1979; the Chicago preacher had exhorted them to repeat his "I Am Somebody" refrain, and in clumsy, heavily accented English the Arabs, grinning broadly, had mouthed the words. To Kulick, watching at home, the whole affair seemed "silly . . . 90 percent of them didn't even know what they were saying." Still, Kulick admitted that the event was charged. "Jackson's charisma was somehow translated . . . really, there was an incredible magnetism," and Kulick had been impressed.

After that, Kulick began to take notice of what Jackson was preaching from his Operation PUSH pulpit. Once more, Kulick applauded. "I mean, here was a guy who was saying to blacks your fate and your future are in your hands. That injustices undoubtedly have abounded for centuries but sitting and griping about it and waiting for whites to compensate you for all that is never going to get you anywhere. . . . That's a message I think needs stressing," Kulick argued.

So Kulick had gone to the 1983 rally with his son and his cousin. Partly because he felt that whites should attend—"I thought it was important to show that it wasn't only blacks who were hearing Jackson's message"—and partly because Kulick wanted to rekindle memories of his own. On that site twenty years earlier he had passed out handbills, had marched with Dr. King, and now he felt that there'd never been a more historic event in which he'd taken part. Then he had been young and idealistic; now he was disenchanted. The upcoming election seemed somehow pointless to him—no challenger could unseat Ronald Reagan, Kulick had concluded—and none of the "serious contenders" seemed to him very worthy: Walter Mondale, Kulick thought, was too weak; Gary Hart, "too superficial, glib." "So I thought, what the hell: let's take advantage of the opportunity to make a statement of some sort, and Jackson was clearly making more of a statement than anybody else." The more Kulick listened at the monument, the more he felt he not only could vote for Jackson but could even feel good about it.

As Lincoln stared down on the crowd from his marble chamber, Jackson bellowed a favorite theme. "He was talking at that point about power," Kulick remembered. "About our time has come, you know. And all those stock things: from the outhouse—to the courthouse—to the statehouse—to the White House." The rhetoric, Kulick felt, was hardly "presidential."

But around him blacks and whites in the crowd, men and women, were smiling, jubilant, some almost delirious. They wanted things to change, they wanted a candidate—and they wanted it now. Slowly the cadence swept over the assembled. "Run, Jesse, run," the voices began, and as the preacher spoke, the chants continued, growing louder with each wave until the crowd was roaring, shouting the phrase again and again. "Run, Jesse, run," Gil Kulick found himself yelling too.

1984. Nachitoches, Louisiana. Like Avery Alexander, Ben Johnson had been poor once, but now he owned a chain of funeral homes (which accepted either Visa or MasterCard) and had become the wealthiest black man in town. Instead of a painted landscape on the wall of his private office there was a color photograph of Louisiana's governor, smiling in a hard hat, hand clasped to a gold shovel, helping break ground at another Ben Johnson mortuary. None of it had come easy. Ben Johnson had even survived the Klan, and the Klan had tried hard to run him out. In the 1960s, hooded Klansmen had burned crosses on his lawn while Ben Johnson and his son lay inside the house, rifles braced to their shoulders. After the nightriders left, Ben Johnson quietly removed the charred wood and went back to work. The Klan returned, and each time Ben Johnson stood his ground, then went about his business, all the while prospering. Finally the Klan gave up.

Ben Johnson had influence now. "Old Ben, why he's sort of the Godfather over there in niggertown" is how one local white politician put it: "used to be in Nachitoches Parish you could go over there and give Ben Johnson a little money, and you'd just pretty well have the black vote. . . . He had 'em for years. Most of your blacks are superstitious, worried about dying and getting buried and all that, you know; if you didn't do what he said, then he wouldn't bury you, simple as that," the politician said, respectfully.

The respect hadn't always been there. Ben Johnson was one of ten kids. His father had worked at a sawmill, his mother was a cook. Even then Ben Johnson had been a worker, picking gallon after gallon of blackberries as an 8-year-old, selling them around town to customers who "would only buy from Ben Johnson. . . . I had the reputation of being the workingest little black fellow that ever lived, and I kept a job all the time."

Even then he was clever—"I was the only black could even play in the front yard of the white folks' house." That is where he had first seen the knife: "I was crazy about this little knife. I always wanted a knife, and one white boy traded me a little poor knife that had a nude white girl on it." Ben Johnson didn't even notice the figure of the white girl on the handle, but the sawmill superintendent who watched the two boys playing didn't know that. "He looked at that little knife, and he caught me by the ears and he picked me up and set me on the counter. The commissaries, you know, they had them long old counters. He says, 'Nigger, if I ever see you again with a white girl, or a white woman naked in your possession, I'm gonna kill you myself. I'm gonna choke you to death.'" Fifty-five years later, Ben Johnson still remembered the incident clearly. And the superintendent. "That stayed with me a long time. Made me hate the man until he died."

The Reverend Thomas Gilmour was also out there. Waiting patiently. Sitting in the living room of his small home in 1985, Gilmour folded his large hands and sighed. "Doesn't seem like much now, but let me tell you—back then, it was something else." He smiled at the memory. He had done the impossible once, and even now, almost twenty years later, it surprised him. Looking back, it all seemed so out of character.

"Back then" was 1966. Then the Reverend Thomas Gilmour was 25, and in those days he preferred to stay in the background, "to move in the shadows," as he put it. But his friends had convinced him that he had to run for sheriff in Green County, Alabama, where no black had ever been elected sheriff before, even though for years more blacks had lived in the county than whites. Devout and apprehensive, Gilmour had prayed over the decision. And had fought against and postponed and dreaded it—but when the time came, he ran. And ran against a man who had played football with the legendary Bear Bryant, no less, and whose family had controlled the sheriff's office for more than half a century. The campaign had been dangerous, sometimes violent, and it had embittered him: "you know, all the stuff that's going on and then you get personally assaulted by the system; and it really cuts into the heart, it makes a man really mean, it really makes you think ugly things." He had wavered, his faith in both himself and his God had been tested, but the miracle had occurred: the black minister had defeated the white incumbent, even though Gilmour's opponents contested the results and fought him bitterly in the courts for years. When he finally took office, he vowed to start a tradition of his own, "to take my ministerial role and mesh it with my sheriff or political role . . . to pastor as a sheriff, kind of pastor the county . . . and I think I did try"; he had tried to meet everyone in the county, black and white, and had done so unarmed, taking off his weapon to set an example, not just to the voters but also to his small sons so they would not "see me having to rely on something like that."

Then and now he considered himself a "hot-blooded southerner . . . in harmony with the ground, with this rough and overworked, pitiful region." He was black, but his favorite politician was white, Huey Long of Louisiana, the Kingfish, Huey Long the populist, not the demagogue. Twice more Tom Gilmour had run and had been elected and each time he had loved it, loved the power and the acclaim, loved it so much it frightened him. And one day after hours of prayer and deliberation Tom Gilmour walked away from it all and accepted a church near Birmingham, where part of the parsonage had been blown away in a 1963 bomb blast. Most of the time he didn't miss the public life; but when he did, the pangs were intense, and Gilmour hated himself for missing it that much, felt it was some kind of addiction he feared he would never overcome.

When 1983 came, Tom Gilmour wanted Jesse Jackson to run for president because he felt that Jackson could inspire blacks, even though Gilmour knew that the campaign would be dangerous. Because Tom Gilmour could never forget the way one man stared at him when he first ran for sheriff. As Gilmour put up a poster over a music box in a bar, one customer glared at him the whole time. "I walked over to him, and I said 'I'm Tom Gilmour, running for sheriff, and I really would like your vote.'" Twenty years later, remembering what he'd seen, Gilmour was still shaken by the hatred confronting him. The huge man at the bar said nothing, "but he looked at me with eyes, well, I don't guess I've ever seen more serious eyes." Neither man moved; nothing more was said until the bartender intervened and broke the silence. But Gilmour never forgot the moment. Or the feeling. Jackson would encounter looks like that too, Gilmour figured. "I'm not so sure Jesse could have come to Green County and run in 1966," Gilmour concluded. "They'd have killed him, or seriously tried." Times had changed, Gilmour thought. But he wasn't sure how much.

Alabama state senator Michael Figures was convinced that the times hadn't changed enough. Black and proud, he had been an aggressive prosecutor and was now a successful attorney in private practice outside Mobile, Alabama. But as he sat in the Senate chambers in Montgomery, Michael Figures seethed. "There is this great frustration. To sit day after day in this Senate—and to watch people move forward in politics in this state and know that I can't. Because I'm black. To know that I'm at least as good as they are—and better. I've tried many cases against Charlie [Graddick, Alabama attorney general]. Won most of them. But he can become attorney general very easily. I have to struggle to be considered even a credible candidate. There's an anger, but it's controlled. I call it a controlled rage." He was shrewd; as a black man in Alabama, he'd learned to control that rage, but he was still looking for a way to strike out against the injustice he felt around him. In Jesse Jackson, Michael Figures thought he had found his vehicle. "I thought the most important thing to do," Figures continued, "was to put the issue of racism on the table. On every American table. To force the American public to look at this man. To look at him and to compare him using the same standards that you use to judge others by. . . . It is more important to remove racism from every house than to get Ronald Reagan from the White House."

Michael Figures wanted to send a message: that black America had waited long enough for equal treatment—and would wait no more. The longer Jackson debated whether to run, the more anxious Figures grew. "Damn, if he'd waited around much longer to announce, I'd have been gone. His waiting around like that almost lost me. . . . What I got out of his running was an opportunity to release all these frustrations I had. . . . I saw him as someone who could help me carry my dreams out. Who could help lift me, show me opportunities I never had before."

Jackson can't possibly win, Figures' friends kept telling him, but Figures wouldn't listen. On December 8, 1983, Walter Mondale phoned and made the same argument. "My answer to him was that there will always be a Walter Mondale around who has a sterling civil rights record—and not be worth a damn. . . . Just because you're not a racist doesn't mean you're a good human being . . . that you'll be a good politican who can best represent my interests."

It is time for principle, not political expediency, Figures concluded. "I don't care what the consequences are," he added.

Other black leaders, though, had to worry about the day *after* the election. They could not afford to invest time and energy merely to "send a message," to fulfill some dream. Tough, successful men, they had cities to run, payrolls to meet, budgets to balance, industries to attract. Men who could read accounting ledgers, they cared more about the bottom line than about noisy road-shows along the way. They were just as proud, just as determined as Michael Figures; but they tended to be a little older, a little more patient. For them the clock didn't seem to be ticking quite as fast. Their targets were different. Just because we're black, they argued, doesn't mean we're obligated to support a black candidate. Especially Jesse Jackson.

Birmingham mayor Richard Arrington typified the breed. Richard Arrington, Ph.D., a man of the laboratory, not the smoke-filled backrooms. A biologist by training, he had chosen an academic life that mirrored his own style: quiet, thoughtful, a teacher first, later a college dean. He was black, but he was no firebrand. Leading marches, waving banners, and organizing boycotts was for others; early on, Arrington had learned when political limits could be stretched and when they could not. Analytical, precise, deliberate, Arrington preferred the background whenever possible. Friends even had to ask him to get involved in politics. After two terms on the city council of Birmingham ("the Magic City"), his intelligence and decency won him respect; in a troubled city, men of good judgment stood out. In 1979, on his first try, he'd been elected mayor of the mostly white city; while his leadership couldn't reverse Birmingham's economic misfortunes—steel mills in town continued to shutter their plants—his reasonable, low-key manner helped foster racial harmony throughout a city much of the world still associated with Bull Connor and his snarling dogs.

In 1984, though, Arrington worried about the direction in which the country was moving. "The social conscience of this country has become somewhat calloused," he said. And he argued that the country would have to make major changes, in its attitudes, in values, in practices. There were, he knew, no panaceas. Slogans wouldn't do the job either. Or emotions. Arrington cared deeply, he said, about "racial pride and identity and advancing the cause of blacks in the country." Jesse Jackson was a friend; he admired Jackson's daring, and he helped Jackson by calling Alabama governor George Wallace to set up an appointment for Jackson to visit. But Arrington—who had rejected racial appeals before—turned away this time too. Richard Arrington deliberated—and spurned Jackson, choosing instead to support the man he expected the party to nominate, Walter Mondale. It was, Arrington said, "a very hard choice."

What he had to decide, he said later, was "what did I consider to be the number one problem politically for this country, this year, this election. And for black America in this election. And for me, the best thing that could happen to black America, if you look at it from that point of view, would be the defeat of Ronald Reagan. That is the number one priority with me. Now that to me in 1984 takes precedence over Jesse running well, when I know that Jesse can't win. I want him to make a respectable showing. I certainly don't want him to be embarrassed. But the number one priority to me was defeating Ronald Reagan . . . as far as I was concerned, everything else flowed from that. That's where I started from."

Some black politicians, Arrington went on, allowed Jackson to stampede them. "A number of black mayors I talked with made it clear that they supported Jackson out of fear. Fear that if they did not support him it would erode their own political base. Their people were excited about Jesse, and they were not going to run the political risk of opposing him. . . . Or they felt that they could buy time. That they could come back once the primaries were over; they knew that Jesse wouldn't be there then, and they could still get aboard the Mondale or Hart wagon."

Arrington had become a political pro. He wasn't condemning anyone; he just knew how the game was played: elections had to be more than ego trips, he insisted. "All those people who voted because Jesse ran, well, that's not good enough. It's good, if it will do something for their image. It's good, if it really brought them into the political arena. It's good, if it said to them that my vote can make a difference. . . . But if it was fueled solely by an emotional response. . . . then it's not going to help us a lot. It's just like having an emotional high and feeling good about something that you know you're not going to win. It's a 'we-showed-'em' kind of thing. That gets you nowhere."

Charlotte, North Carolina, mayor Harvey Gantt had been "nowhere" himself, and he had no intention of going back. At 40, his life had been tightly disciplined, and it had paid rich dividends: his architectural firm was flourishing, and he had recently moved into an upper-income, largely white community. Tough-minded, resourceful, respected, he had a bright professional and political future.

Some Charlotte blacks grumbled that Harvey Gantt tried to hide his blackness, but Gantt had a ready answer for them too: when times had been tough, he had earned his stripes. He had been a pioneer when it counted: in January, 1963, he had been the first black to enter—and later, the first to graduate from—Clemson University in South Carolina; less than twenty years later, he had been elected the first black mayor of mostly white, conservative Charlotte.

Harvey Gantt knew what it was like both to make symbolic gestures and to win. And Gantt decided he much preferred winning. That, he concluded, was what mattered. Gantt played hardball. The cause had to be more than noble—it also had to have a reasonable chance to succeed.

As a black man, Gantt felt the pull toward Jesse Jackson, a friend and a former South Carolinian. But he would not give in to sentiment. "No," he said after the campaign, "I was not caught up in the emotion. . . . I wanted to keep my options open, because I wasn't convinced that Jesse was the candidate to win . . . I never believe in getting in something unless you're going to go for the whole damn thing. Win. . . . I didn't go to Clemson simply to say I was the first to go—and then be out of there in three weeks. Bullshit! Who wants to be symbolic! Well, some people might want that. I'm talking about my perspective. I don't."

Gantt thought the Jackson effort was too much grandstand, too little substance. Long on gesture, and short on what Gantt called "believability." Harvey Gantt would be hard-nosed. "It's one thing to admire a pioneer like myself who went to Clemson. 'Cause there's some reality there," he argued. But in Jackson's campaign, "I saw no victory," said Gantt.

His decision—to straddle the fence, endorse no one in the primary—was not popular in Charlotte's black community. Several Jackson supporters tried to get him to make a commitment. Even "my kid said, 'Dad, why aren't you supporting Jesse Jackson?' And I sat down and told him that I thought Jesse was doing some good things but that I didn't know that he would be the best candidate for our party. And that simply because the candidate is black is no ultimate reason to say you're going to support him. . . . it's a little bit unfair to anyone to simply say because we've got a black man out there running that I should be automatically for him; that borders on a little bit of irrationality," Gantt concluded.

Something else bothered him. He sensed a softness in the campaign, in the candidate too. It was the difference, Gantt felt, between enrolling in Clemson and sticking around only a few weeks—and toughing it out, mastering the course load, then graduating. Jackson wasn't getting a degree, Gantt argued. "You got to be a pro and you got to be charismatic too. This is not a camp meeting. It's not a spiritual revival," he said. Gantt felt that Jackson was too much the evangelist, too little the tough-minded candidate. A political realist would have met quietly with Charlotte's mayor, Gantt said. Would have tried to get the mayor to commit. "Because that's what a pro does. I mean, you get down to it and you say, 'Look, I need your support. I gotta have it. And if I don't get it, well then all these bad things will happen.'" Only Jackson had never done anything like that, Gantt complained. "He never put the muscle on me. Seriously. No one ever knew that. In fact, that was a big surprise of mine." Someone with toughness, Gantt concluded, would have tried.

Joe Reed, black executive director of the Alabama Democratic Caucus, didn't care to tilt at windmills either. Like Harvey Gantt, Joe Reed cared mostly about results. Now 45, he had arrived in Montgomery in the late 1950s, when blacks were only observers at the Democratic National Convention. In 1984, 40 percent of the delegation from Alabama was black, and Joe Reed had helped bring that about. Just the way he had lobbied for—and helped get—two new federal judges for Alabama. Black federal judges. Results are what counts, Joe Reed said. Not intentions. Not motives.

After nearly a quarter century of fighting for civil rights, for the rights of blacks in the deep South, Joe Reed felt he knew a thing or two about progress. About when to hold fast—and when to cave in. "Hell, some folks were afraid to stand up to Jackson," he said after the campaign. "They were too weak . . . a lot of your stand on Jackson had to do with your own security. Politically, no one in America has a better record on civil rights than I do," he continued. "You can't call Joe Reed an Uncle Tom."

But many black officials, Joe Reed argued, felt they somehow had to demonstrate, sometimes even prove, their blackness. And many of them, he felt, couldn't meet the standard he set for himself. "Many folks acted on how secure, or how insecure they were. . . . You can tell people what they want to hear, or you can tell them the truth. . . . I went through this thing [should Jackson run, or shouldn't he] over and over again, yes sir. I know what we did in backing Mondale was politically right. Except for the fact that Jesse was black, what did we do wrong? Nothing. So when you narrowed it all down, the issue came down to race. If you're black, do you owe it to Jesse?" No, Joe Reed answered. No, you do not.

Jackson had learned from his travels that there were many in the country who would not be as sympathetic to his running as Avery Alexander and Gil Kulick and Ben Johnson and Michael Figures—who would be even more difficult to reach than Joe Reed or Richard Arrington or Harvey Gantt.

Some of the others, he knew, would stand along the sidelines and thumb their noses at him. Or turn their backs. Would laugh at what he was trying to do. Even derive satisfaction from seeing Jackson fail.

They were not necessarily bigots, mean and close-minded. Some even insisted that as Americans they were perfectly willing to give everyone a chance, to give an underdog a break. They were more a part of mainstream America than Jackson sometimes cared to admit, and in 1984 many of them were feeling ignored, passed over, resentful. Kenneth Hamm was one of them.

Kenneth Hamm had been an underdog—and he had made it. In 1961, he had run away from home, but twenty years later he had come back to Nachitoches, Louisiana, and had bought the filling station where he'd worked as a kid. During those years Kenneth Hamm had covered a lot of ground and had learned a few lessons along the way. "The underdog, all he has to do is get on his feet, you know. My damn bulldog over there at the house, he had two broken legs, and he's just a puppy, and a big old German shepherd down the street come down there three mornings in a row picking on that damn bulldog and finally he got tired of it and he tore that German shepherd's ass somewhere he couldn't walk for three days. It's a matter of guts, you know; people ought either to be somebody or not be somebody. And in America, if you're not somebody, it's your own damn fault."

That approach had worked for Kenneth Hamm. His father had spent nearly all his paychecks on liquor, so Hamm had grown up a poor white boy on the other side of the tracks; hating it, he'd dropped out of high school at 15, had lied about his age to get a job peeling shrimp and potatoes on an offshore rig in the Gulf of Mexico; drafted, he'd fought in Viet Nam and then spent twelve years working for the phone company, where his native intelligence ("when I was in the army, they told me I had an IQ of 138. I said, 'I can't believe this shit,' you know, 'cause my teachers told me I couldn't even pass") helped him land a high-paying job; finally, at age 35, he chucked it all, especially the phone company bureaucracy he hated, and headed back home. He was a redneck once who felt now that he'd outgrown racism, and he was ready to settle down.

"In '67, I tried to borrow money to open a Kentucky Fried Chicken 'cause I'd seen one in Oklahoma, best chicken I ever had, and there wasn't anything such as fast food in Nachitoches. And they wouldn't loan me the money and six months later one of the prominent men in town got the idea and had the largest grand opening in the history of the franchise, you know, and right here in Nachitoches, he made a million." When he couldn't get the loan, Hamm took his savings and his wife's too and bought the filling station; no one had given him a thing, he had done it on his own.

Now he came to work before sunup and left well after the sun went down and during the day spent a lot of time grousing over the long hours and the paperwork and the taxes he was forever paying, all the while loving every minute of it and wanting nothing more. Exhilarated by the freedom of being able to come and go when he pleased, Hamm loved being the boss, loved doing what he wanted and not what somebody else wanted for him; this, he felt, is how America is supposed to be—every man a king. Barely 40, he was a throwback to simpler times of sturdy virtues and blunt talk when men were men and the dollar was worth something and nobody, but nobody, he said, pushed this country around. He liked Ronald Reagan ("'cause he's got balls, internationally . . . aren't you prouder to be an American now than you were four years ago? I damn sure am") and hoped Reagan could stop things before they got completely out of control. Surely none of the others would even try, especially this guy Jackson "this loudmouth, so-called preacher":

> Jackson has no qualifications. Other than he's just a political activist. He just gets out there with his dreams. Well, them dreams don't work. We all got dreams. But hell, actions is better. They don't believe that you can make it in America by working. And I happen to believe that you can. 'Cause I did. . . . For a long time, I was a classic bigot. In that I thought that uh, well, we went from discrimination to reverse discrimination, I think that probably almost every white American has had to pay for something he didn't do. Hell, I didn't work no slaves, I didn't have none. Hell, my daddy didn't have none—he was a grease monkey! So why should I have to pay for what somebody else did? . . . I think in your older people, if you get the ones who are set in their ways, they'll never change. They've got the stigma of racism in them and all that kind of stuff. But I think in my generation—and those a little older, a little younger—there's no such thing anymore. We're all human, you're human, the black guy's human. . . . You know, I can understand how you can be born poor in America but I can't understand how you can stay that way. If you got the will to win, a little positive thinking, and a little energy, you can make it. Color matters not, I really believe. . . . They're always looking for the freebie, the American people are, I guess I'm coming out of the mold, as a bit eccentric, I don't mean to—basically in America we've made it so easy, we've subsidized laziness so damn much that where's the work ethic any more? . . . Hell, the formula is to go out there and *make* your damn money and quit your bitchin'. . . . Jackson? We have *arriiiiived.* Our time has *cooooome.* [He mimics Jackson's delivery.] Well, hell, his time has always been here, same as mine has. Get out there and work for it, you know, don't wait for somebody to give it to you. . . . Black kids got heroes, they got ballplayers, they got all kind of people that have really done good. If they're using him for a hero, they picked a poor one. What's he a

hero for? A hero is usually someone who's accomplished something. What the hell did Jesse Jackson ever do? Besides make a speech.

So voices throughout the land conflicted wherever Jackson sought counsel. "Run, Jesse, run," said the Avery Alexanders and Tom Gilmours and Gil Kulicks. "Forget it," said the Arringtons and the Joe Reeds. "Who the hell do you think you are?" the rednecks sneered.

But more went into Jackson's deliberations than just the voices. He knew there were also numbers in black America. Cold, hard, irrefutable numbers as raw as the passions that greeted him. And in deciding whether to run, Jackson would seize upon the numbers the way he seized emotions.

"Color is not a human or personal reality; it is a political reality," James Baldwin wrote;[5] in 1984, more and more people were starting to count. The numbers couldn't be ignored. "Of us 235 million Americans, 25 to 35 million are of African descent, more than 17 million are eligible to vote; in 1966, 4.4 million voted; by 1980, 8 million . . . ," Theodore White noted.[6] They were numbers too great for politicians to dismiss or take for granted. And the numbers were growing fast.

Celia Anderson, 69, was one of those numbers, but she had spent too many years chopping cotton on Karl Weil's plantation to settle for being some drab statistic. "Folks forget where they came from," she said. "You gotta remind them once in a while how white folks always trying to put you back there. . . . We should be glad we have this privilege [to vote] we used not to have, to make a better situation for ourselves. It's time we should be getting what we want," she continued.

Celia Anderson lived in Port Gibson, Mississippi; her county, Claiborne, was 72 percent black, but for years Claiborne County blacks had neither registered to vote nor voted—nor counted for much politically. Slowly that was changing; black registration totals were spiraling. In March, 1984, Celia Anderson and her neighbors headed off to the Port Gibson firehouse to take part in what for many was their first primary election. Like many other blacks in town, Celia Anderson hoped she'd have a chance to vote for Jesse Jackson. She felt that then maybe those white county commissioners would sit up and take notice of a few things. Then, she hoped, maybe Claiborne County blacks would start getting a fairer shake. And start making up for lost time.

Celia Anderson was too busy taking care of the future, though, to worry much about the past. "You got to plant the cotton, hoe it, chop it, swing that sack over your shoulder, pick it, boll by boll. And when you're done, the white man got it all. Two hundred pounds a day. Can't be no more days like that. Sun's getting hotter, so it seems," she told a visitor.

The numbers—represented by hundreds, thousands of Celia Andersons—tantalized Jackson. Four years earlier, Ronald Reagan's margin of victory in sixteen states had been slight: less than 5 percent of the votes cast in those states. If the black vote increased roughly 25 percent, and Reagan's share of the white vote stayed the same as in 1980, Reagan could lose eight of those states.[7] Organize those who had not voted, register them, get the Celia Andersons and all her neighbors to the polls—and in all sixteen states, maybe more, the balance could shift. North Carolina, for instance: Reagan had carried the Tar Heel state by just 39,000 votes. But North Carolina had nearly 1.3 million unregistered voters, and over half a million of them were black. Or Massachusetts: Reagan's 1980 margin there had been just 3,800 votes, and the state had 1.1 million unregistered.[8]

The numbers became part of Jackson's standard litany: "in 1980, I looked at Reagan's victory. He won by the margin of our despair," he'd tell audiences. "He won Virginia by 200,000, more than 400,000 blacks unregistered. Rocks, just layin' around. He won Tennessee by 4,710 votes; 160,000 blacks unregistered. Rocks, just layin' around. . . . He won eight southern states by 182,000 votes where there were 3 million unregistered blacks. *Rocks, Little David, just layin' around.*"

But there were other numbers concerning black America that told a different story: not of potential strength—but of impotence. These were numbers that spelled out the misery of black America, its despair. "For them, the poverty rate during the Reagan years has risen from 32.5% to 35.6%, representing the addition of one point three million people. The total listed as poor included nearly fifty percent of all black children. The black unemployment rate under President Carter was an average of 12.4%. Under Mr. Reagan, the average is 16.2%. Not counting the effects of inflation, the median family income for blacks has dropped by more than five percent from 1980 to 1983."[9] At every income level, according to the nonpartisan Urban Institute, ". . . the average black family has less disposable income and a lower standard of living today than it did in 1980. . . . Today the average black two-parent family in which one parent works has two thousand dollars less in income than four years ago."[10] The rich were getting richer, but more of the poor, and more blacks, were going hungry: ". . . of black families headed by women, 56.1% are officially [by government definition] poor. Of the nation's black children, 46.3%—nearly one half—are in poverty. . . ."[11]

If the arithmetic of politics was promising for black America, for many blacks the arithmetic of economics was not. The former made a black candidacy possible, Jackson argued; the latter, he insisted, made it imperative. No one else dared make so bold a claim. And Jackson wasn't finished. His genius wasn't simply putting the two sets of numbers together—his masterstroke was in convincing hundreds, thousands, that he, more than anyone else, could capitalize on that combination: that no one else could inspire more people to register, and that no one else could better rally the forces of poverty, of despair.

In the summer of 1983, he crisscrossed the South one more time. A black whirlwind, he would touch down in some backwoods community, fire up his believers, then rush on at breakneck speed to another delta hamlet, another bayou church. Shouting, waving his arms, pleading, he would denounce what he said were violations of the Voting Rights Act of 1965. "Nails in our flesh," he would cry. He demanded, and he got, a team from the Department of Justice to make on-site inspections; after an emotional tour, he grabbed the hand of the department's civil rights division chief Bradford Reynolds, a conservative white who had questioned whether the trip was even necessary, and the two men joined in singing "We Shall Overcome." As guerrilla theatre, it was spectacular: implausible, bizarre, totally unforgettable. Once again, Jackson was improvising, he was performing, he was making things happen; he was also presenting his credentials, getting confirmation, creating a mandate. And everywhere he went, the crowds were chanting the same refrain: "run, Jesse, run." Like peals of thunder, the chorus surged forward, washing over the speaker and ricocheting off the walls.

"There's a freedom train acomin' but you got to register to ride," he would wail.

"Amen. Tell it, preacher," the congregation would shout.

"Run, and you can win your self-respect. If you run, you may lose. But if you don't run, you're guaranteed to lose," he would tell them.

"Run, run, run," they would cry.

"From welfare to our share . . . from the slave ship to championship. . . . Hands that once picked cotton can now pick presidents," he would cry.

"Run, Jesse, run," their chant would rock the hall.

"Weeping may endure for a night, but joy will be coming in the morning. Suffering breeds character, character breeds faith, and in the end faith will not disappoint. Our time has come. *Our time has come. Our time—has come.*"

The crowd would be on its feet as the speaker sagged back on the stage, his clothes bathed in sweat—and the mighty voice would shout in unison: "Run, Jesse, run."

Electrifying: no other word describes that 1983 southern crusade. Jackson preached passion, and the congregations caught fire. Their deafening roar could not be muffled, ignored, refused. "Damn Straight! It's Time for a Black Presidential Candidate," read the button Jacqueline Jackson began wearing. Some political pros watched the proceedings and shook their heads in exasperation. And in envy. "No one anointed him. Jesse just reached out there and grabbed it for himself," said Ron Brown of the Democratic National Committee much later. "Nobody else got out there," said Carl Holman of the National Urban Coalition.[12] "He just stampeded the process," said Joseph Lowery of the Southern Christian Leadership Conference.

The combination of the dreams of black Americans and the numbers and needs of black America was powerful. Some reservations about a black candidacy, especially *his* candidacy, wouldn't go away—for instance, wouldn't registering more blacks trigger a white backlash?—but now there were new answers to counter the skeptics: the word went out that savvy black political operatives like Ivanhoe Donaldson (a key strategist for Washington, D.C., mayor Marion Barry), Ernie Green (who'd worked in Washington for the Carter administration), and Preston Love (who'd worked for Atlanta mayor Andrew Young) would assist the Jackson effort and that 40,000 black churches could raise $250 each for what some Jackson aides insisted could be a campaign war chest of $10 million. The momentum, the enthusiasm grew. And no other figure stepped forward and tried to stop him.

By autumn, 1983, the question wasn't whether Jesse Jackson would announce—but when. Black reporters, who'd been traveling with him for weeks to make sure that they found out first, met with him in late October; you'll be the first to know, Jackson assured them. They learned on October 30 along with 40 million others who turned on CBS's *60 Minutes* and heard Jackson declare his candidacy to Mike Wallace. Four days later, in a rousing 3½-hour extravaganza at the Washington, D.C., Convention Center, Jesse Jackson made it official.

2.

THE EARLY CAMPAIGN

He was the last candidate to enter the race, and by that time all the others had raised money, assembled staffs, and opened campaign offices in many of the primary states. He hadn't done any of that. At that point he didn't even have a campaign manager. "Oh my God, what a mess," Arnold Pinkney thought in early November as he watched the campaign pull into a Columbus, Ohio, motel well after midnight. A few hours later Jackson offered Pinkney the campaign manager's job. (In May, 1985, Pinkney was convicted of having an unlawful interest in a public contract and sentenced to one year's probation.) Pinkney, who'd twice helped Carl Stokes get elected mayor of Cleveland and who'd also been part of Hubert Humphrey's run for the presidency in 1968, promptly agreed. He had no illusions. "We had to start from scratch," he said.

At first the problems didn't seem to matter. Crowds the first month were large and enthusiastic. No other black candidate had mounted a national campaign before, and the audiences applauded his daring. Some were curious. Some were proud. Many had never seen a presidential contender, let alone a black one surrounded by mainly white security guards.

Like the night in early December at a Holiness Church in Tyler, Texas. Campaign aide Gene Wheeler remembered the scene:

> . . . it held about three hundred people and it was jam-packed. The Secret Service was in front of the pulpit,

standing all around the room. The pastor was talking about their son returning home. This was a very impressive night, you got to remember, because coming to the church, we came in this motorcade, with these sirens and these red lights, all these local police and motorcycles and stuff. . . . it took a lot of people around this country by storm, well, it did these people too. They were just so happy.

And this preacher was going on and on and on. Jackson was being taken care of and all by the Secret Service all over the place. You could see all this pride exuding through the place, just coming through the walls.

Then Jesse started speaking. All of a sudden, we began to notice a change. The people started getting apprehensive; they started whispering. They were not as enthusiastic about Jesse's speech anymore.

I was in the back, you see; I used to work the crowd, go back there, see what they were selling, listen to what people were saying. Nobody knew who in the hell I was, you know what I mean? Then Lamond [Godwin, another campaign advisor to Jackson] comes tiptoeing up.

"Hey, something going on," he says.

I said, "Yeah, I thought it was just me."

Lamond says no, he noticed it too. I said I better go up and check with the SS because maybe there's a rumor or something people are hearing. [Secret Service detail leader Dwight] Ellison says everything is under control, don't worry about it.

Jesse, you know Jesse, he picks up the drop of a pin. He notices something. But he just keeps talking, talking. So I went and got Lamond and said we better go find the pastor; maybe he knows.

Lamond finally got the pastor and he came back to the back of the church, to his office, and he told us what was happening: he said the people were very proud of JJ, they were really proud that President Reagan had allowed the SS to protect him, but then in the course of the evening, they got word around to each other that they were not the best SS men, they were rejects, they were also-rans. The reason they felt that was because, the pastor said, "Reagan, those white folks, would not do right by us; they will not treat us right. They gave Jesse protection and gave him all men who had disabilities."

We asked, "What's that, Reverend?"

And he said, "They're all wearing hearing aids."

Remembering the incident several months later, Wheeler burst out laughing again. "When Jesse came off the pulpit that night and we told him, he laughed so hard I thought he'd die. We were laughing about that for days."

For Jackson, black churches like the one in Tyler, Texas, were a sanctuary and launching pad. Mondale might have Big Labor, he joked, "but we have Big Church." The black church, he knew, had always been a special place for black Americans. As he told one interviewer after the election, ". . . the church was the one institution that kept reminding us that we were not brought from Africa to be white people's slaves. But perhaps were sent here by God to save the nation."[13]

Certainly that's how the Reverend T. J. (Theodore Judson) Jemison looked upon his role. President of the 7-million-member National Baptist Convention, USA, the portly Jemison brooked no interference from dissenters. Or anyone else for that matter. "I don't know if I speak for all Baptists, but I speak for so many, the number I don't speak for don't matter," Jemison told a January, 1984, convention of Baptist ministers in Baton Rouge, Louisiana. "I love Negroes, and when one can represent us, and be a Baptist preacher, I'd be an ingrate or a foolish man not to support him. The people are with him," Jemison thundered, to cheers. "We are behind him in numbers, in spirit, and we are behind him—in sugar [money]," he added, rubbing his hands together as convention delegates roared their approval.

Jackson could count on the network of black Baptist ministers, but the political challenge facing him was awesome. He had little money, a meager staff, few political resources—and black skin. Unlike the other candidates, he also had to run weighted down by ghosts of the past. Despite black America's need for a political hero, the old shibboleths, the old fears, died hard.

Brutalized, some blacks had grown fearful. The murderous eyes Tom Gilmour had seen in an Alabama bar, the death threat to Ben Johnson over a two-bit knife, a grandfather humiliated while the young Avery Alexander watched—moments like those would never be erased. And since white America expected so little of them, some came to expect less of themselves; exploited, some became defensive. Terror stalked even their few miserable triumphs. Coming together round a radio to hear Joe Louis fight, and win, they celebrated joyously—and then trembled; after cheering the Brown Bomber, they spent the night with friends rather than venture back home, because in the South then, as Maya Angelou recalled, ". . . it wouldn't do for a black man and his family to be caught on a lonely country road on a night when Joe Louis had proved that we were the strongest people in the world."[14]

Some southern blacks hated the conditions, chafed under them, tried to rebel. Many, though, felt that rebellion was pointless. Afraid that whatever they might do would make things worse, they did nothing. The apathy reinforced their powerlessness. The struggle was not to achieve—but to survive; given the odds, they began to define winning differently. Wisdom meant learning they could never be strong, meant accepting their weakness. "I'm 43, going on 100," said Tom Gilmour, worn out fighting the region's past. "It's more than the way people are accustomed to think," he continued. "It's the years of living a certain kind of way—it's a kind of conditioning. And it's affected all of us. . . . Few of us can dream and really think that the dreams are possible."

H. M. "Mickey" Michaux knew the odds. He'd battled them himself. In 1982, the articulate black lawyer and former U.S. Attorney from Durham, North Carolina, had finished first in a crowded primary contest for North Carolina's second congressional district seat (mostly rural and small-town, with the exception of Durham, almost 50 percent black). But in the subsequent runoff election, called a "second primary" in the nine states that required them when no one candidate received a majority in the first election, Michaux was outpolled by a white candidate (former state legislator and state Democratic chairman, Tim Valentine). Michaux was "living proof," said Jackson, of "the evils of the second primary"—how the system was rigged, Jackson claimed, to keep blacks out of power.

Mickey Michaux knew all about how the system worked in the South. He warned Jackson that while southern politics was on the verge of a new era, the legacy of all those Mr. Greenwich episodes lived on: "Black folks, from baseball players starting with Jackie Robinson to lawyers, politicians, and would-be presidents have first to convince black folks that they're credible, that they're good as white people, and that it does no harm to support them," Michaux said later. "That the black person can do as good a job as a white person doing the same job. Stated simply, that the black man's ice is just as cold as the white man's ice," he continued.

Breaking through that barrier wouldn't be easy, Michaux felt. And there were other obstacles erected by blacks, he argued: blacks who felt that a great deal had been achieved, who sensed resentment building in white America—and who now wanted to move cautiously. Michaux called it "a complacency mind-set." "This 'hey, we got everything going our way, these folks are going to look out for us.' It's the paternalistic instinct that whites have for blacks. In other words, that old 'you don't have to worry about it 'cause I'm gonna look out for you. That whatever happens, you my nigger.' And blacks," Michaux concluded, "have a tendency, even now, to get comfortable with that because they say 'hey, regardless of what happens, I know Mr. Charlie is gonna look out for me.'" That mind-set will be a real problem for you, the would-be congressman told the would-be president. "Frankly, Jesse," he added, "I'm not sure there's too much you can do about it."

Shackled by the past, Jackson still had to figure a way to follow the first law of the political jungle: deliver your own—or perish. "Experience has shown that unless a candidate is carrying a reasonable number of his own [that is, black] constituents, then the whole community tends not to believe that she or he is authentic," said AME Bishop H. H. Brookins, an early Jackson booster. A Gallup Poll might rank Jackson as the most-admired black man in America, but Democratic party power-brokers would treat him as a political force only if he got his supporters—especially those who had not registered, or who had rarely voted—to the polls. It would not be easy. There was no such thing as a monolithic black vote. And sizable numbers of black voters were scattered in pockets throughout the country: of 435 congressional districts, only 86 had populations that were 25 percent or more black.[15]

Political geography was against him—and so were rules the Walter Mondale–Edward Kennedy dominated Democratic National Committee had adopted for the 1984 campaign. In most cases, a candidate had to get a minimum of 20 percent of the vote (the so-called threshold) in a congressional district to qualify for one delegate. That was the party's way of making sure that long shots—and fringe candidates—didn't clutter up the primary field. Jackson's man (Gary mayor and DNC vice-chairman) Dick Hatcher had not objected when the 20 percent threshold rule was being adopted in the precampaign days of 1982. But Jackson was complaining bitterly now. "Got to get 20 percent to get any! Get 19.9 percent—and get none. That's not right. That discriminates against that 19 plus percent. It disenfranchises them. They get shut out."

Once blacks and other minorities try to play the political game, he went on, the powers-that-be change the rules: "we can win in the Olympics because there everyone can see the starting line and the finishing line . . . Joe Louis could win because everybody could count to ten. And see who was still standing." But not in politics. There decisions are made behind closed doors "where no one can see. . . . No telling what might have happened if they made Joe Louis fight behind closed doors." It's time to change the rules, he insisted, "it's time for the old wineskins to make room for the new wine."

And the threshold requirement wasn't his only headache. Several electoral-rich states (New York, Illinois, Pennsylvania, Ohio, even Florida) had adopted versions of a winner-take-all scheme. In those states the top vote-getter in a congressional district would get all the delegates. Even if Jackson got a heavy black vote there, and ended up second or third in the voting, he would end up with no delegates.

So circumstance dictated his strategy. He would concentrate on nine states with large black populations, most in the South (Alabama, Georgia, North Carolina, for instance), as well as the major northeastern cities with large black populations. And he would try to get the party to change its rules. Even at the eleventh hour.

Starting late, he would have to move quickly; there was little time for subtlety. "I think Jackson had to be 'unabashedly black' from kickoff because he had no political structure anywhere," said California assembly speaker Willie Brown. "He had to go to the black disenfranchised as his first source. And the only way you address them is to make them know you are super black. And that you are their super hero." The appeal would have to be an ancient one: to blood, to class, to religion. As former congresswoman Barbara Jordan put it, "the effort itself had to be raw."

Ethnic groups had done that for years in America. "Jews in New York, the Irish in Boston, the Italians in New Jersey . . . got their power through pulling themselves up through the power of the ballot box," conservative publisher William Rusher conceded. "It is the tradition of American politics," said columnist James Kilpatrick. "You had the Jewish vote, you had a Catholic vote, a farm vote, a labor vote, at one time a Masonic vote. . . . we've had one factor after another emerging," he continued.

Some observers found that appeal troubling. "The whole notion of appealing at a national level to the black vote is very very divisive. It sets black people apart," said Walter Williams, a conservative black economist at George Mason University in Virginia.[16] But many political pros understood what Jackson was doing and found criticism like Williams's unwarranted. "I went through fifty years ago what Jesse's trying to go through today," said House Speaker Thomas P. "Tip" O'Neill.

For some, O'Neill's analogy of blacks and the Irish didn't hold up. For many Americans, progress had been too swift; it had, they felt, been rammed down their throats. Many balked. Blacks ought to slow down, quit pushing so much, they argued. By 1984, attitudes had hardened. Words that inspired some incensed others. Jackson's "Our Time Has Come" chant, for example. Many blacks who heard it took heart; many whites seethed. "Nobody wanted to admit that when Jesse Jackson gets up there on network television, and there are ninety million people out there watching, and he says 'Our time has come, Our time has come,'—nobody wants to say 'fuck you, Jackson, your time has not come.' But that's what they're thinking. Because if *your* time has come, then what has happened to *my* time?" said Al Vorspan, a vice-president and director of the Social Action program of the Union of American Hebrew Congregations.

The white policeman in Baton Rouge chose each word carefully. Something was bothering him that chilly winter morning in Louisiana when Jesse Jackson left his motorcade and walked into the Capitol Hotel. A disgusted look flashed across the policeman's face, and his body seemed almost to bristle with rage. "What does this guy know about budgets . . . what does he know about running the country?" he asked, lip curled.

The policeman illustrated Jackson's paradox, and the paradox was crippling. Jackson had to run black, but the more he ran as the black candidate, the greater the likelihood that whites would be offended. Black hope created the foundation for his campaign, but white resistance, and in some cases hate, imposed the limits. What made the campaign possible set off forces that doomed it. He was driven, yet he was confined. The paradox would torment him throughout the campaign.

Far from the chanting congregations, and untouched by sentiments in big city housing projects or in delta shanties, hardheaded political realists made their calculations. No one expected Jackson to win. And many expected him to do poorly. "At best he will end up at the Democratic National Convention with fewer than three hundred of a total of 3933 delegates," Harvard University professor Martin Kilson wrote to the *New York Times.*[17] Thomas Cavanaugh, of the Joint Center for Political Studies, made an estimate for the campaign that was not much brighter: around three hundred delegates, not much more. And these were two of the rosier forecasts! "Rival strategists believe that Mr. Jackson will be hard pressed to get more than seventy five delegates. . . . To achieve the two hundred delegate level, Mr. Jackson would need an almost monolithic black vote, and public opinion polls indicate that would be hard to achieve," the *New York Times* concluded.[18]

December 5, 1983. Beirut. "Eight U.S. Marines were killed and two wounded Sunday night in a massive barrage on their compound here hours after U.S. airstrikes on Syrian positions in which two American jets were shot down. . . . The A-8, a two-man jet, crashed into a mountainside near the village of Kfar Selouane in Syrian-held territory. The pilot, Lt. Mark A. Lange, 26, of Fraser, Michigan and Lt. Robert O. Goodman, Jr., 27, of Portsmouth, New Hampshire, his bombardier-navigator, ejected before the plane crashed, but the Syrians said they took only one of the two airmen prisoner. . . ." (*Los Angeles Times*).

The A-8 Intruder was strewn wreckage, and pilot Lange was dead. Robert Goodman, knocked unconscious when he parachuted to the ground, was quickly surrounded by jeering Syrian soldiers and bundled off to a military prison in Damascus. Beaten by his captors the first day, he was eventually put in a large room, brought books, and fed three times a day; an official of the International Red Cross was permitted to make several visits.

Lieutenant Goodman's release is a high priority, President Ronald Reagan told a news conference a few days later. Special U.S. envoy to the Middle East Donald Rumsfeld was dispatched to Syria. But upon his return, Syrian officials let it be known that Rumsfeld hadn't even inquired about Goodman. An embarrassed White House admitted that Rumsfeld had been under orders not to bring up the subject first.

An irate Jackson—hinting that a white airman would have been the subject of more intensive efforts—announced on Christmas day that he would be part of a "rescue mission" going to Damascus. Critics scoffed. Why would Syrian president Assad, who had ordered the execution of an estimated 20,000 of his countrymen to crush a 1983 insurrection against his regime in the city of Hama, release one black airman as a humanitarian gesture?—especially when keeping Goodman might discourage Washington from sending more reconnaissance flights over Syrian positions in Lebanon.

State Department officials were skeptical. They hinted that the Jackson effort might scuttle delicate negotiations the department insisted were underway. President Reagan would not accept or return Jackson's phone calls. Some of Jackson's detractors felt that this time the grandstanding Jackson had gone too far. Even Goodman's father suggested at one time that Jackson stay home; and as Jackson met with the downed airman's mother at New York's Kennedy Airport before his scheduled departure for Frankfurt and Damascus, one network correspondent told his evening news audience: ". . . what some regard as an election stunt is great for getting Jesse Jackson exposure. The question, of course, is whether it will do any good in getting results: the release of Lieutenant Goodman."

Trying to put Goodman on the front burner of the Reagan administration did succeed in putting Jesse Jackson on front pages, but politically the gamble was enormous. At the least, Jackson exposed himself to charges of meddling in government business; at the worst, he would come back empty-handed—and look foolish. Several campaign advisors urged him not to go. Jackson tried to silence the critics by describing the pilgrimage as humanitarian, not political. He was part of an interdenominational religious group, he said, including the Reverend William Howard, former president of the National Council of Churches, Unitarian minister Jack Mendelsohn, and Louis Farrakhan, leader of the Nation of Islam, a Black Muslim sect with headquarters in Chicago.

Before leaving, Jackson called Don Hewitt, executive producer of the CBS *60 Minutes* program, and asked for advice. "It doesn't look right. Try to take along some prominent white churchmen. Try Billy Graham, for God's sake," Hewitt urged him.

"He's too sick; he can't go," Jackson replied.

"Well, then, try what's-his-name, the president of Notre Dame, [Father Theodore H.] Hesburgh," Hewitt countered.

"Good idea," Jackson told him, but Hesburgh couldn't go either.

When the delegation arrived in Damascus on December 30, there were no guarantees the members would even get to see Goodman—much less President Assad, who had refused to meet with Rumsfeld a few weeks earlier. In fact, Syrian foreign minister Khaddam told Jackson that many in the government were dead-set against the prisoner release. Still furious with the United States for the overflights, they felt that keeping Goodman would both punish Washington and perhaps discourage other reconnaissance missions.

At first Jackson's talks with the government seemed to be going nowhere. The only positive sign came after the American group met with Syrian religious leaders. When Jackson asked Farrakhan to close the session with prayer, and Farrakhan responded with an Islamic prayer in Arabic, the Syrians were visibly pleased. "It was very, very clever on Jesse's part to have Louis there. He was an enormous asset," said Mendelsohn much later.

On New Year's Eve, the Assad government permitted Jackson to visit Goodman; for thirty minutes, reporters and cameras clustered around both men. "I'm fine . . . given more food than I can eat," Goodman told the horde, adding that when his excited Syrian guards told him that "Jackson" was coming, his first response was "Michael—or Reggie?"

The next day the waiting resumed. Marking time, the irrepressible Jackson swept into a Palestinian refugee camp outside the city where few residents spoke English and even fewer knew who he was, even though his staff photographer busily handed out black-and-white photographs. The lack of recognition hardly slowed Jackson. As cameras recorded every move, he led the Palestinians in a spontaneous chorus of "I Am Somebody. . . . I may be poor, but I Am Somebody. I may not have a job. But I Am—Somebody." Then Jackson began to preach: "Just because it rains, you don't have to drown. You may have been born in a slum, but the slum was not born in you. You are special, you are royal. Keep dreaming. Keep hoping," he exhorted the crowd of onlookers, by now thoroughly puzzled.

Late the next day, Sunday, Assad sent word that if Jackson would postpone his scheduled departure, the president would see him on Monday. After cooling his heels all morning, Jackson was summoned. Secret Service agents traveling with him jumped into action, preparing to accompany him, but Syrian bodyguards blocked their way; with just a few aides, Jackson rode off to one of Assad's homes outside the city.

"Mr. President, I'm just a simple country preacher," Jackson said he told the canny leader. "You can break the cycle of pain" that binds the United States and Syria, he argued—if you release Goodman. Keeping him, Jackson continued, made Goodman "warbait" and was "an incentive to escalation of the conflict."[19]

They talked for nearly two hours, and participants felt that Assad never once tipped his hand. Later, students of Middle East diplomacy concluded that Goodman as a prisoner had outlived his usefulness for Assad; that Goodman's detention had not produced any tangible results for the Damascus government; that if Goodman remained, and something happened to him—if he became ill, for instance—he could become a problem for the regime. Releasing Goodman, the observers reasoned, would seem magnanimous—and would clearly embarrass Washington. Especially releasing him to an upstart contender for Ronald Reagan's job.

The government is divided over this issue, Assad finally said. We'll have to meet and thrash things out. "Mr. President, if I had to choose just one lawyer in this country to plead my case, I'd pick you. . . . I'm told that people here have a way of coming around to your point of view," Jackson told Assad. Returning to his hotel, the normally voluble Jackson clammed up. "Our appeal is being deliberated upon. These deliberations are signs of hope," he said through a spokesman.

The waiting ended on January 3. In a mid-morning ceremony

at the Foreign Ministry office, Goodman was released into American custody, a beaming Jackson at his side. Within minutes the two men sped off for a news conference—and live appearances on all network morning programs in the United States. The flight to Frankfurt in a U.S. Army plane landed in time for a second round of live interviews, this time on the network evening news programs. And the final leg of the trip, in an Air Force jet provided by the White House, ended at Andrews Air Force Base just as the next day's morning news programs were going on the air.

President Reagan invited Goodman and Jackson to the White House. In a crowded Rose Garden ceremony, Jesse Jackson gestured where Reagan should stand. "We all congratulate the Reverend and his successful mission," said the president before Jackson took over the microphone.

The political world stood up and took note. "Certainly it's a net plus for Reverend Jackson and his campaign," said Democratic National Committee chairman Charles Manatt. "It is impressive, yes," Walter Mondale concurred. Jackson had gone from a laughingstock to international negotiator. While other candidates had debated what might be done, Jackson had taken a risk and had brought home the goods. "The brother went and got the brother out," a Washington, D.C., taxi driver exulted on the day of their return. Black America rejoiced too. Jackson had pulled it off during a holiday period when other news was scarce; for more than a week he had dominated the airwaves and headlines. Asked about the impact of the trip on his campaign, Jackson replied, none too modestly: "There will be a reward by people who respect courage and intelligence that were displayed." He had clearly gained credibility, and crowds treated him with new respect. They were larger now, seemed louder and more enthusiastic.

The Damascus success, however, could not be translated into votes at the January 20 meeting of the Democratic National Committee in Washington, D.C. Southern party chairpersons balked at a compromise worked out by Mondale forces to lower the burdensome 20 percent "threshold" needed to win convention delegates in a district to 15 percent. But even in losing, Jackson managed to control the proceedings; all afternoon he kept southern leaders waiting to see if he'd personally return to argue his case—or, as some of his detractors were hinting, stalk out. He chose to stay away from the meeting—"I'm daring; but not suicidal; I'm not masochistic. I don't like pain"—but to stay with the party. There would be no hotheaded gestures, no angry walking away. Accepting defeat graciously—"I would rather have a broken heart than a broken party"—earned him praise from all political quarters.

Jackson didn't let the DNC setback slow him down. His post-Damascus mood was upbeat; more money than before was coming into his campaign headquarters; the candidate was charged up, his standing in the polls was climbing. A *Boston Globe* survey in mid-January said he might draw as much as 16 percent of the vote in the upcoming New Hampshire primary. The *Globe* poll showed him in third place, behind Mondale and Glenn, in a state where the black population was only 1 percent.

Then on January 25, in a private moment, Jackson sat down with two reporters in a cafeteria at Washington's National Airport. "Let's talk black talk," he told them, launching into a discussion of the primary in New York state. In the conversation he referred to New York Jews as "Hymie" and to New York City as "Hymietown."

After that, the campaign would never be the same.

3. "HYMIE"

Well hell, they had been calling us 'nigger' every day for years and when Jesse turns around and calls one of them—what is the word, a 'Hymie'?—why then they jump on him and never let up, never.

(Robert Faulkner, Jackson's college roommate, November, 1984)

Mr. Hymie had a store too, and he gave a lot of credit and he screwed people too, OK? Every time we saw a Jew, it wasn't like we saw him on an equal basis with us.

(Greenville, South Carolina, native and campaign aide Gene Wheeler, October, 1984)

. . . on the scale of insults, 'Hymie' isn't a yellow star pinned on your sleeve. The irony is that . . . it's what's opened up for somebody like myself the opportunity to be heard on a dimension of Jesse Jackson's character. . . .

(Anti-Defamation League executive director Nathan Perlmutter, November, 1984)

February 26, 1984. Temple Adeth Yeshurun, Manchester, New Hampshire. The campaign, and the candidate, were at a breaking point. Ramrod straight, Jackson strode to the front of the synagogue, his fists clenched tight at his sides, his eyes darting warily across the tense crowd. "Daniel, in the lion's den," he would say later, but in some ways it was also Greenville all over again, thirty-four years ago when he was 8 and had whistled in the white man's grocery for service and the owner had pointed a loaded .45 pistol at his head to teach him his place;[20] then, as now, Jackson found himself cornered by his own pride. This time he had poked fun at Jews by calling them "Hymie" and New York City "Hymietown," and what he'd said had been quoted and condemned in the *Washington Post.* At first he had tried to deny the remarks; then, turning street fighter, he had tried to put Jews on the defensive, accusing them of making him the victim, target of a Jewish conspiracy to ruin his campaign. But the counterattack hadn't worked, and day by day the furor had grown. As Jewish groups denounced him, white liberals began deserting his campaign; as editorial page writers sniped away, reporters hounded him with questions. In the polls he was slipping, and less money was being given to his campaign. Within two weeks his historic run for the presidency had nearly collapsed, and Jackson was trapped: there was no other choice now but to swallow his pride and own up to his mistake.

The temple crowd waited. Thirty minutes, one hour, an hour and forty-five minutes. They grew restless; some angrily demanded that Jackson appear immediately. Another slight, some whispered, unaware that behind the scenes in a small office just a few yards away a tense drama was coming to a climax.

For the past several days Jackson had been "literally torn apart," as one aide put it, trying to find his way out of the "Hymie" minefield. The controversy had done more than throw his campaign off-stride—it had also changed Jackson. "It put him on the defensive, made him go almost into a shell; he was not the same, positive, outgoing person," said campaign manager Arnold Pinkney. "He disintegrated," said longtime Jackson loyalist Frank Watkins, worn down by pressure and all the conflicting advice he was getting about how to defuse the issue. The advisors were bitterly divided. A few, like Watkins and Unitarian minister Jack Mendelsohn, an old Jackson friend from Chicago, wanted Jackson to come clean: to admit that he'd blundered, that he'd said something stupid in an unguarded moment but that he'd meant no harm; get it out of the way, they had argued, get it behind us—then go on. That felt right, Jackson once conceded, but he just couldn't bring himself to do so, at least not yet; to admit such a thing could wreck him politically, he reasoned, could tarnish his standing as a moral leader.

Besides, many close to him were telling him just the opposite, to stonewall, to stand firm against the critics, especially the Jewish critics. "They're trying to derail the campaign, you know they are," the Reverend Herb Daughtry told him. "There was a real feeling of 'fuck the Jews,' it was pretty intense," said one who took part in the debate. Deputy campaign manager Preston Love appeared so upset that some staff members felt he'd quit if Jackson apologized, and Jackson's wife Jacqueline was so adamant that he not apologize that she packed her bags and flew immediately to New Hampshire to argue her case in person. Don't admit to anything, she told Jackson. She cited history: "I've heard many Jews refer to Washington as 'Chocolate City,'" she said, and there had been no outcry then. She also complained about what she felt was a double standard in the press: when Jewish militants had disrupted Jackson's presidential announcement, when they had offended him, there had been no editorials. "To dig up something that you don't know when you said it and no one is being truthful enough when Jesse Jackson said 'Bring me my accusers,' I don't believe in admitting to anything that you are confused about when you said it or when you did it," Jacqueline Jackson said, growing angrier as she spoke. "And the arrogance of the press to say—did you say it? When? Who said? And yet for two or three weeks our campaign was haunted and plagued . . . it was a conspiracy. It was unfair. And my husband pined over this particular situation and it hurt him deeply and it was the most unfair situation I ever witnessed during the campaign . . . I felt it was like a crucifixion."

What became so explosive started quietly. No one seemed to pay much attention to the "Hymie" and "Hymietown" quote when it was first published on February 13, 1984; the words, after all, had been buried deep in a long, thoughtful *Washington Post* article in paragraphs 37 and 38 of a 52-paragraph story, prophetically entitled "Peace with American Jews Eludes Jackson." According to the *Post*, "In private conversations with reporters, Jackson has referred to Jews as 'Hymie' and to New York as 'Hymietown.'" "I'm not familiar with that, that's not accurate," the newspaper then quoted Jackson as saying.

"I knew they would become controversial," said reporter Milton Coleman, who had supplied the quotes to the *Post*.[21] But many readers apparently missed the words; even the *Post*'s editorial page editor, Meg Greenfield, admitted later that she hadn't read that far into the article.[22] For others the words simply didn't set off alarms. "When the 'Hymie' thing first came to my attention, when I read the original *Washington Post* piece, I literally thought he meant me, that he was talking about me, that that was his teasing way of saying the Hymies, you know. Obviously it wasn't. And by the way, even though my name is Hymie, at least my mother called me Hymie, nobody has for some time, I had never heard of 'Hymie' being used in that way. . . . It was not known to me and to almost all of the people that I associate with in the New York area. They never heard of 'Hymietown,' they never heard of 'Hymie,'" said Hyman Bookbinder, a prominent Jewish spokesman in Washington.

But *Washington Post* editorial writer Michael Barone was incensed; confronting Meg Greenfield, he insisted that the *Post* "do something" about Jackson's slurs. Leonard Downie, then the *Post's* deputy national editor, agreed with Barone; after checking, Downie concluded that the words were "something Jackson says all the time."[23] Four days later, on February 18, the *Post* lowered its editorial boom. Labeling the words "ugly . . . degrading . . . and disgusting," it demanded from Jackson "an explanation and an apology" for saying something the newspaper said is "not typical, we think, of the way any large number of Americans usually talk and certainly not of the way they want political leaders to talk."

Asked about the *Post* editorial the next morning on the CBS News broadcast *Face the Nation* (co-produced by the late Joan Barone, whose husband Michael had written the scathing editorial), Jackson denied making the slurs. "It simply isn't true, and I think the accuser ought to come forth," he told interviewer Leslie Stahl. But the answer satisfied neither Stahl nor waiting reporters who descended upon Jackson outside the CBS studio and demanded clarification. Their persistence became a pattern that continued all week. The hounding angered Jackson, and he charged a Jewish conspiracy; just as he was climbing in the polls in New Hampshire, he said, came stories that his income in each of the last three years exceeded $100,000 and that the Arab League had contributed to one of Jackson's Chicago-based foundations. The timing of those disclosures, he argued, was no accident. Jackson didn't stop there. Not only did he complain that the Anti-Defamation League had inflamed the situation by leaking to reporters a 19-page memorandum listing all the statements he'd made that had been critical of Jews, but on February 21 he also accused the American Jewish community of not doing enough to stop the harassment of his campaign by Jewish extremists; the incidents, he told a Washington news conference, were "too orchestrated to be accidental." (The next day, the American Jewish Congress issued a statement that flatly denied Jackson's charge: "We have in the past and we repeat now our denunciation of any undemocratic tactics or other abuse that Mr. Jackson may have been subjected to. These actions do not in any way represent mainstream Jewish America. . . .") And the press, he went on, isn't playing fair either: ". . . obviously the same reporter who thought he heard ['Hymie' and 'Hymietown'] also had seen the attempts [by Jewish militants] to disrupt my campaign, knew about the threats against me, knew about the pickets of my house, knew about the ads [in the *New York Times*] against me, knew about Jews Against Jesse, knew about the Ruin, Jesse, Ruin campaign. But apparently that's not offensive," Jackson complained to columnist William Raspberry.[24] "There were no big stories about that, no editorial demanding that be stopped, or even commending me for staying above it," he went on. Jackson refused to back down. "What's happening is condemnation without a trial and it's totally diversionary and it distorts the facts . . . I have no recollection of it, and from my point of view, it is a denial," Jackson told reporters in New Hampshire on February 24. "There is in fact documented evidence now that many Jewish leaders and rabbis as well as the Jewish Defense League in fact have assumed the responsibility to hound this campaign," he charged two days later in Chicago.

But as Jackson continued to counterattack, he was digging himself in deeper, and the controversy was accelerating; on February 25, Black Muslim minister Louis Farrakhan warned Jews "if you harm this brother, it will be the last one you harm" (for more on Farrakhan, see chapter 7)—and Jackson, standing just a few feet away, had said nothing, had neither repudiated the remark nor tried to distance himself from it. The storm was threatening to sweep away everything, and Jackson could no longer deny it; flying from Chicago to Manchester on the morning of February 26, he was met by aide Frank Watkins, who convinced him that the political damage was enormous. At the airport Jackson decided to apologize. "I said I'll deal with this today," Jackson said later. "The shortest distance between two points is a straight line. Shit, I'll do it tonight," he told Watkins. It would be humiliating, but there was no other way. Nothing else had worked.

That afternoon at the University of New Hampshire he closeted himself with advisors Watkins, Mendelsohn, Barry Commoner, and *New York Daily News* columnist Earl Caldwell, an old friend. Slowly he began to outline his thoughts; as he talked they jotted down his words, which Watkins would spend the rest of the afternoon organizing and typing. That did not end the debate. Until just a few minutes before he appeared, Pinkney and Love were trying to turn him around; the statement, they argued in the office of Rabbi Arthur F. Starr, is much too strong—at least wait until after the primary Tuesday before conceding anything. But Jackson, already annoyed because a typed copy of his speech still hadn't arrived, was in no mood for any more arguments. In a burst of anger, he barked at Pinkney and Love: "I don't want to hear any more of this. Everybody, clear out of the room." And everybody did, including the rabbi, as Mendelsohn recalled with amusement much later. Alone now, Jackson first spoke by phone to his wife, then studied the long-delayed text. And a few minutes later he walked into the temple to confess. His message was conciliatory, but his voice was cold.

"In private talks we sometimes let our guard down and we become thoughtless," said Jackson grimly. "It was not in a spirit of meanness, an off-color remark having no bearing on religion or politics . . . however innocent and unintended, it was wrong." Adding that he was shocked "that something so small has become so large that it threatens the fabric of relations that have been long in the making and must be protected," he asked for forgiveness. He also denied that the words meant what his critics insisted, that they proved Jackson was an anti-Semite: "I categorically deny allegations that there is anything in my personal attitude or my public career, behavior, or record that lends itself to that interpretation. In fact, the record is the exact opposite."

Some Jewish leaders were willing to accept Jackson's apology. To be sure, they had found his remarks offensive, but they had also been disturbed by the severity of the attacks on him: too harsh, too shrill, they felt; after all, they confided, Jesse Jackson isn't the only one using ethnic terms. "I can recall and can empathize with a thousand conversations, not one but a thousand, that I regard as parallel," said Al Vorspan of the Union of American Hebrew Congregations. "Happens to me every day, as a matter of fact. In which someone from the Jewish community will hear me talking about race relations, or black-Jewish relations, or whatever it is I'm talking about and will say to me, not up on a platform, very off-the-record, just kind of schmoozing around, something about—'Well, you know the schvartzes' [the Yiddish word for "black," often used pejoratively], or 'you know how the schvartzes are'—it's said to me all the time. And obviously in saying this I'm acknowledging that there's plenty of racism in the Jewish community. I'm not saying that what Jesse is doing is unique in the world and that therefore we all ought to go crazy."

But some Jews would not forgive; instead they would scoff at Jackson's apology in the Manchester temple. An apology made "belatedly" that "doesn't acknowledge the gravity of his language," said Rabbi Alexander Shindler; "a minimalist apology," *Village Voice* columnist Jack Newfield called it.[25] And if the president of the Union of American Hebrew Congregations concluded that "this matter is now behind us," others like the president of the American Jewish Congress, Howard Friedman, urged Jackson to do even more, "to examine other statements he has made in the past . . . that have caused anguish not only to the Jewish community but to the general community." What Jackson would later call "a casual mistake" seemed to prove what his critics had been saying all along: that the man who stands in the pulpit is a closet bigot, that in private moments he really doesn't like Jews. In earlier disputes Jackson had always found a rationale for his statements that had caused pain, but this time there was no real defense; this time he had been caught red-handed, and his *mea culpa* confirmed it: "he could light candles every Friday night, and grow sidecurls, and it still wouldn't matter . . . he's a whore," Nathan Perlmutter almost hissed.

Hadn't they been listening in Manchester? Jacqueline Jackson asked later. "He said I will go before them. I will answer every question. And I will make the apology and ask for forgiveness. And my God, it made no difference," she complained. The Jewish hard-liners would never be won over; there was nothing, the candidate now felt, that he could do or say to placate them; ultimately, he said, they feared his Middle East policies and despised him for saying that Jews are no more special than Jordanians. Or Iraquis and Saudis. Deep-down, he thought, they probably hate me too.

But he also felt that many Jews were open-minded, and he

would try once again to reach them. On March 4, one week after Manchester, he addressed a gathering sponsored by B'nai B'rith in Framingham, Massachusetts. It would not be pleasant; as he arrived, Jewish militants screamed that he was a "murderer"; inside, one listener called him a "goddamn dirty Nazi" and had to be dragged off; the rabbi on the panel that interrogated him was also openly hostile and revealed how explosive even conversations between blacks and Jews had become. The rabbi, Alfred Friedman, said, "If you forgive the expression, you're the fair-haired boy of the Arab World," and Jackson bristled, responding in cold fury: "I'm not anybody's boy, I'm 42 years old." For weeks afterward the memory of the slight, of the unfeeling language, enraged him; the rabbi countered that he meant no harm, but that merely confirmed the point: the exchange showed that the flash-point was very low, exposed again the raw-nerve quality of the relationship between blacks and Jews.

Still, Jackson tried to appease. He was proud ("I stand before you this day bloody, but unbowed"), but he also made what he thought was another apology for his "Hymie-Hymietown" references ("while I deeply regret any pain I may have caused at any time"), again condemned anti-Semitism and called for the survival of Israel, and for what seemed to him like the ten thousandth time explained that embracing Yasser Arafat did not mean embracing Arafat's policies. But the performance made few converts.

He had tried, and the effort had fallen short. "I'm not really sure he heard us," Rabbi Friedman said afterward; "he never conceded anything." Some wouldn't accept his apology, and others argued that whatever Jackson said now wouldn't make any difference. "I'm afraid an apology really isn't going to change the way he feels—and that's what concerns me more than anything else," said a local resident, Richard Forman. And Jackson knew all that. Months later he compared his relationship with his Jewish critics to a marriage of twenty years where one partner seizes one episode to dissolve the partnership. "Marriages aren't like that," Jackson argued. "It's a series of compromises, of ups and downs. You don't just find one 'gotcha' after twenty years—and end it. A marriage is a whole series of 'gotcha' this and 'gotcha' thats, a whole twenty years of 'gotchas.'" Jackson had a glimpse of all that in Framingham. "What more do they [his critics] want," he wondered later, shaking his head and suggesting that trying to talk with most of them was pointless. "It has made no difference. . . . What can you do? Do they want us to act like dogs?" his wife asked.

The *New York Times* definition was prim, almost Victorian. "Hymie," it reported, "is a shortened form of Hyman, a name once relatively common among Jews; using the nickname to refer to Jews in general might be likened to referring to an Irish person as 'Mick.'"[26] But "Hymie" was more than just some nickname: for those who'd developed their own private language to shield themselves from an unfriendly world, "Hymie" was also code, the street's shorthand for the landlord or merchant who so often held an economic hammerlock on blacks in the South or urban North.

"Non-insulting, colloquial language," Jackson called it, and some no doubt would intend it that way. But Jackson was wrong, dangerously wrong, if he thought it was only that: "Hymie" also had an edge to it, especially for those who lived with a heritage of persecution and for whom buzz words had often been a prelude to menace. "Let's talk black talk," Jackson said to Milton Coleman, signaling that he thought his remarks were off the record. He was naive to think that ethnic slurs coming from a presidential candidate wouldn't be published; he was naive to assume that Coleman would not report the words. Mostly, though, Jackson blundered by thinking that he, of all people, could use those words about Jews and get away with it. For him that wasn't possible. In 1984, wounds from the past were still too deep.

Yet he tried. He explained what he'd meant to *Newsweek* editors: "I think the first time I heard it was when I got to Chicago about 20 years ago. There's a place down off Maxwell Street called 'Jewtown.' Understand? 'Jewtown' is where Hymie gets you if you can't negotiate them suits down, you understand? It's not meant as anti-Semitic . . . if you can't buy suits downtown, you go to Jewtown on Maxwell Street and you start negotiating with Hyman and Sons . . . and if Hyman and Sons show up, they're called Hymie. There's no insult, even to them."[27]

Some accepted that. Rabbi Balfour Brickner, a leader of American Reform Jews, thought that Jackson had said something dumb, not bigoted. "I've said this to Jesse, 'You're not an anti-Semite, you've just got foot-in-mouth disease. You sometimes don't know when to shut the hell up,'" Balfour continued. "And I don't think calling somebody 'Hymie' is by definition enough to suggest that the man who used that statement is anti-Semitic, any more than if I say schvartze that I'm anti-black," Brickner added.

But some Jackson critics felt that the liberal Brickner had too short a memory. They felt Jackson had been able to "weasel out" of some harsh statements he'd made earlier about Jews. For these critics, "Hymie" was a red flag; if he used crude terms about Jews, then he must have some pretty crude thoughts about Jews too, they reasoned. "There's an irony with 'Hymie,'" said Nathan Perlmutter, executive director of the Anti-Defamation League of B'nai B'rith:

> . . . the irony is that Jesse Jackson for many years gave public expression to statements that were clearly anti-Semitic; cumulatively they made the portrait of an anti-Semite, and while this was all of record, the anti-Semitic dimensions of Jackson simply were not reported in the general press. . . . Then comes a private conversation and the statement "Hymie," which isn't nearly so anti-Semitic as standing before audiences and reminding them that the Ku Klux Klan didn't bring the Bakke case or the Weber or DeFunis cases [court cases that attempted to strike down affirmative action programs in hiring and education]. . . . So on the scale of insults, "Hymie" isn't a yellow-star pinned on your sleeve. The irony is that somehow this "Hymie" item, the least of a dozen public expressions of anti-Semitism, it fit a headline, it's easy to dramatize. And it's what opened up for somebody like myself the opportunity to be heard on a dimension of Jesse Jackson's character that heretofore simply had not been reported in the press.

Harvard psychiatrist Alvin Poussaint, a close Jackson friend, had to agree. "'Hymie' gave the Jewish community a weapon to smear the Reverend Jackson with. . . . He provided them with some very potent ammunition."

As his advisors Bill Howard, Gene Wheeler, and Herb Daughtry later conceded, Jackson often used the term "Hymie" and had often spoken of other groups as well in a flip, street-wise way. Some of the advisors worried that Jackson's tendency to run on at the mouth might catch up with him. His Brooklyn friend the Reverend Herb Daughtry frequently tried to slow him down.

"To tell him to keep his mouth shut. He just talks, talks, talks. Never stops. You know, that's part of his relaxation I guess. You know and everybody telling him, man, you got to be quiet. You got to keep still. You know, you got to shut up. But he talks, talks, talks. And sometimes, he starts cussing. And so that was Jesse. That was part of his, a part of what he is." Frank Watkins, with Jackson since 1969, said, "You know, he just talks like that. For example, there are a lot of Italians along the waterfront area in, what is it, San Francisco? Right. Well, Jesse calls them 'Jap-talians.' Or we'll be driving along and he'll see a black man who's been drinking, staggering along. And he'll say, 'Oh look, there goes Old Moz.' Or Old Mozella, if its a woman."

"He has words for everybody . . . blacks, everybody," said campaign aide Gene Wheeler, who also grew up in Jackson's hometown, Greenville, South Carolina. He argued that "it's a tradition that people in our community call people by nicknames . . . Hymie? It's a derivative of Mr. Hyman . . . and you name a guy by the way you feel about him. For instance, Mr. Hyman was not necessarily a great guy with us. It was a bitter-sweet relationship. I mean, he was kind enough to give us credit, but he was not such a good guy that he would treat us fairly in the repayment of the credit." The words, Wheeler insisted, should not be taken at face value. "For instance, we had black characters we'd name—Moz and Mozetta, that was any black person who was acting a certain way. . . . We'd be in a neighborhood [he got up from his desk and jive-walked across the room], riding in a car and see someone and say, 'Oh boy, Moz is on his way somewhere,' . . . or a guy trying to jive talk us out of something, we'd say 'OK, come on Moz, give it up.' Or we might say something like, 'Boy, I sure like to have some of Mozetta's pie,' and that just meant we wanted some black woman's cooking. *We could use it in both a positive and negative way . . . good, bad, interchangeable*" (emphasis added). Wheeler concluded:

> I never heard JJ use the word ["Hymie"] except on the plane, and I heard him use it a couple of times. . . . I never heard him say "Hymietown," just heard him say "Hymie." And when he even said "Hymie" in my presence, it just didn't register because I knew—see, I'm from Greenville too—I knew he was talking about Mr. Hyman, just like we talk about Mr. Rhodes, who was a

> big farmer back home, Mr. Rhodes, old man Rhodes, who had a general store that sold everything. . . . I don't know whether Mr. Rhodes was Jewish or not. He was white. But we always referred to him as "Rhodie boy." . . . What I'm saying is, out of that experience came a certain attitude that wasn't necessarily racist in the traditional sense that people think is racist, but said as a defense mechanism, to get back at him, not the whole race.

So a nickname could fit the circumstance. What seemed unkind needn't be. Context meant everything, as an old southern lawmaker made clear. "I've punched a few guys in the mouth about that, calling me 'nigger,'" said Louisiana state representative Avery Alexander. "I had a friend and we were working together, and he came down and said, 'Alexander, let's get one thing straight right now.' He said, 'Now I'm an American of Italian descent. So you just as well may call me a "dago" if you want because I'm sure gonna call you a "nigger."' And he and I just laughed about that. There wasn't anything to it. Now he could put it another way. And it would have been a fight. . . . It's all in how you use it, or what you mean," Alexander concluded. "Good, bad, interchangeable." The defense could be stretched: "Moz" and "Mozetta" were the same as "Japtalian," the same as "Rhodie boy," the same as "Hymie," many blacks felt.

Jewish critics scoffed at all this. Come off it, they countered—"Hymie" is different; there is no way the word can be "neutral." We know you, they told Jackson, we know what you meant; the way you used it was derogatory. Black supporters scoffed right back: "If Jesse wanted to offend [Jews] . . . there are plenty of other words he could use," the Reverend Herb Daughtry countered.

So the dispute raged, Jackson defending himself and many Jews simply not believing, and much of black America getting angry: their man was being drawn and quartered for talking the way many of them talked, a victim of the black idiom, "crucified" for using nicknames just like everybody else did, even the Jews with their references to "schvartzes." His campaign—and their aspirations—were being sandbagged by two offhand remarks for which he'd already apologized. Black America had learned a thing or two about words: language had always been freewheeling, an antidote to the drab surroundings, a verbal buffer against despair. Words were also the vehicle of escape from all that was mean; if there was little promise and even less money, then words would have to spark, would weep and rejoice, like black America's music. Everything got a name, labels came and went, no quarter spared, no mercy shown.

Often the words didn't travel very far. "Hymie"—why a word like that could get lost in the shuffle. "I don't believe the average black person had ever heard the word 'Hymie,'" said the Reverend T. J. Jemison, president of the National Baptist Convention, USA. "When it came out in the paper, I said, 'Well now, that's a new word for me.' I had never heard of it. And I spoke to several people, they had not heard or knew what the word meant. And I had several people ask me, What is a Hymie? What does it mean? And I could not intelligently discuss it until I met with my rabbi friend and had him to tell me about it. 'Cause the dictionary didn't give you enough to go on. And I really wanted to be intelligent about it so I had to ask him. And he told me it was just like your word *nigger.* He said it's offensive to us just like that's offensive to you."

The problem, of course, is that the speaker may intend one meaning—but the listener might "understand" quite another. For example, take the argument of Dr. Jemison: "The word 'nigger' to us is more offensive than it might be to some other groups, than 'Hymie' or cracker or redneck because in general they have made such progress. . . . Now, we use the term among ourselves. I use it . . . affectionately with us. I say 'Man, you're a bad nigger.' But I don't want nobody else to use it like that." Jemison, however, couldn't understand why Jews got so upset when a black called them "Hymie." Al Vorspan, of the Union of American Hebrew Congregations, thinks a distinction like Jemison's doesn't hold water. "We all have the same rationalizations," says Vorspan, adding that the connotation of "schvartze" is also "invidious—it's at least insensitive, in any context. . . . Each group knows the code words for bigotry against it. I would not presume to tell blacks which of the things that are said by other people are really anti-black; they know. They know it. They can feel it. And so can Jews. . . . and I feel the same way about 'Hymie.' The context in which he used it, I felt was anti-Semitic."

No other incident in the campaign revealed more about the character of the candidate than "Hymie." Misjudging the impact of the remark had been a miscalculation; failing to defuse the controversy sooner had been cowardly. He had listened, he said later, to those who told him what he wanted to hear rather than to his own instincts. Maybe, he allowed himself to think, maybe those who told him to ride out the storm were right. They weren't of course; he had sprung the trap himself—only he could get himself out. Had he acted sooner, much of the damage could have been prevented. But he had been stubborn, and the delay was devastating.

Damage control was a technique Jackson had mastered years earlier. He had been cornered before in his public life, and sometimes he had not handled pressure well, but at least there had always been a way out: he would simply strike back, that's what he'd learned growing up. Striking back had always worked before. In the Greenville, South Carolina, restaurant where he'd worked as a boy he could spit into the plates of food ordered by white diners; in school he could silence those who doubted him by getting more As on his report card or by scoring more touchdowns or by dating a new girl. When stymied as a civil rights leader, he had always been able to call for another protest march, give another speech, find another target. For Jackson, retaliation was natural; submission was alien. At the age of 42, there was still a lot of Greenville in the presidential candidate. Only he needed a target. And this time there wasn't one. Only him.

His campaign never fully recovered from the beating it took over "Hymie." The controversy not only hurt Jackson with Jews—it undercut his position within the Democratic party. "Hymie" hurt him with some liberal whites who wanted to support the nation's first serious black presidential candidate but who now had to wonder about his sensitivity. And increasingly, his credibility. Finally, "Hymie" angered many of Jackson's black supporters; they felt he was being persecuted by Jews and the media, both, they felt, overreacting to off-the-cuff remarks that none of the critics would let be bygones—and that much of black America regarded as harmless.

The incident did something more—it turned the national spotlight on Jackson's past relations with Jews, which had never been especially good; he had become almost a metaphor for black-Jewish relations, so the scrutiny was intense. And it tore again at the fragile links that bound blacks and Jews together.

Months after the "Hymie" controversy, a few Jackson defenders remembered *that* letter on Operation PUSH stationery to the Pentagon:

November 14, 1974

General George S. Brown
Chairman, Joint Chiefs of Staffs
The Pentagon
Rosslyn, Virginia

Dear General Brown:

One of the most critical challenges facing the leadership of this country is to work tirelessly to reduce tensions and misunderstanding among the world's peoples so that economic justice and world peace can be the fruits of this work. As Chairman of the Joint Chiefs of Staff you are in a particularly relevant position to make a constructive contribution towards the achievement of these two pressing needs. In view of this your remarks to the Duke University Law School Forum as reported in the nation's press this week to the effect that the "Jews own the banks and newspapers in this country" are a disservice to the public. As we all know this kind of distortion of economic reality was widely used by Hitler's propaganda machine to produce fascism and World War II.

It is quite easy for you to confirm the fact that such giant banking institutions as the Chase National Bank, the First National City Bank which is part of the Jay-Pierpont Morgan financial empire, the Mellon National Bank of Pittsburgh and many others are not "Jewish" institutions. As a case in point, Chase National Bank is owned by Vice President–designate Rockefeller, who claims his religious affiliation to be Baptist.

As for the canard about Jewish ownership of newspapers in the country that sounds like a variation on the Agnew theme that the newspapers in America are too liberal.

Given your position of authority and the access you have to public media, to be careless in your public pronouncements is to be irresponsible. That there is a pro-Israel lobby in Washington is a fairly obvious fact, but to associate that fact with an exaggerated reference to the Jews owning the banks and the newspapers is really to spread ignorance. I hope you will take very seriously the import of your remarks and consciously avoid a repetition of such an unfortunate incident in the future.

Sincerely,
Rev. Jesse L. Jackson
National President

Later Jackson argued that he had walked the extra mile. Not only had he written a tough letter in 1974 dressing down the chairman of the Joint Chiefs, he had worked closely with the Jewish Urban Affairs Council in Chicago, had taken his family into predominantly Jewish Skokie, Illinois, to protest against a march held there by Neo-Nazis, had gone into synagogues and temples, and had spoken movingly to survivors of concentration camps. As he told Jewish leaders whom he'd invited to a 1974 Chicago conference: "we share the common mandate . . . we of the black and Jewish communities have become necessary to each other." True, he conceded, there are "serious strains in the relationships between black and Jewish communities"; but the task now, he told them, "is to rise above the rhetoric of the past few years, which has too often been abrasive and tended to divide us and share a common vision of social change in this country. . . . Today's challenges call for a coalition of equals to be cemented."[28]

Only it had not worked; no "coalition of equals" had emerged. Even then, suspicion about Jackson had persisted; some who had worked with or watched him felt that something wasn't quite right, that the public utterances were too contrived, too self-serving, that he would help them only if he felt they could help him in return, do what was good for Jesse Jackson and not necessarily what was good for the Jews. "The local people in Chicago, the business types . . . local hard-nosed guys, they said don't touch this guy with a ten-foot pole; it was not just that they thought he was a hustler; they thought he was also anti-Jewish; he'll use you, he'll use you, they said, but he's not a friend of the Jews. I mean, that was a deep instinct," said Al Vorspan of the Union of American Hebrew Congregations.

For example, former presidential envoy Sol Linowitz remembered an offhand comment Jackson had made at Camp David in July, 1979, when the two men (along with AFL-CIO president Lane Kirkland, Clark Clifford, Common Cause president John Gardner, Wellesley College president Barbara Newell, and other leaders) had been summoned by President Jimmy Carter; in a celebrated nationwide address afterward, Carter had complained that the country was suffering from what he called a "malaise." Linowitz recalled that he and Jackson had been assigned to sleep in the same cabin that Egyptian president Anwar Sadat had used when he had come to Camp David to negotiate with Israeli prime minister Menachem Begin. "It had two bedrooms, one big and one which was much smaller," Linowitz told one of the authors (November, 1985). When the diplomat and Jackson entered the cabin, they paused: who would get the more spacious quarters? Linowitz suggested flipping a coin.

"Heads," Jackson called as the coin fluttered down. It was tails.

"Well, looks like I win," Linowitz said.

"Yeah, you Jews nearly always do," Jackson replied, with a smile.

But years later when he told the story Linowitz did not smile. And when the "Hymie" controversy erupted, Linowitz remembered. "No," he said, "I was not at all surprised."

It wasn't just the angry words Jackson had traded with Jewish merchants, accusing them of stocking dirty stores with overpriced, stale goods; there had been long sessions and ugly boycotts that would never be forgotten. Nor was it that he kept taking potshots at "Jewish slumlords" and "Jewish fight-promoters." It was more a gut feeling among some Jews that beneath those flowing public words about brotherhood there was something other than a street-wise operator—that here was the soul of a bigot, a real hater. They couldn't prove it, of course, but there were signs, they felt, even then. "I think he did have a negative feeling about Jews. There were too many references to me as 'the little Jew.' After a while, I did not take it as a joke," says Chicago attorney

Bill Singer, who worked with Jackson to unseat a delegation headed by Mayor Richard J. Daley at the 1972 Democratic National Convention in Miami. "He was willing to be very critical of Jewish businessmen. Let's put it this way. I don't think Jesse Jackson is objective on these questions. I think it's part of a bias he harbors. He also saw his bread buttered by it. He preaches civil rights and harbors a great deal of prejudice, especially when it comes to Jews."[29]

Singer's opinions are shared by others. Al Vorspan once liked and admired Jackson; the two, however, parted company after a mid-seventies march in Washington went badly and Jackson blamed Jewish groups for the failure. "If Jesse doesn't get what he wants, he really isn't interested in this relationship," Vorspan concluded. "And I thought what Jesse wanted was two things from the Jewish community: one is money, because he thought this was the ultimate geyser, there's got to be a geyser there, and if we can work together, there ought to be Jewish money. And two, there ought to be a really significant response of Jewish bodies to the things that Jesse wanted to do. And neither happened. [After the march fizzled] I got the distinct impression that Jesse said 'Who needs 'em' . . . it fizzled and he thought that we were a useless ally, weak reed, no money there, and he concluded that Jews really don't care about that issue, that's not their issue, they're so locked into Israel that they're useless allies. . . ."

There were also the barbed inflections that signaled a hidden bias to a people taught by history to fear verbal slights. Here, after all, was a Christian minister who hinted of Jewish control of banks and the media (*60 Minutes,* September 16, 1979), who denounced Andrew Young's resignation as "capitulation" to the Jewish community: "the Klan didn't move on Andy," he grumbled. Jews bridled at being lumped with the Klan and also winced when Jackson wrote: "there are tensions in the labor movement, where blacks constitute a large percentage of the workers at the bottom but Jews dominate the leadership at the top. . . . Tensions between black renters and Jewish landlords are just a few recent historical events that have brought to a head the present state of affairs. . . . When there wasn't much decency in society, many Jews were willing to share decency. The conflict began when we started our quest for power. Jews were willing to share decency, not power." That charge drew blood; Jews were infuriated. As the Reverend William Sloane Coffin put it later, "Jews think they've cornered the market on suffering and along come Jackson and blacks and say to the Jews, 'Look, you're oppressing us.' A Jew hates to be thought of as an oppressor."

Troubled by what he'd read and heard, Hyman Bookbinder (Washington representative of the American Jewish Committee) remembered confronting Jackson at a White House dinner late in 1979:

> I told him we can disagree on quotas or rights of Palestinians, but I said "Jesse, when you talk of Jewish slumlords, you drive me up the wall. . . ." I said "Jesse, you're talking about slumlords, you're not talking about Jewish slumlords." [He said,] "Well, what's the difference, they're Jews." I said, "Jesse, don't you know the first ABCs about bigotry and prejudice. . . . Are they slumlords because they're Jews; why do you point out their Jewishness? They're also white, they're middle-aged, they're all men. . . ." [He said,] "I don't know what the hell you're getting at, what's the point you're trying to make?" I said, "Jesse, you evidently need an ABC lecture in the nature of bigotry. Let me tell you what it means when you attribute to a group, to a segment of life, bad attributes of an individual or two, you are being bigoted, you are saying Jews are slumlords." He then repeated something like I don't know what the hell you're talking about. . . . There was irritation in his voice because I was trying to teach him something.

Bookbinder too was getting angry; Jackson, he thought, was either exceedingly inflexible—or very ignorant. Remembering the incident later, Bookbinder became agitated again:

> I kept repeating, "Why don't you understand what I'm saying to you?" I found myself having to say things like—"Do you get angry when you read stories about black rapists? They're not black rapists—they're rapists. And anytime we see references to black rapists, you and I should get very angry about it, that's what I'm talking about. . . ." It did not register. Either it did not register or he did not want to concede that it registered because if he conceded it, it would be conceding that

> he'd made a major mistake. . . . If Jesse Jackson allows himself into modifying his language by a Bookbinder, or a [Rabbi David] Saperstein, he has to say to himself, in effect, those goddamn Jews, they conned me into a reversal again, they're really on top, they really are dictating to us what we should say and we should believe, and I'm not going to let them do it, I'm not going to let them do it.

The problem, Bookbinder felt, was more than stubbornness. Or pride. Instead, he concluded, Jackson "has a thing against Jews, he is suspicious of, resentful of, jealous of, I don't know which words are the most appropriate." A kind of blindness, a peculiar insensitivity: that was what Bookbinder felt he had witnessed, and he was not alone. Rabbi Robert Marx, a social activist who had marched beside Jackson, reached the same conclusion. For Marx, the last straw was Yasser Arafat. The way Marx learned that Jackson was going to visit the PLO chieftain in 1979 was unsettling enough; he and another rabbi were in Jackson's Chicago office discussing another matter; when they emerged, the three found local reporters and television crews waiting. Jackson, flanked by the two rabbis, used the forum to tout his upcoming trip to meet Arafat. The rabbis were appalled and furious. "No doubt about it, we were used. We were used. It was a very unhappy occasion," Marx recalled. But Marx did not give up. As a worried friend, he went back to Jackson's office later and tried to explain why Arafat was such a hated figure for Jews, how Arafat embodied all that Jews detested. For two emotional hours he argued, pleaded, even begged—and Jesse Jackson was not moved, Marx thought, was not moved at all. "You know, it was like talking to a recording . . . everything said seemed like it was being deflected; the criticism wasn't getting through. . . . It was like he was not listening. . . . Here's a man who's so sensitive to personal slight who could not hear the pain I felt."

Two months later, Marx was still angry—and hurt. Once he had genuinely liked Jackson. In the early 1960s, they had marched side by side in Selma, Alabama, and in the racial battleground of Chicago's Marquette Park. Marx concluded then that Jackson was blessed as few men are and that, with his eloquence and keen mind, he could attain greatness. But now Marx sensed that the talent was being abused. Slowly Marx grew disillusioned; now he felt almost betrayed.

In a private letter to Jackson (October 15, 1979), the rabbi tried to explain why. "In my heart of hearts," he wrote, "I believe that you are not an anti-Semite. But some of the things you have said are the words used by anti-Semites through the centuries. . . . One expects dark hints about a Jewish power structure to be found on the lips of malicious and vengeful bigots. One does not expect them coming from the lips of the Reverend Jesse Jackson . . . words of accusation, words of stereotype, of hate."

Angered by the criticism, Jackson wrote back (December 29, 1979) and immediately went on the offensive. "I must frankly state that I am appalled at the reaction I have received," he told Marx. "I have been picketed and viciously heckled at places I have lectured, animal heads were left on the doorstep of our offices in the Crenshaw community of Los Angeles. Yes, and I have been the victim of assassination threats—and nothing publicly has been said. At the very least I expect you and others to oppose, on principle, the acts of the Jewish Defense League who picketed us with bats and other instruments of provocation and violence."

It was, Jackson seemed to be warning, a new day: ". . . we have grown and things have changed. The fundamental fact must be recognized, if our relationship is to be of any value." Improving matters, he concluded in the letter, ". . . will not be easy. It must at least be premised upon a level of trust which I sense does not exist at this time." For Marx, the rupture was complete. After the exchange of letters, the onetime allies rarely saw one another again. "Hymie" lay four years down the road. When that controversy erupted, Robert Marx said he was very saddened. But not surprised.

The litmus test for Marx and many other Jews, especially those who didn't know Jackson well, was his 1979 Middle East trip. Rabbi Balfour Brickner of New York City's Stephen Weiss synagogue explained it this way: "Israel colors every relationship that Jews have with every group or force; as an item it has poisoned Christian-Jewish relations and it poisons and inhibits black-Jewish relations. . . . Israel colors everything, damn it. . . . Jews want to know where a guy is on Israel, first and foremost. He can be any other place he wants to be on other issues, church-state, polar bears, whaling." Jackson flunked the test—the 1979 trip was a disaster.

"I am sick and tired of hearing about Holocaust," Jackson was quoted as saying; nothing would undo the impact of that quote, even though he vehemently denied making it and much later the source of the statement, *Israel Today* publisher Philip Blazer, conceded that what Jackson really said was "it's about time American Jews stopped putting Americans on a guilt trip about the Holocaust."

It wasn't just the disputed quote. Or what some thought was his callous behavior at Jerusalem's Holocaust Museum. (Mrs. Paul Weltman of Chicago, who had been honored as a woman of the year by PUSH, happened to be visiting the site, which often reduces visitors to tears. She watched Jackson with amazement: "he seemed completely unmoved . . . he looked bored." She and other visitors were also stunned when Jackson suggested to his tour guide that Jews were partly responsible for the fate of the victims.) In addition to all that, there was also a picture taken a few days later in Beirut: Jackson and Arafat, arms entwined, the two men smiling broadly. Nothing, not all the words Jackson used later—"embracing him is what you do in the Middle East. It doesn't mean you embrace his politics; it is more a cultural gesture"—counted as much as that picture; with it, all Jewish doubts were confirmed, and it haunted him throughout the campaign; in the center of the November, 1984, ad his detractors put in the *New York Times* was that picture, the two men linked forever.

Looking back, the relationship between Jews and blacks—all blacks, not just Jackson—had been precarious. Even when necessity forged an alliance, the pairing was tentative. In the good moments and the bad, there had always been tension. The two had once been victims, had shared poverty, known discrimination. Even so, Ralph Bunche wrote in 1942, ". . . it is common knowledge that many members of the Negro and the Jewish communities of the country share mutual dislike, scorn and mistrust."[30]

James Baldwin explained it from the black side: ". . . growing up in Harlem, our demoralizing series of landlords were Jewish, and we hated them. We hated them because they were terrible landlords, and did not take care of the buildings. . . . The grocer was a Jew, and being in debt to him was very much like being in debt to the company store. The butcher was a Jew and yes, we certainly paid more for bad cuts of meat than other New York citizens and we very often carried insults home, along with the meat. . . . All of them were exploiting us, and that was why we hated them all. . . ."[31] As Baldwin put it on another occasion, ". . . Jews in Harlem are small tradesmen, rent collectors, real estate agents and pawn brokers; they operate in accordance with the American business tradition of exploiting Negroes, and they are therefore identified with oppression and are hated for it. I remember meeting no Negro in the years of growing up who would really trust a Jew, and few who did not, indeed, exhibit for them the blackest contempt. . . ."[32] And Harlem, as Gene Wheeler had noted, wasn't unique.

Still, blacks and Jews became allies; for more than fifty years theirs had been "a special relationship." Hyman Bookbinder of the American Jewish Committee recalled, "Blacks and Jews of my generation remember vividly the signs that said 'Niggers, Jews, and dogs—stay out.' That brought us together. . . ." Jews played a prominent, often crucial, role in the civil rights movement of the fifties and sixties; as Bayard Rustin noted, ". . . Jews have played a major—and at times the principal—role in most of the civil rights groups. Had it not been for their financial efforts and labors of dedication, there is no question that the American Negro's freedom struggle would not have reached its present stage. . . ." Dr. Martin Luther King, Jr., agreed with that assessment.

The relationship had been effective, but it had never been equal. Blacks supplied the numbers; Jews provided the money, the expertise. The masses, on the one hand; the brain trust, on the other. "Jews and blacks were always of unequal status, with the Jews clearly dominant and blacks subordinate," one Jewish study concluded.[33] "Relations were inherently unequal, not peer to peer," an officer of the Union of American Hebrew Congregations conceded. Rabbi Harold Schulweis remembered hearing of a Watts resident who complained that Jews ". . . put the NAACP stickers in the windows and they pat us on the back and they say 'We know how it is to be persecuted.' But every day they put the money in the sack and get in their Jewish canoes—those damned Cadillacs—and drive away to Beverly Hills."[34] Rabbi Balfour Brickner, a veteran of the sixties struggles, put it even more harshly: "the Jewish community used the black community to further its aims in the labor movement, to make unions and break bosses. Blacks went along with that because they had nothing else to do but lose their chains. And that created an image of black-Jewish friendship. It was only an image because it was patronizing. It was *noblesse oblige.* It was the Jewish brain using the black hand."

Chafing at their role as the junior partner, at their inferior status, some blacks grew resentful at what they felt was belittling treatment; some, like AME Bishop H. H. Brookins in Los Angeles, an early Jackson supporter, openly criticized their one-time Jewish partners:

> . . . although there's been a black-Jewish alliance for years, but always a black-Jewish alliance on Jewish terms . . . that we are your older, bigger, more educated, able brothers. So we'll patronize you. We'll bring you along but for God's sake don't sit on the same seat and don't step ahead and take the front seat. Understand you come along as we say you come along. We'll dole it out. And of course the new movement was that, look, we don't need you to give us a lesson in the struggle. Don't patronize me. I don't need that. If you want to help, help. But don't come up and know it all. I might know a little something myself.

Temporary, fragile, unbalanced, the relationship had to crumble; not only were the two groups growing in opposite directions, their needs were also changing. "Coming out of different social worlds, they saw themselves and others—and each other—through very different lenses," according to Peter Rose.[35] As the two groups changed, their needs were also changing. Jews, more secure, more prosperous, felt the need to consolidate, to protect their hard-earned access to professional schools and jobs, to turn away from the universalism of the civil rights movement toward a more conservative, interest-group philosophy. Blacks, on the other hand, with fewer material achievements and access still denied, felt they had not yet arrived and kept wanting to thrust ahead. While Jews were turning "inward," blacks wanted to keep reaching out; the agendas of the two groups had diverged. The former partners had by now become competitors and often bitter rivals, ". . . for scarce jobs, as teachers or social workers, as well as scarce positions in graduate schools."[36] Everywhere blacks tried to surge forward they found, or felt they found, Jews blocking the way; ". . . the increase in black education and the expansion of the black middle class have brought blacks into greater competition with Jews. Blacks seeking to gain entrance to and advancement in the professions, business and government have been coming up not simply against whites but often against Jews who happen to be a step or two above them. . . ."[37] For their part, Jews, looking back over their shoulders, felt blacks coming on—and wished they would be more patient; ". . . to many accustomed to seeing blacks as supplicants, this new aggressiveness is disturbing."[38]

The conflict of interest was real, so the friction was genuine; Jews felt that blacks were encroaching on inroads Jews had just made and were threatening gains Jews had barely been able to enjoy; on the other hand, blacks resented being left behind, felt stymied because they had a smaller share, not just of wealth, but also of political power, which they felt Jews had. Blacks also felt abandoned by their onetime allies. As the *New York Times* reported in 1979, "Jewish organization support of the DeFunis and Bakke lawsuits, which challenged affirmative action in education, and much more limited support in the Weber case, which challenged affirmative action in employment, strained black patience almost to its limit."[39] When the Bakke case reached the Supreme Court, the American Jewish Committee, American Jewish Congress, and Anti-Defamation League of B'nai B'rith were opposed to the NAACP, Urban League, and other black organizations. Although a 1977 Gallup Poll showed that 83 percent of the American people—and 64 percent of nonwhites—opposed preferential treatment for minorities, the Jewish position came under heavy attack by many black leaders. Writing in the *Amsterdam News,* Louis Clayton Jones declared that the Jews were already, through the state of Israel, "the greatest beneficiaries of preferential treatment in the history of mankind. And were now trying to prevent others from benefiting from the same process." And one of the loudest voices was Jesse Jackson's. In 1979, he said "in the economic struggle to move up (equity and parity, shared power) Jewish resistance to affirmative action and minimum quotas of inclusion for blacks into law, medical, and other professional schools—which Jews historically viewed as a means for their own exclusion—has put black and Jewish interests in conflict. Thus Jewish intellectual and legal opposition to black upward mobility in the DeFunis, Bakke, and Weber cases . . . was, and remains, a source of irritation." The resignation of United Nations ambassador Andrew Young in August, 1979, was one "source of irritation" too; many American Jews were outraged to learn that Young had met privately with a representative of the PLO, and many blacks felt that Young had been forced to step down because of Jewish pressure. The incident triggered a historic meeting of 200 black leaders at the NAACP headquarters in New York, where they released a statement that not only condemned the opposition of Jewish groups to affirmative action but also complained that Jews had supported blacks in the past only when "it was in their best interest to do so."

Clearly, Jews had rubbed many blacks the wrong way, and in the process the attitudes of black Americans toward American Jews had hardened. After querying 53 national black leaders for the National Conference of Christians and Jews, Lou Harris concluded that ". . . blacks hold attitudes toward Jews which are considerably less tolerant and sympathetic than is the case with the rest of the non-Jewish public . . . blacks tend to be more anti-Jewish than any other group."[40] (Black leaders were even more negative. For example, 56 percent of all blacks polled agreed with the statement "When it comes to choosing between people and money, Jews will choose money," compared to the astounding figure of 81 percent of black leaders who agreed. And while only 41 percent of all blacks polled felt that "Most of the slumlords are Jewish," 67 percent of black leaders polled felt that way. The Harris poll also found that "Younger blacks were more anti-Semitic than whites their own age.") And a 1981 study for the American Jewish Committee ("Anti-Semitism in the United States," by Yankelovich, Skelly, and White) found the same pattern, namely, that anti-Semitism across the country was "more widespread among blacks than among whites"; while this survey concluded that part of the reason is "a specific expression of a more general conflict between the haves and the have-nots," the study also attributed part to the feeling of many blacks "that Jewish people own and control everything and that it is the Jewish community that keeps blacks subjugated economically."

Judging by his own public statements, Jackson shared many of those beliefs. "We are on different sides of the table . . . there is a brokenness" is how he described black-Jewish relations on *Meet the Press* on August 26, 1979. He had grown wary himself not just because the two sides had parted company on several important issues, but also because he personally felt betrayed. His sense of history was strong: Jews had shouldered the burden when many whites would not, they had been friends, they knew better; more was expected of them. "The truth is, blacks hold Jews to a higher standard," one Jewish commentator complained.[41] And Jackson was no exception. His disillusionment with Jews can be understood partly in terms of those expectations. "Jackson has the opinion . . . that the Jews are simply out for themselves," one of his most perceptive advisors, the Reverend Bill Howard, once put it. Howard likened Jackson in this case to a jilted lover: "when you are black, and have had a certain expectation or assumption that the Jews are your natural allies, and you woke up one day to discover that they were out to do you in like everybody else, then you become even more angry about them." Jackson had trusted them once, he said. But now the feeling of betrayal was deep; trust was no longer possible.

Jackson may have felt betrayed, but he was hardly paralyzed with grief. He knew a potent bargaining chip when he saw one. When it came time to announce his candidacy, he wangled a live appearance on *60 Minutes;* no candidate in any election had ever had an audience that large. But at the last minute there'd been a snag—the CBS News vice-president in charge of the program, worried about setting a precedent, had balked, and the invitation was very much in jeopardy. The next thing Mike Wallace knew, Jesse Jackson was on the telephone, talking about a 19-page memorandum circulated by the Anti-Defamation League and stopping just short of accusing the network of knuckling under to B'nai B'rith pressure. Jackson argued that he still should appear but that he was no fool and could understand the odds: the network was caving in. Wallace, who'd never even heard about the memo, was perplexed—and annoyed. Let me get back to you, he said. When he did, the invitation was still there; Jackson would get his live appearance after all. (The memo did not get Jesse Jackson on the air—*60 Minutes* executive producer Don Hewitt had screamed and pleaded with the company vice-president and had won.) The episode proved that the candidate who could complain so bitterly about Jewish opposition wasn't above trying to use that opposition to help his own cause.

In fact, Jackson knew as he began the campaign that Jewish opposition cut both ways—while it was a lightning rod for black support, it could also be fatal for any serious political effort. So the opposition would have to be blunted. And carefully: public gestures could be misconstrued, could make him look like a supplicant, weak, could make his constituents think he was kowtowing to the Jews. So shortly before his formal announcement on November 3—at a time when Jewish opponents were beginning to mobilize—he sent out feelers. Word came back that Jewish leaders would meet privately with him: Thomas Dine, who headed the powerful Jewish lobby in Washington, and Irving Levine and Rabbi Mark Tannenbaum of the American Jewish Committee in New York. In November, 1983, Jackson met with each, talking privately and exchanging views, and tried to clear up any misunderstandings. It didn't work—there were no misunderstandings, each side understood the other perfectly well. The Dine meeting was a standoff. The session with Levine and Tannenbaum was terrible, at least so the Jewish participants thought. Tannenbaum came to the Berkshire Court Hotel meeting determined that it would be no mere exchange of pleasantries; within minutes he confronted Jackson with several quotes attributed to him that Jewish groups had found offensive. Tannenbaum said that he told Jackson "if you genuinely want the support of Jews, you're going to have to show repentance . . . you're going to have to confess, in a public way, that you've sinned against the Jewish people." According to Tannenbaum, Jackson was stunned by the demand, "got agitated . . . began huffing and puffing. . . . There's no question but that he got upset." Jackson did not apologize, Tannenbaum added, even though the candidate did complain that his earlier statements had been misrepresented and that he regretted any "misunderstanding." The rabbi, disappointed and even more suspicious, considered Jackson's performance "hostile." Jackson, asked later for his version of the breakfast meeting, insisted there had been no fireworks, no unpleasantness or tension. And while Jackson was perhaps insensitive to Tannenbaum's concerns as a Jew, Jackson's version was supported by another participant in the meeting. Protestant theologian Howard Schomer, Jackson's former teacher at the Chicago Theological Seminary, who'd helped arrange the session, later described it as "a very calm meeting . . . there was a real effort on both parts to find a common ground . . . there were no angry tones and no outbursts."

Hyman Bookbinder, who was briefed on the sessions, says that they "contributed to a feeling that maybe meetings with him would not be useful, that is, that maybe face-to-face meetings will really not serve any purpose, that he'll abuse it, take advantage of it, that he'll attribute things to it; there was a kind of basic suspicion. . . . Things that he said were sort of hostile. He indicated a kind of hostility . . . they were left with some negative feelings, that's why they didn't immediately say let's meet again two weeks from now, they wanted to think it through, he was not prepared to pull back on some statements."

"Funny," said Rabbi David Saperstein, shaking his head, "We could have done so much." Saperstein was thinking back on the months he had worked feverishly to set up meetings with Jackson and Jewish groups, the letters and the phone calls, the countless arrangements, the on-again, off-again agreements; even thinking about them seemed to exasperate him. Saperstein was a Jewish lobbyist on Capitol Hill, he had learned from political masters about delays and backsliding and missed connections, but he had never experienced anything like dealing with those Jackson people. A small man, wiry and intense, Saperstein's energy was almost legendary—no one around him worked longer hours, no one darted in and out of more meetings; he even talked fast, the words tumbling out in rat-a-tat bursts faster than most listeners could absorb them. Saperstein wasn't a quitter; once he'd taken on an assignment he'd always guide it safely home to completion. But this business with Jackson's people was different—all that failed, all the time and energy, all the maneuvering and pleading and cajoling went nowhere; the meetings so earnestly sought would not be held.

Some close to the candidate felt the efforts ended before they even began. "Jews saw Jesse as a devil against the Jews," Gene Wheeler said. While Wheeler's rhetoric is exaggerated, many Jews had grave reservations about Jackson. Not only had he said some harsh things about Jews, not only did he support quotas that Jews opposed—many Jews found his positions on the Middle East, especially his demand that Israel and Arab nations be treated the same, totally unacceptable, even alarming. "U.S. foreign policy in terms of the Middle East has been, Republican and Democratic, absolutely consistent for the last forty years," said Peter Straus, incoming president of the American Jewish Congress;[42] in that context Jackson was a radical, perhaps even a dangerous one. "Jackson," Straus went on, "is saying something different. It's not an illegitimate position. It is not one that has ever been expressed by any candidate in a presidential campaign; and I think that's what, seeing it raised to that level, is what concerns some Jewish people and Jewish groups."

Joe Reed, the executive director of the Alabama Democratic Caucus and no Jackson ally, felt Jackson's stand on the Middle

East was the crux of his ongoing problem with Jews. Many observers agreed when Reed said, "the 'Hymie' thing is just a front to attack him on the Middle East; if he changes on that, they'd forget all about 'Hymie.'" "Hymie" had not just poisoned the way many Americans thought about Jackson—it had also poisoned the whole debate. "How can anyone," columnist William Raspberry asked, "ascribe worthy motives to a man who . . . refers to Jews as 'Hymies'?"[43]

The incident certainly made Jackson's life much harder, David Saperstein agreed. "After that, everything seemed to fall apart," he concluded. Sitting in his Washington office late on a November, 1984, afternoon, Saperstein tried to analyze why meetings between Jackson and the Jewish groups never happened. An old fable, he decided, summed up the entire proceedings—the blind men and the elephant: "for Jews, Jackson was the archetypal foe of Israel, the friend of Arafat, the champion of the PLO. That for them was all that mattered. That was all they could see. Nothing else. They were blind to anything else." He went on, "On the other hand, most blacks could care less about the Middle East. For them, Jackson was a symbol of their aspirations, that was the extent of their perceptions—that was all that counted for them. They too were blind."

Despite all the animosity and failed attempts to get Jackson to sit down with Jewish leaders, efforts continued until the Democratic National Convention in July. Longtime friend Jack Mendelsohn and a former president of the National Council of Churches, the Reverend Bill Howard, spearheaded the efforts for Jackson, while Rabbi David Saperstein served as a liaison for various Jewish groups. Others tried to help. In Washington, Hyman Bookbinder discussed possibilities with Washington, D.C., representative Walter Fauntroy and Howard University professor Ron Walters. From Mississippi, Jackson advisor Victor McTeer contacted some of his Jewish acquaintances, as did the Reverend John Collins and the Reverend William Sloane Coffin in New York. The attempts were earnest but they collapsed; the suspicion and distrust on both sides were too great.

From the start, each side was wary. No one wanted a recurrence of the session with Tannenbaum and Levine; no one wanted to be burned again; the arrangements dragged on, all agreements were verbal, tentative. "There was a feeling that we should make it appear that the meeting just magically happened so it wouldn't appear we were pursuing him. Or vice versa. Each side was very concerned about its image in all this," Saperstein recalled.

Logistics were another obstacle. Since the Jackson campaign was so chaotic and fast-moving—sometimes to destinations that were not certain until arrival—phone calls frequently went unanswered, letters got lost, and tempers flared. Lines of communication were never clearly defined and kept changing; "you never really knew who was talking for Jesse," lamented Saperstein. There were conflicts in scheduling, problems with dates, and seemingly endless discussions over format. Would Jackson appear alone? Would he be accompanied by supporters?—if so, how many? Would the sessions be public or private?—a combination of each? Would there be a panel of questioners? Who would select them? Who would make statements afterwards?

Ordinarily questions like that could be resolved, but in this case the atmosphere was too charged. Jackson was surrounded by advisors who felt, as Bishop Brookins put it, that "the Jews were laying in wait for him." The Reverend Herb Daughtry was almost fanatical on the subject of Jews. Daughtry, who had complained that "Zionist racist pressure" had forced Andrew Young from office, once demanded that a United Nations peacekeeping force be brought into Bedford-Stuyvesant to calm tensions between blacks and Jews.[44] He certainly felt that the Jewish groups could not be trusted, and he kept telling Jackson to keep his distance. "Some members of the Jewish leadership had been after him from the beginning. . . . There was a continuing attempt on the part of Jewish leaders, most Jewish leaders I think I could say . . . to derail his campaign," Daughtry argued, and others kept warning Jackson too. One of his closest friends, Gene Wheeler, felt Jewish groups were trying to "sidetrack" the campaign: "the more we tried to get away from the one-issue campaign, which was Jewish, the more it was thrown back in our faces." He told Jackson it was "useless" to talk to the Jewish groups: "they weren't really serious about making peace with Jesse." Wheeler felt what the Jewish groups really wanted was "to shut Jesse's ass up." Other advisors, said Dr. Ben Chavis, told Jackson that Jewish minds had already been made up, "that the deck was stacked against him . . . that meeting with them would make matters worse." Rabbi Balfour Brickner agreed; many Jews, he conceded, were gunning for Jackson. Brickner was even more caustic when describing Jewish groups that refused to meet with Jackson:

"they feared that they couldn't get anything out of him . . . and they didn't want to meet with him, they just wrote him off, they assumed that the man was just bad on Israel—therefore he's no good, no reason to meet with him, period. I'm talking about the Jewish establishment, such as the American Jewish Congress, such as the NJCRAC [National Jewish Community Relations Advisory Council] and all its constituencies."

But the liberal Brickner had never been in the mainstream, and most Jewish leaders felt that Jackson was dragging his feet. The longer he delayed meeting with them, the more David Saperstein burned. Finally he lost control of his temper and began screaming at Jack Mendelsohn, a man he genuinely respected. "You're cutting us off at the knees, you're insulting, you're embarrassing us. We're not getting straight answers from you . . . you people are crazy," Saperstein recalled hollering. The outburst changed nothing. By now momentum had turned against Saperstein. Jackson had apologized in Manchester but had found that many had not accepted his words; he had also gone to Framingham, and there too he had seen his effort fall short. Jack Mendelsohn made one more try. Mendelsohn was no Pollyanna type, but he remembered Houston in 1960 when John Kennedy had gone before the Baptists and had silenced their doubts; maybe that could happen this time as well. He watched Jackson closely and saw the look in his eyes; the fight simply wasn't there. "I just can't do it, Jack," the candidate finally said, and the old Unitarian minister, a veteran of many civil rights crusades long before they'd been fashionable, walked away, dejected. "He just doesn't have the stomach for it," Mendelsohn thought. Politically, he felt Jackson was making a mistake; personally, he was crushed. For Mendelsohn it was the lowest moment of the campaign. David Saperstein was disappointed too. He felt that Jackson had become a symbol for black-Jewish problems and that only Jackson could help set things right. Jackson, he felt, had passed up a golden possibility: "he could have said 'Look, I've made my apology, let's put it all behind us.' He could have issued a call to action to his people. . . . He could have thrown the ball right back into the Jewish court," Saperstein said. "It could have been quite a moment."

There would be one final chance for Jackson to mollify Jewish feelings and help mend the rift between blacks and Jews. It happened quietly, on the eve of the Democratic National Convention in San Francisco. Months later, Cuyahoga (Ohio) county commissioner Tim Hagen remembered the incident very clearly: Sunday, July 15, 1984, San Francisco's Hyatt Hotel on Union Square, just before midnight, Jesse Jackson's bedroom on the thirty-second floor. In just a few hours the convention would officially open on what could be a stormy session. A group led by Ohio congressman Edward F. Feighan and Rabbi Marvin Hier wanted the party to adopt a resolution condemning anti-Semitism and racism, but Jackson was firmly opposed. This was just one more attempt to revive the "Hymie-Hymietown" controversy and the Farrakhan disputes, a not-so-veiled effort to embarrass us—we're the target of that resolution, not anti-Semitism, Jackson argued. Hagen felt that Jackson didn't understand the issues. What was needed, the commissioner felt, was the direct approach, one-on-one, to convince the candidate that the resolution made good political sense, that hate—not Jackson—was the target. So the commissioner went to the candidate's hotel room. "The Reverend had already retired; he was lying on his bed, in his pajamas, silk pajamas I think . . . his head was propped up against the pillows . . . sort of like the emperor holding court, in his PJs," Hagen recalled, chuckling. As the lights of San Francisco twinkled below, the commissioner pleaded his case.

Hagen carried his Irish name proudly. He had prospered in a brawling, shot-and-a-beer town and was accustomed to speaking bluntly, so this would be no ivory-tower lecture. Besides, the commissioner had been a victim himself, one of fourteen children who'd grown up on the wrong side of the tracks in an Ohio mill town. His grandfather had called himself Joe Miller for forty years because back then the name Matthew DiLoretto wasn't acceptable; back then his mother simply couldn't bring herself to admit publicly that her mother was a Navajo Indian. He was no johnny-come-lately on civil rights, the commissioner argued to Jackson. Hagen's family had marched with Dr. King, he had earned his stripes.

Remembering the scene later, the commissioner gave his presentation high marks: he had covered all the bases, had been precise, even analytical, tough-minded yet impassioned. Maybe, he found himself thinking, maybe this is sinking in. "Reverend," Hagen found himself almost begging, "you once asked how you could tell a black kid in Hough [a black area in Cleveland] to support a party that condoned racism. I want you to tell me, Reverend, how I can tell a kid in Shaker Heights [a predominantly white, upper-class Cleveland suburb] to support a party that doesn't denounce anti-Semitism."

But Jackson wasn't impressed. This guy's used his friendship with [campaign manager Arnold] Pinkney to maneuver his way into my room—and now he's trying to use the resolution to maneuver me into making a conciliatory convention speech Tuesday night. Go easy then and we'll forget all about the resolution: that's what Jackson heard Hagen saying. Jackson felt strong-armed. And he was angry. The speech for Tuesday night was nearly written and contained an apology. But Jackson would not give Hagen the satisfaction of telling him that. No, he would not support the resolution, Jackson told the commissioner. "You should derive no pleasure whatsoever from this meeting. . . . You cannot leave here with any satisfaction that you have influenced anything I'm going to say," he added. He got off his bed and strolled over to where Hagen was sitting. "You Jews are much too sensitive," Jackson said, nonchalantly patting his Irish-Italian visitor on the arm.

4. FORNWOOD

March 3, 1984. The lady of the mansion swept down the mahogany stairs and extended her hand to the honored guest waiting below. Briefly their worlds touched: she in jewels and gown of white lace—he in a cheap jogging suit and running shoes. She was the perfect hostess and a proper smile accompanied her words of welcome, but the eyes had already betrayed her; as she'd made her grand entrance she had seen his costume and had immediately turned away, burning in anger and disbelief.

He alone did not fit in the sparkling tableau. Fornwood, 110 acres of antebellum southern graciousness outside Birmingham, Alabama, owned by one of the city's leading black families, had been decorated especially for his visit: its fenceposts topped with gay lanterns, its mantels decked with blinking white Christmas tree lights this warm night, its kitchen bustling with two dozen women in their Sunday-best suits presiding over the preparation of steaming platters of fried chicken and ribs, sweet potatoes and black-eyed peas, cornbread, cobbler, and punch, the provisions steadily filling the dining room of freshly polished wood, with expensive china glistening on the starched white table linen.

Earlier that day he had arrived so late in the city that a five-mile benefit run for which he had changed on the plane had already ended, and he'd been running late ever since. Still, there had been time to change clothes. For this candidate, appearance was important. Tonight would be no different, except that at

Fornwood, where one hundred of Birmingham's most prominent black professionals and their well-attired spouses were being entertained, his appearance was designed to send a different message: not that he could dress better than they did—but that he didn't have to, that they would have to accept him as he was, on his terms. So the running garb stayed; it was a calculated choice, neither forgetful nor lazy, instead a cold, deliberate snub. He reveled in the contrast. Dressed "inappropriately," he shook their hands, gave them a speech, and then asked for their money—all very mechanically, with no passion. The speech itself was flat, uninspired, with none of the flourishes crowds so loved, none of the magic he could summon almost at will. And shortly afterward he left them, relieved to be going.

Later, as his luxury charter jet climbed into the night sky over Birmingham, the candidate turned toward the window and stared into the darkness. Slowly he remembered Birmingham in the old days, the danger and the violence, when the righteousness of a cause had united a people and infused them with a sense of joy—and community, despite the defeats and pain. Somehow, he was saying, back then seemed better: back then, every town had its own special places, its own character, spots where everyone knew to hang out, 110th Street in Harlem, Gaston's Motel in Birmingham, the place to go if you had new shoes, for instance, and wanted to be noticed, "to get confirmation." Nowadays, he complained, all that was gone; progress had taken a toll. In just twenty years, America, even the South, was more homogenized—desegregation had eroded a sense of blackness; mass culture and television had introduced sameness. Even the local atmosphere had been diluted, confused; Gaston's had been sold to the Ramada chain, he lamented.

The people at Fornwood had reminded him of all that. You could never count on them back then, he was saying, and you can't really count on them now. They had other priorities, different values. He would mingle with them and break their bread and take their contributions, but he would let them know he was not the way they were. The running suit and shoes had been silent evidence of his scorn. "Blueberry Hill," he sneeringly called Fornwood. "These people live in the twilight zone: too black to be white, too white to be black. . . . They're the equivalent to upper-class whites. They send their kids to Juilliard, if not that, then to West Point; they take trips to London each summer . . .

shit, they didn't have no part of the action back in the sixties, no way," he concluded, failing to mention that he sent his sons to an exclusive boys' school in Washington, D.C. It was a question of identity, he went on; theirs had gotten mixed up. He wouldn't let that happen to him. It wouldn't be easy—he could make money whenever he wanted to, lots of it too, could easily become lionized in some white circles. But he would guard against it. They had surrendered something precious. He would not.

5.

SUPER TUESDAY

February 24, 1985. Jackson had been asked about "Hymie" again at another New Hampshire rally; frustrated now, he was showing his anger. "We're being hounded and persecuted," he snapped at reporters, accusing them of keeping alive an issue he insisted was of no interest to most voters. "Of course he's depressed. You would be too, with all that carping," said his man Frank Watkins. "I am not an anti-Semite," Jackson said firmly, not once but three different times during the candidates' second televised debate at St. Anselm's College on February 23. The defense was eating up valuable time and sapping his spirit. "I don't operate so well when my back's to the wall," he complained to Watkins. The rhythm of the campaign was broken; compared to earlier performances, Jackson seemed almost mechanical, his attention somewhere else; the spark that ignited crowds earlier was missing.

The Manchester confession should clear the air, he argued the day after he'd made it. Certainly he felt better—the burden had been lifted. "I made an error, but thanks be to God I feel a personal sense of relief and a sense of redemption and forgiveness. And we're going on to higher ground," he gamely told reporters standing in the snow outside a high school in Nashua.

Many Granite State residents seemed willing to accept his apology. "It takes a big man to admit his mistakes. I give him a lot of credit. Up here we get a lot of slurs. I wouldn't be surprised if he's even heard a few himself," said chemistry teacher Neil

Cascadden. "What he said back then doesn't bother me in the least," said Bea Gifford, a nurse.

But echoes of the controversy lingered. Politically, the question now was which would hurt Jackson most: his thoughtlessness in a private moment at a Washington airport in January—or his candor in Manchester. "Don't you think you ought to drop out of the race, Reverend Jackson?" yelled a man at the Littleton (N.H.) Opera House the day after the confession. Jackson didn't flinch. People don't keep dragging up "ethnic purity" remarks or other verbal indiscretions of former presidents Carter and Ford, he countered, because everyone knows those comments weren't consistent with their true character. The same should happen here, he went on. Then he turned to the Bible. Let him who is without sin throw the first stone. "If there is anyone among us who can throw a stone, based upon perfection, those rocks will stay on the floor," he added, and the crowd roared its approval. One woman in the audience picked up the cue. "I'm a Hymie—and I can't throw stones," she said, and the candidate laughed. Slowly, his exuberance was returning.

But politically he'd been wounded. The results of the New Hampshire primary were much less than his staff had hoped. The big crowds early on had teased—and misled—them. Either the *Boston Globe* poll had overstated his strength at 16 percent—"I kept telling everybody that poll couldn't possibly be right, no way. But no one wanted to hear that," Jackson's Northeast coordinator, Mel Reynolds, complained—or New Hampshire voters had changed their minds. Jackson polled 5.3 percent of the vote, finishing a mediocre fourth place behind Mondale, Glenn, and Hart—but ahead of McGovern, Cranston, Hollings, and Askew.

Typically, Jackson tried to cast the situation in a bright light. The vote shows that front-runner Mondale hasn't wrapped up the nomination and is coming back to the pack, Jackson opined. John Glenn (former astronaut) "is parachuting back to earth." Gary Hart, he hinted, had taken votes that otherwise would have gone to him. Why was Hart able to do that? "He's white. He had the inside track," Jackson shot back. Then he boasted: a former presidential nominee (McGovern), a former keynote speaker at the Democratic National Convention (Askew), and two sitting U.S. senators (Hollings and Cranston) had finished behind the Country Preacher. "Done shot past them," he chortled. Privately he conceded that "Hymie" had been devastating. He tried to boost the spirits of some staff members who felt he'd been done in by the media—and Jewish critics. "We went through a week of crisis and trauma. And we survived. Spiritually and politically," he told them. The South, he went on, would be better.

February 28, 1984. The snow kept falling and the airport stayed closed and the press corps stayed cooped up inside the tiny waiting room. A story in that morning's *Boston Globe* suggesting that black reporters had been cozy with the candidate was passed back and forth around the room.

"How 'Hymie' Became Page One News," the headline read. It was the wrong day for this to happen. Tension rose in the small terminal. Words flew. Eyes darted. In the last ten days the candidate had been caught slurring Jews, had denied calling them "Hymies"; reporters had dogged him for the truth, had watched him grow surly and withdrawn. They'd reported his accusations of a Jewish conspiracy against him; they'd listened to Nation of Islam leader Louis Farrakhan threaten retaliation. They'd packed into a crowded synagogue to record Jackson's confession.

This day they were supposed to escape. Head south, to Augusta, Georgia. Sun. "The homefield advantage," Jackson was calling it. Perhaps a slower pace, a less volatile candidate. Then came the snow. And the *Boston Globe* story. "Beset by extraordinary attention because of the novelty of his campaign," wrote the paper's Curtis Wilkie, "Jackson was more comfortable dealing with black journalists, according to press sources, and enjoyed holding court with them." That's how "Hymie" came out, Wilkie suggested.

The implication was clear, blacks on the Jackson trail felt. "Bullshit," said one, slamming the newspaper down on a bench. The pressure of the last few days finally exploded in one torrent. For days blacks covering Jackson had been under a microscope. Why did Jackson feel free to say "Hymie-Hymietown" in front of blacks? Why did only Milton Coleman report it? Was there some kind of unspoken pledge among some blacks not to sabotage the nation's first serious black presidential candidate? Were they going easier on him than on other aspirants?

Questions. Innuendos. Professionals with years of experience scrutinizing others were now being scrutinized themselves. Finally a white reporter, Curtis Wilkie, came along and—without interviewing any of the black reporters regularly assigned to cover Jackson—wrote about the comfortable relationship the candidate had with blacks in the press entourage.

The griping in the airport soon moved away from Wilkie to white journalists in general, to their inadequacies, their inability to cover this campaign: how could whites understand the subtleties of the civil rights movement—or black religion? How could they hone in on the nuances? Sort out the emotions? Separate symbols from substance? Truth from hype? White reporters were in earshot as the black reporters debated.

"That's bullshit too," one white responded. "I've been covering black stories since before you were born," added another. For days it had been hidden, escaping only occasionally, on a long ride in a cramped van, in a hallway. A slight sneer. A cold stare.

Blacks said they felt a double standard was being used to judge not only their work—but Jackson's campaign. Some felt that Jews were being allowed to exploit the "Hymie" remark; some felt that white reporters—under fire for not being tough enough themselves on Jackson—were using "Hymie" to even the score. Some aimed their anger at Coleman, accusing him of reporting an off-the-record comment and then burying it, in a cowardly way, in somebody else's story. Many blacks were angry that the white-dominated media were not treating Jackson as seriously as the other candidates. Was it because he was black? Because he couldn't win? Weren't those two synonymous in their minds?

The bickering in the airport was turning ugly. No questions were being answered. The differences were profound, and the gap was widening. The reporters were beginning to wander off when Jackson walked to the center of the room and began talking to a small group. Gradually others moved back within hearing distance. Talking softly and slowly—the preacher now, not the politician—he tried to mediate with a metaphor. The first black campaign for president was like a birth, he said. Keep that in mind, he went on, it might help. "Like when the baby comes out, there's all the blood and pain and suffering. . . . There's a dynamic going on that hasn't gone on before . . . we're all going through changes." Reporters nodded. There were a couple of half-smiles. A couple of handshakes and shoulder pats. Not a change of minds. But a change of moods. Then the snow let up, and the plane lifted off.

It was the first public squabbling within the Jackson press

corps, roughly half of which was black. It was also the last. "We're all going through changes." Each wanted to believe that was true. There would be occasional flare-ups in private, a crack, an unthinking barb. But some air had been let out of the taut balloon that day in the Manchester terminal; new margins had been drawn. Blacks and whites on the press bus still differed, sometimes widely. But now at least each had a better understanding of why.

Jackson was going back to his roots. Back to what he called the "land of cracklin' corn bread," pitchers of lemonade, and coconut cake. What he called "serious eating," rubbing his hands together and grinning at the prospect. On this turf he would depict the front-running candidates as carpetbaggers. Greenville, South Carolina's native was the rightful heir here, he'd say. "I am running as a son of the South, blood of your blood, flesh of your flesh," he told crowds in Georgia and Alabama and Florida.

He would go on the offensive in the black Bible belt, where the numbers gave him a fighting chance in a crowded primary field. The voting lists in Georgia and Alabama were nearly one-quarter black (21.9 percent and 22.5 percent, respectively), and the black vote could provide up to one-third of the expected turnout. Let the other candidates divvy up the rest of the pie, he figured. With that base, "we can win Super Tuesday," he exhorted his crowds.

But there were problems, big ones. Early on, Mondale had courted and won such powerful allies as Birmingham mayor Richard Arrington, Alabama Democratic Caucus chief Joe Reed; in Atlanta, Mrs. Coretta Scott King and black councilman John Lewis were supporting Mondale; and Andrew Young was leaning in the same direction. The potential white vote for Jackson was limited. In one Gallup Poll, nearly one white voter in five said he or she would not vote for any black candidate, and politicians assumed the real number was much higher.

Nor was the black vote simply hanging there like some overripe berry waiting to be plucked. It was not organized and not accustomed to supporting black candidates. Georgia's population was 30 percent black, for example, but none of its officials elected statewide was black; nor were any of its 159 sheriffs. Only 5 of 67 sheriffs in Alabama were black. And while 19 blacks did sit in the Alabama legislature, the real number could be twice as many—if the black vote matched the percentage of the black population. "He could not take the black vote for granted. We had to bust our asses to get the vote we got," said Michael Figures, Alabama state co-chairman for Jackson.

Jackson's southern workers were enthusiastic but largely untested in political campaigns. "They had a bunch of us who were minor leaguers playing in a game with some of the guys who had been up in the big leagues," said the Reverend Thomas Gilmour, who worked tirelessly for Jackson in Alabama. There never was enough money either—only $50,000 for Georgia, Alabama, and Florida, deputy campaign chief Preston Love estimated, a fraction of what Mondale was spending. There was no money for television or newspaper ads, just a few bargain-basement radio spots. As before, Jackson would have to keep passing chicken buckets and pleading for contributions from the pulpit. All the $5 and $10 bills the black congregations could spare. And the $20s—"Jacksons for Jackson," as the staff liked to say.

Earlier, in the Northeast, Jackson had played down his color. "I'm not Santa Claus from the North Pole. I'm your brother from next door," he told one Providence, Rhode Island, audience. In the South, though, he stressed his origin and kinship. Appeals for a Rainbow Coalition were secondary. Securing the black vote took precedence. He would try to revive the crusade of the previous summer. He would appeal to his own. To their sense of history, their dignity, their blackness.

February 19, 1984. Brown's Chapel, Selma, Alabama, the starting point for many of Dr. Martin Luther King's 1960 marches, was packed. "Resurrection is upon us now. This is a new day. . . . One glad moment is not too far away. We're moving toward one fine morning," Jackson told the overflow crowd.

A small woman stood by him on the stage. That morning she had announced that she was running for assessor of Dallas County. Since Reconstruction, blacks had never held that position even though they had long been a majority in the county. Jackie Walker was 35, a community worker of modest means, with no political staff—and little political experience. Many of her friends thought she was wasting her time running for any office, much less assessor.

But something Jesse Jackson said earlier, she recalled, had hit home. "He made black people feel they could make a difference. . . . that really helped make up my mind. . . . The enthusiasm and the excitement he created for running was really inspiring," she said. In the steamy auditorium she listened to Jackson again. "In 1965, we could hope for a change," he was saying. "Now we can vote for a change. That is the fundamental difference."

Listening to him in Brown's Chapel, Jackie Walker felt she could win. Despite the odds. Never had she felt better, or bigger. "I was standing next to him, and I'm really short and all, four feet eleven inches. And when he raised my hand, I felt like I was going right off the ground. . . . It was an electrifying moment. . . . The air was jumping. You could just feel the energy." (Jackie Walker was elected assessor of Dallas County. In February, 1985, however, before she could take office, she was killed when her car skidded off an icy county road.)

He told southerners not only that he was one of them—but also that he was better than the other candidates. That he had earned their support. "There are eight men running. One of us has marched the longest. One of us has climbed the right side of the mountain. There are eight of us running and I got the best record on civil rights. Give me a chance, give me a . . . ," and the crowd would drown him with applause. He repeated the theme in churches, civic centers, courthouses. "In the heat of the day, I've got the best record on civil rights . . . I earned your vote, I paid my dues. . . . I led the march to Mobile and Montgomery. . . . Mondale is a good man, but I'm a better man." Mondale and Hart were his chief rivals, he thought, so he trained his fire on them. "Hart has no history of struggle in this land. I have knowledge of the terrain. Walter Mondale wants to pick fruit from trees he didn't plant. I have earned your support." And again: "Hart and Mondale seem to believe in the right thing, but they've never done the right thing . . . they have no plan of action . . . I understand action . . . don't tell me what you did in 1965. Tell me what you've done lately."

The location changed, but his message did not. He would ask a crowd a question—and then answer it himself.

> Somebody says why do I talk about working people so much more than Mondale and Hart? Because I'm a working people. I'm one of the working people. They never had to cut no grass and rake no leaves for a living. They never had to get no hundred pound sack of cement and seventeen shovels of sand to make mortar. They never had to

> cut no new ground on the farm, they never had to wait tables and hop curbs. They never had to face being called 'boy' when you was a grown man. They never had to fight for the right to use a bathroom downtown, or fight for the right to vote. They don't really understand struggle except as a theory. In my life, it's real. I understand life from the bottom up. I come from the bottom up. I understand.

From the pulpit his voice would begin softly, slowly, gaining momentum and volume, like some huge locomotive heading down an open track, steaming ahead, sparks flying; the more he talked, the richer the language, the more resonant, the more emotional the appeal. "Keep on preaching, people will get well. Keep on preaching! Demons will *come out*," he'd tell the murmuring congregations. For shepherd and flock it was a holy communion. "When I'm up there preaching, the people and I are engaging in a spiritual rendezvous, energizing each other," he said. They knew what he would tell them, they even knew that the spell wouldn't last. But they wanted to hear. "You're not *junk, God didn't make no junk*," he'd proclaim, and they'd holler "Oh yes, Jesse . . . tell us, brother. . . . Amen, Jesse. Speak preacher, make it plain," as they fanned themselves in the sticky heat. He kept the message simple, direct, affirmative: "you can rise from the manger to the mansion—if your mind is made up. . . . there's nothing more powerful in the world than a made-up mind . . . you can be whatever you want to be; you can do whatever you want to do," he would speak to the poorest in a town, and for a few moments they too would make themselves believe. "Don't just hang around the graveyard talking about the crucifixion," he'd say, "Roll the stone away and look to the resurrection, to new hope." They don't want policy, he once said. They don't care about programs. They just want something to believe in. They only want hope.

Then he would ask them for their money. "Let me have your attention, please. This will only take a few minutes. Please, no one move. Everyone be absolutely still," he would say, his large preacher hands motioning the crowd to be seated and silent. "You asked me to run for president. You didn't ask me to run for alderman. This takes some serious money . . . don't put any chump change on the freedom train."

"Freedom isn't free," he'd remind them. "A hundred of your

friends at ten dollars apiece, or ten at a hundred. Any combination of ways, you make it. If you really want to make this campaign work, you got to give till it hurts," he would shout as they started to line up in the aisles.

> One sister is standing, one brother is standing. Come down here please. Come right on down. . . .
>
> Ushers, I want you to stand right there in the aisles. Now, if your church, your business, your sorority, your fraternity can raise one thousand dollars, just raise your hand. Stand right where you are. Please don't make any noise. . . . This won't take very long; we need names and addresses and place of employment—and hopefully a check tonight. You know, pledges get cold. . . . You know, this is how we all survive, Nancy. . . . [In the audience activity had slowed; no one was proceeding to the front. Timing himself perfectly, Jackson continued.] Anyone who can give five hundred dollars: please hold up your hand. Or stand wherever you are. Five hundred dollars to help this campaign. If you want to play, you got to pay. Please don't make me sound like I'm begging; I'm trying to sound presidential. Make room for these people, please come forward. . . .
>
> I need your help. I want those with Right Now money to raise your hand, just raise your hand. . . . Don't anyone else move. . . . If you've got twenty-five dollars, I know it's a sacrifice, but we need the money to keep our movement going. . . . Just sit right there; please, don't anybody leave, we're almost finished. Before I'm done I'm going to get down to welfare checks, and food stamps. . . . [to an usher] We need a bucket over here. . . . Those with money, don't put it in the bucket—drop it in. This ain't no currency exchange.

The pattern never varied. After the last to give had filed past and the hall once again started to get noisy, he would lead them in prayer.

Eugene Wheeler usually kept the details to himself. Like the day one of the engines on the campaign's chartered plane failed in midair somewhere near Columbus, Ohio. Or all the times when there weren't enough seats for reporters who'd paid to ride aboard the "Rainbow Express", and who were forced to stowaway in the plane's bathroom during take-offs. Wheeler remained sphinxlike through all that. And during those post-midnight scenes in backwater southern motels when forty or so members of the traveling press slapped their credit cards on the front desk and waited for room keys—when the campaign had neglected to make reservations for any of them. On those occasions Eugene Wheeler would walk off into an elevator, smiling, still jaunty. "We're checking on it right now," he'd say.

Wheeler, the dapper and resourceful chief of operations for the Jackson campaign, had realized early on that this operation would not be business-as-usual. Don't let yourself get all worked up, he'd decided. He had become wealthy, and a little bored, running a Los Angeles medical clinic and pharmacy, and now he was on the ultimate adventure—Damascus, Syria, one day, Washington, the next—helping his old buddy "JJ" run for president.

On March 7, 1984 Wheeler stood in the lobby of the Book Cadillac Hotel in Detroit. "This is not going to be a great day," he kept muttering, but few paid much attention. They were too busy scrambling out of the hotel for the bus which would take them to the Detroit airport. In seventeen degree cold and a biting wind, the reporters waited—and waited, but there was no bus. The company was trying to gouge him by charging three hundred dollars, Wheeler explained, and he wasn't going to stand for that. No one would take this campaign for a ride, he fumed. It was the only snafu he would explain all day.

Wedged into cabs the disgruntled reporters raced to the airport—and then waited some more. The heater in the campaign-chartered turbo prop didn't work, and the part needed for repairs couldn't be found. It was the latest in a string of malfunctions, and pilot Allen Heasley was angry. When a stewardess complained that one of the reporters had been rude, Heasley erupted. His face beet-red, the veins in his neck bulging, he grabbed the reporter and threatened to throw him off the plane. "Uh oh," said one passenger, "Captain Crash is going to make us suffer today." They had dubbed him "Captain Crash" weeks earlier when two reporters had walked to the rear of the plane and Heasley had come careening down the aisle waving his arms wildly and screaming that the plane was going to tip over. Tip over then and there if the two didn't vacate the premises immediately! "I've seen it happen once, uh two, no—three times," he bellowed. "Boys, we got us a real ding-dong," said one of the Secret Service agents, laughing and at the same time shaking his head. Ten months later the laughter stopped and the moniker became chillingly real when the same plane with "Captain Crash" at the helm went down just outside Reno, Nevada killing Allen Heasley and seventy others on board.

Ice caked the inside of the cabin window on the trip to Chicago. Trying to get warm, a shivering Jackson hustled up to the cockpit and nestled down in a jumpseat. Most of the passengers sat huddled under blankets and overcoats, teeth chattering, hands too cold to work.

An air of frivolity began to spread through the refrigerated chamber. One huge cameraman, draped in a blanket, began shimmying down the aisle. "When cameramen wear blankets, we're moving on up," he chortled, mimicking the candidate, dragging his wooly shroud behind. "Moving on up, moving on up," the passengers chanted the campaign refrain in unison.

Two taciturn Secret Service agents walked to the rear of the plane and glared at the reporter who'd angered the pilot earlier. "We can't have this. You're under arrest," one intoned sternly as the other snapped a pair of handcuffs on the reporter's wrists. Turning quickly, the agents walked away before the stunned reporter could see either of them grinning. "My Lord, things have really gotten out of control," one Jackson staff member murmured, falling for the prank.

The plane landed at Chicago's Midway Airport thirty minutes after the day's first event was scheduled to begin—in Waukegan, Illinois, more than an hour away by bus. But there were no buses at this airport either, no reception committee, no motorcade, no security. All that was waiting across town, at Chicago's other airport, O'Hare.

It was only 9:00 A.M., and already the day was being frittered away. Reporters, thawing out inside a hangar, were mutinous. Staffers were sullen. Ordinarily Jackson ignored complaints about his haphazard campaigning. The grumbling, he said, showed a lack of character by persons who were used "to having too much." He, on the other hand, could roll with the punches. "I came up on the rough side of the mountain," he never tired of reminding listeners. This day, though, he did apologize for the cold plane ride. "They're very hard-nosed about the money," he said of the charter company. "But not very hard-nosed about the heat." No one chuckled.

On most campaigns reporters relished, even reveled in wacky moments along the way. But no one had ever endured anything like this. This, they grumbled, was setting records as the most mismanaged, most inept road-show of all time. And for the privilege, reporters groused, the campaign was charging them one hundred and fifty percent of a first-class fare. So the traveling press began to gripe. Daily, sometimes hourly. To Jackson. And behind his back. But it did no good. Nothing changed. "It's better for the press and the Secret Service to adjust to the rhythm of the people than for the people to adjust to the rhythm of the press and the Secret Service," Jackson hissed when cornered. "You guys are just too soft," an aide sneered.

Telephones, for example. Other campaigns routinely provided telephones so reporters could file stories; other campaigns budgeted time for filing too. Not this operation; most days it allowed for neither. Part of a reporter's day therefore was spent looking for a phone. And a reporter might find one—in a pastor's study, outside a washroom, or at a filling station half a mile away—only to look up and see the candidate's motorcade go roaring by, stranding reporters in places with neither taxis or rental cars and often no clear idea of where to catch-up with a campaign that could change hourly according to the candidate's whim. They complained that he wasn't just making it hard for them—but that he was also hurting himself. "None of what you do has much impact if we can't write it up and tell anyone about it," one frustrated reporter told Jackson. "I'm not going to let you break my spirit," the candidate snapped back. "I'm running and you're writing—and at some point we may come together."

They never did. And certainly not that March day which began before dawn in the bitter winds of Detroit and which ended twenty-two hours later in Starkville, Mississippi as the chartered plane landed on a darkened runway and pulled up in front of an empty fire department building. Again, no buses. Or reservations at the motel. From the side of the lobby, Eugene Wheeler surveyed the scene as the weary crowd plodded in. He smiled, went behind a door and closed it tight. Again Wheeler spared everyone the details.

The chaos was intentional, Jackson insisted. "You may not

understand it, but there is a sense of order in this confusion. I like it. This is the way I want to operate," he told one bewildered Secret Service agent. He alone knew where the campaign was going because he made all the decisions. Each morning he would personally approve every appearance, sometimes throwing the schedule hopelessly behind by adding stops at the spur of the moment. "Ole Jesse, he runs on rhythm, not on timetables," said Lew Armstrong, who tried to manage the candidate in Mississippi. In a new town Jackson would suddenly remember an old friend in a town nearby—and off the campaign would roar in that direction.

Detractors sneered that he was taking himself on a political joyride. Even his friends agreed that it was impossible to conduct a campaign like that. "I told him in Tallahassee, Florida—Jesse, how in the hell can you be running for president—and scheduling your own damn time. I said you just can't do that, man," Michael Figures told him. "You got to have somebody in your organization who can do two things: who can command respect of your organization—and who can slap the shit out of you when it becomes necessary to do so." Nobody could do either, of course. The criticism had gone nowhere, Figures admitted. Nothing changed. Fifteen, sixteen hours a day, from early morning until well after midnight, the campaign lurched across the South: a caravan of history fueled by the hopes of black Americans and the ego of the candidate. By his sense of mission and sometimes by his whims.

By now, though, black America was starting to pay closer attention. It had a candidate performing centerstage, holding his own, proving that he belonged. Even some people who felt the effort was hopeless rallied behind him. "It doesn't matter if he don't win. Just so they have somebody to look up to. Just so we have somebody to idolize," said a Rocky Mount, North Carolina, school teacher standing near her class. "It is black pride. I should put that to the nth degree. *Black pride!* Those who felt that Jesse Jackson did not have a chance to be successful, knowing that he would not be president of the United States, were proud that there is a black person seeking the presidency. That I think underlies, undergirds everything that black people have done by way of participation in the Jackson effort," said former congresswoman Barbara Jordan. "He's us. That's all" is how a nurse in Chattanooga put it.

The more that black Americans whooped it up, the more Jackson poured it on. Some complained that he was speaking now with two voices: one white, the other black. "Can you imagine, if Ronald Reagan addressed black audiences saying 'I Am Somebody' or 'from the outhouse to the White House' or 'from the guttermost to the uppermost'? He'd be run out of town on a rail. He'd be considered a racist. But Jackson, when he talks to black people, speaks in this stupid, mindless cant. When he talks to white people on *Face the Nation,* he speaks the King's English," Professor Walter Williams, a black economist and Jackson critic, concluded.[45]

While some criticized him, others worried. They saw that the audiences now were mostly black, that whites were staying away. They knew that Jackson's florid style was scoring points with black listeners—but they conceded he might also be driving off potential white supporters.

AME Bishop H. H. Brookins, an early Jackson advisor, watched the crusade weave its way through the South. Jackson's performance, he concluded, might be costing him dearly—but it was also saving him: "Jesse frightened people. The way he came across to the white person who doesn't know anything about blacks other than a house maid or butler or something—you know, to let a nigger this smart get up that high, that was the attitude—so when he came on like he did, he was intimidating. . . . Jesse was a bit much for them to take. . . . I'm saying that many of the non-black people saw Jesse as an anathema. See, he registered something in them. He sparked something in them that turned them off. And turned them on him. . . . that was frightening to most white Americans." But to blacks, Brookins went on, the performance was revolutionary. "They empathized with it, they identified with it," he said. For now, Brookins and other Jackson advisors felt, the price was worth paying. It might be costly in the future, he conceded. But Jackson didn't have that luxury, Brookins insisted. Jackson, he said, had to secure the black vote. And do so quickly.

Jackson complained that some of his problems in "reaching out to whites" stemmed from the way that reporters presented his campaign. "The news media says every night 'Jesse Jackson, black leader.' It never says Walter Mondale, white leader. Gary Hart, white leader. The reinforcement of the blackness almost makes whites feel excluded, unwelcome, and that's a double standard. I mean, why should the media keep referring to me as a black leader? My blackness is self-evident."

The media, he protested, spent too little time discussing the issues he raised (the impact of the second primary system on black candidates, for example), too little on his own accomplishments—and too much on stereotypes Jackson said were distorted and unflattering. "It happens all the time, every day. Local TV, national TV, all the time. See the media deals with blacks in about five deadly ways every day. It has an isolating impact. . . . it's cultural bias. Blacks tend to be projected as less intelligent than we are—less hard-working, than we work—less patriotic than we are (no black person in this country has ever been convicted of treason, not one)—more violent, less universal."

The basic problem, he concluded, was that too many editorial decisions about blacks were being made by white reporters, producers, and editors who didn't understand the black experience. And who were, he thought, weighed down by stereotypes: "it's the reason why some might say that black reporters on this trip are less professional than white reporters. No one ever accused white reporters covering Hart and Mondale of being unable to cover them as professionals. . . . No white reporter's professionalism or integrity has been challenged covering Hart and Mondale. It's a double standard."

Many reporters watching the spectacle decided this was a campaign where reality wore many disguises. Very little was what it seemed. At times, very little made sense. A week before the crucial Super Tuesday primaries, for instance, Jackson had left the south and gone barnstorming in Michigan, where his prospects were, at best, dim. He'd always come up with a reason: "It's important for the people there to see me too," the candidate had replied when asked why he'd gone. Nothing and everything seemed to fit, from the aging Jewish carney-barker in the tattered red sportscoat who followed Jackson around the country hawking campaign buttons to the Secret Service agent with the Uzi submachine gun slung over his shoulder on the murderously hot airport Tarmac who warned everyone within earshot, "Don't mess with me. I'm armed and extremely dangerous. This thing goes through anything. I'm scared to death for my right foot."

It was a madcap fantasy voyage, and the passengers made up rules as they went along. "Your attention please! There will be a news conference sometime between three and six A.M. Thank you." A voice boomed through the bus. A network cameraman, giddy after a day that had begun seventeen hours and hundreds of miles earlier, had seized a microphone and was prattling on. Some on board laughed. Others scribbled down the time so they wouldn't be late. Out here, nothing was impossible; nothing could be taken for granted. Not even that those who were in charge of going somewhere knew where they were going. In Dayton, Ohio, a bus rumbled along for several miles in the wrong direction. It was late, the end of another long day. "I'd like some truffles," someone said softly as the vehicle sped on the wrong way into the dead of night. "Yes, truffles . . . that would be lovely . . . yes, truffles in Dayton."

Reporters traveling along with him knew even then there had never been a campaign quite like it. Already it was legendary, and they relished the bit parts they were playing. Jackson called them "alligators"—after "all those allegations you people in the press keep making"—and it became their trademark. They filled the plane with stuffed alligators, pasted alligator posters on the walls, bought every shirt, every hat and pin, they could find with an alligator emblem. And around their necks they wore brightly colored toy alligators with metal snaps. It was part souvenir, part badge of honor. It signified the bond they had forged in all those hours together, black and white strangers united by a child's plaything. Gleefully they would click away whenever Jackson would enter a room, from the stuffy Commonwealth Club in San Francisco to the presidential palace in Panama City. Even Secret Service agents carried the clacking toys; when they wanted to get the reporters' attention, they'd click away too.

It became a crazed endurance contest, and they would not leave. Even when their home offices ordered them to take a break, Jackson regulars chose to stay with the doomed caravan, keep on winding down the backroads, keep cradling against the worn-out pews. Let other campaigns have the fancy hotel rooms and regular meals. They were going other places, seeing other things they had not seen before: tears of joy in dingy slums, sweet-singing choirs in dirt-poor country towns. It was more exciting than anything most of them had ever done. And moving, hopeful. "Historic," the candidate would yell. "Hysterical," they'd reply, and each knew the other was telling part of the truth.

"Lord, help me to hold out—until my Saviour comes," the

140-voice choir, resplendent in light yellow robes with green trim, sang in another Shiloh Baptist Church that could have been anywhere he stopped. "It takes grits, grease—and greenbacks for Jesse to get elected. So dig down deep in your pockets," the minister implored the congregation. One church member who'd written songs for Muhammad Ali and for the American Bicentennial sang one she'd written for Jesse Jackson:

> . . . you're a brave man,
> You loved God and you took your stand.
> You know we are meant for more,
> More than we have had before. . . .

"Thank you, sir," said the local deacon who introduced him, "for giving us back our self-respect."

"There is an emerging spirit," Jackson told them. Then he shouted: *"Don't matter how dark it is, there is a sunny side, somewhere.* Don't tell me the glass is half-empty. I say it is half-full."

"Damn, the man sure can talk," said one new reporter walking out of the church.

"Yeah, but I hear the motel tonight is a real dump," one of the tour regulars replied.

It was part crusade, part carnival, part grueling trek. It was also a death watch. No one could forget that. "It was something around him you could almost feel," Democratic vice-presidential candidate Geraldine Ferraro told one of the authors several months after the 1984 election. Recalling campaigning with Jackson in several southern cities in October, Ferraro said that she "had never been so afraid . . . I've been on stage with [Senator Edward] Kennedy lots of times too, and he's always a target, but that was nothing like this. This was just a feeling that something was imminent, something menacing. I've never felt anything like that before. In fact, I told my kids [who were traveling with the campaign], 'I don't want you anywhere near.'" And the three kids stayed away from Jackson, Ferraro added. The threat of violence never disappeared. Even the camera crews chasing him wore bullet-proof vests. Late at night, off-duty Secret Service agents would sink down on a bar stool and unload their fears. "When I hear someone in a crowd say 'Come over here, Jesse,' my blood runs cold," said one veteran bodyguard who'd been with George

Wallace the day Arthur Bremer opened fire. The Service asked Jackson repeatedly not to plunge into crowds, but he ignored the requests. Please, they pleaded, look at the tapes we have of the Wallace shooting; that way you'll understand our problems, our procedures. He refused to look. Of course I worry about getting shot, he once conceded. I'd be crazy not to. But I won't let it paralyze me. Publicly he discussed the threat of assassination only once, near the Memphis, Tennessee, motel where Martin Luther King, Jr., had been gunned down. "I'm sensitive: I want to live as other people do. I want the conveniences and comforts of life as other people do," he said, staring for a moment at the building where James Earl Ray had hidden. "There's danger and I know there will be more blood spilled because there's still a lot of meanness and violence," he said quickly, then steered the conversation into another direction. But some of those who guarded him weren't convinced. "There's nothing this guy would like more than to get a nice wound that doesn't hurt too much," one agent said.

Everywhere they expected trouble. Sensing a threat, they slammed into a man carrying a bag of knives and forks in snowy Montpelier, Vermont; in Helena, Arkansas, they asked local police to remove a well-known town character when he stood up in a rally and motioned toward Jackson; on an Alabama highway agents pulled his van over to the side and quickly transferred him to a waiting sedan and sped away after getting reports about a man with a rifle up ahead; in Hartford, Connecticut, where Jackson wanted to walk several hundred feet from a newspaper office to an insurance company office, agents instead hustled him into his bullet-proof limousine and drove him on a longer, round-about way: another death threat had just been received. There were others, over three hundred Jackson once insisted; while the Secret Service would not provide numbers, agents admitted that there were more threats against this black candidate than against all the other candidates combined. It could happen at any moment. That too was why reporters were there; one network (CBS) provided two camera crews to watch him at all times. "It's my job to stop it—and yours to see it," said the agent, taking one more sip of beer in the hotel bar.

"We are very impressed with our gains on this night [March 13] . . . each campaign we get more numbers and more support,"

Jackson told supporters in a Birmingham hotel as the Super Tuesday votes were being tallied. He made it sound like the sweetest victory. But he had not won a single state. Or even come close. Indeed, in many black areas, he'd been relatively weak. Mondale, with Arrington's muscle, had squeezed by Jackson in Birmingham. Macon County (Alabama) was 84 percent black, but Jackson had barely gotten 60 percent of the vote there. Overall he'd limped home with 19.6 percent of the vote—fourth, in Alabama, behind Mondale, Hart, and the faltering Glenn.

Still, his 21.6 percent showing in Georgia placed him in a solid third (behind Mondale and Hart). And it was above the 20 percent showing required to keep matching federal campaign funds. In all, he had carried four congressional districts in the South, including Atlanta. The 350,000 votes he won in the region were nearly double Ronald Reagan's margin of victory (180,000 votes) in five southern states in 1980. The implication, Jackson's aides said, was this: the Jackson factor could tip the scales for the Democratic party ticket in November, 1984.

Whatever the facts, the interpretation is what counted, and Jackson announced he'd survived Super Tuesday: "in 1972, when I was fighting for a seat at the Democratic National Convention, George McGovern was the presidential nominee . . . [Reuben] Askew, the keynote speaker. I shot by them." The crowd in the ballroom cheered. "Alan Cranston, powerful four-term senator from California. . . . Fritz Hollings, governor of South Carolina when I couldn't even use the bathroom in the state capitol; him sitting high, looking low. . . . well, I shot by them." And the crowd cheered again. "John Glenn, up there orbiting the earth." Here Jackson's hand made a slow sweeping arc, up and slowly down. "While I was out walking the country roads, trying to scrape two coins together to ride the bus. *Well, done shot past him,*" he thundered, arm thrusting upward as the crowd roared its delight.

Super Tuesday had done more than help set him apart from the others. It also helped him light a fire in black America. "The Rainbow Coalition will be in this race until San Francisco—and beyond," Jackson had shouted, and now more people would have to take the words seriously. The next morning a black Birmingham cabbie savored the prospect: "he ain't gonna win, but he ain't gonna quit either."

Hollings, Cranston, and Askew had dropped out of the race

after New Hampshire. After Super Tuesday, Glenn and McGovern called it quits. As the 1984 presidential campaign headed back north—to Illinois, Pennsylvania, and New York—the eight-man Democratic field had been narrowed to three: a former vice-president of the United States, a United States senator—and a black preacher who'd never held a public office in his life.

6. POWER

April 1, 1984. Sunday morning. New York City. In a grey drizzle, the armor-plated car jerks to a halt outside the New York broadcast center. The neighborhood is nearly deserted, but the well-muscled agents spring from their cars. The candidate steps into the street. As always, he is late. In just three minutes, he is scheduled to appear live on a national interview program. For that kind of exposure most politicians arrive early. Jackson chooses not to. He has been in a hurry all his life, but now they can wait for him.

Inside, the broadcast executives are getting nervous, snubbing out cigarettes, swearing. "Where the hell is Jackson? Who does he think he is," one mutters. As their anger builds, the candidate outside straightens the bullet-proof lining of his blue raincoat and glances at his watch.

"Reverend, we better hurry up," the nervous company employee tells him.

"Did I cut it close enough?" Jackson grins. Strutting into the lobby, he stops outside a bathroom. "I think I got time to go here," he says to no one in particular but loud enough for all to hear. A few minutes later he strolls into the studio. The show has already begun. Like Lilliputians, stagehands swarm all over him, lashing him down with microphones and cables.

"Good morning, Reverend Jackson," the interview starts, and it goes just the way the candidate has imagined—just the right combination of fact and indignation, just enough of the well-rehearsed phrases sprayed round the studio like machine-gun fire—but with the proper dollop of humor, the confident smile. Firm yet relaxed. Tough, smooth, electronic-cool, just as he wishes.

When the program ends, the broadcast staff thanks him profusely: "it really was a fine interview, Reverend. Thank you so much for interrupting your busy schedule to be with us." They shake his hand good-bye but curse his arrogance as soon as the door closes behind him, knowing then what he has known all along: that even with their sophisticated hardware and access to millions of people, control for the moment has belonged to this descendant of slaves who is running for something that he, better than the others, knows is beyond reach. Power. The illegitimate son from Greenville had accumulated a kind of power all right, and he was spending it almost as fast as he got it. This too he understood. Funny, isn't it, he once mused, how precarious it is, how quickly it can all slip away.

7.

FARRAKHAN

April 2, 1984. Jackson was leaving a fund-raiser at New York's posh Tavern on the Green restaurant, and his mood was sour. "I didn't say it, I didn't inspire it, I don't condone it," he snapped at reporters. He had spent fifteen minutes on the telephone with *Washington Post* executive editor Benjamin Bradlee—and he hadn't scored too many points. Bradlee considered him an old buddy, but now Bradlee was furious. Who does this guy Farrakhan think he is? he fumed. The Black Muslim leader had threatened "to punish with death" *Post* reporter Milton Coleman, and Bradlee was indignant. "We're taking this goddamned thing very seriously—a man's life could be at stake," he stormed. Jackson, on the defensive, said he would talk again with Farrakhan. He also suggested that Coleman and Farrakhan sit down together. Bradlee wasn't buying any of it. Coleman was off the Jackson campaign, effective immediately. "I'm really disappointed in you, Jesse," Bradlee added.

Some two dozen reporters and cameras were stationed between the door of the restaurant and Jackson's car. Minutes before, Farrakhan had ducked out a side entrance after meeting with Jackson and his supporters inside, and the reporters were in no mood to be given the slip again. "No comment" wouldn't be enough this time. Was he going to repudiate Farrakhan—or wasn't he? "I discourage violence or intimidation or threats or the implication of it anywhere, any time," he told them. But do you repudiate Farrakhan? they repeated. The more they persisted, the angrier he got. "Why are you talking around the point?" one reporter asked. "You know what Farrakhan said." "That's a lie," Jackson shot back, getting into his car and driving off.

The two men did not appear together in public again, but the firestorm did not subside. Jackson would not back down—he would not repudiate Farrakhan. "That's selling out," he said, slamming his fist down for emphasis. The pressure and outrage built, but Jackson would not give in. Privately he counseled Farrakhan: "I've advised him how to say 'no comment.' Or how to preach away from the storm, don't hit everything head on." Jackson's friends, Chicago attorney Thomas Todd and former Manhattan borough president Percy Sutton had also tried to intercede with the Muslim leader. So had another Jackson counselor, Harvard Medical School professor Alvin Poussaint. In June, after Farrakhan labeled Judaism a "dirty" religion, Poussaint at Jackson's urging spoke again to Farrakhan by phone and told the Muslim leader that he would be "doing the Reverend [Jackson] a real favor" if he would temper his future remarks—and apologize for language that had so outraged Jews.

"You know, Poussaint, everything you say makes sense," Poussaint recalled Farrakhan answering. "That's good politics. But that stuff is for politicians. It's of this world. I'm not a politician. I'm a prophet. And prophets never apologize," Farrakhan told the exasperated Harvard psychiatrist. "How do you deal rationally with someone who thinks like that?" Poussaint asked a visitor long after the phone conversation. "You don't," he answered his own question.

Jackson knew that efforts like Poussaint's and Sutton's would only partially succeed. Farrakhan was Farrakhan; he won't be muzzled for long, Jackson told aides. "He's brilliant . . . but he's also naive," Jackson sighed. He was beginning to sense that Farrakhan was bound more to his own crusade than to Jackson's. Each outburst that caused whites to gnash their teeth also brought Farrakhan enormous notoriety—and greater cachet in the black community. During one controversy triggered by a Farrakhan statement, an annoyed staffer asked, what's wrong with this guy—is he crazy? "Like a fox," Jackson replied.

What is it that I'm saying that engenders fear in the hearts of our oppressors? Just to mention my name, it strikes terror in the hearts of some white people.

(Louis Farrakhan, March, 1985, Chicago)

He lived in a quiet neighborhood where most of the residents were white, and at night in his living room he liked to play Mozart on the violin. Born Louis Eugene Walcott, and Episcopalian, he'd grown up in Boston, in a Jewish area that was turning black. His neighborhood had been tense, but he'd had no trouble with the angry whites who were leaving. Except when, at the age of 12, he punched a white boy for no reason. "And I lived with the pain of that for years. . . . because it was unjustified . . . that young boy never said a word to me, he never bothered me. . . . It was wrong to inflict pain on any man without justification," he said much later.[46]

In high school he was an honor student and track star; in church, an acolyte. In the marriage of thirty years to his high school sweetheart, Betsy Ross, there had been nine children. She had encouraged him to become a musician, and after nearly three years at a North Carolina teachers' college he had turned performer, full-time: "Calypso Gene." "The Charmer," the billboards read, and that career had been promising.

When he abandoned it for religion, the money quickly ran out, and he became little more than an urban scavenger, so poor that "my wife and I would go to Boston's Haymarket Square at the end of the day on Saturday and pick up discarded produce that was in good condition. . . . Rejoicing, we could go home and feed our family."[47] By then he had dropped the "slave name" of Walcott and was a fervent Black Muslim, calling himself "Louis X." In 1965, the leader of the Nation of Islam, Elijah Muhammad, changed it again—to Louis Farrakhan, "a very modern name of God," Muhammad told him. The old man promised to tell more about the name; but a few days later Elijah Muhammad died, and years later Louis Farrakhan still wasn't sure what the word meant.

He don't need you as a maid no more, black woman. He got boat people from Europe that are cleaning his toilets. He got European boat people now making his nasty beds, they don't need you any more.

(Chicago, April, 1984)

He didn't welcome white visitors at the stone house with the clipped lawn on Chicago's south side. White America would hear only the imprecations, would see only the clenched fist and the "Fruits of Islam" bodyguards who surrounded him, stone-faced men in bow ties (they feared that long ties could be turned into a deadly choking weapon). The enemy is everywhere, Farrakhan told them, and the Fruits of Islam were poised to strike; a paramilitary elite in scrubbed shirts and "shabazz" haircuts, they scanned every crowd to protect the minister who saw himself as an Old Testament prophet. Words were his only weapons, white-hot, sometimes apocalyptic phrases sent screeching into the darkened lives of his believers like rounds of artillery shells, whining overhead and lighting up the skies and exploding all around, boom boom, boom boom, pounding away, leaving them dazed and trembling and, Farrakhan hoped, aroused, their torpor broken. He declared war on "the blue-eyed white devils," and whites in turn regarded him as some oddball fanatic who prowled through the garbage of America's ghettos, fomenting rebellion and predicting race war. It was a caricature, cruel and twisted, but it was also an image he wanted, one he nurtured. It set him apart and brought him attention and respect.

The black man in America's death is not permanent. He can be risen from this death, and this is exactly why they fear these words coming from my mouth. Because the words in my mouth have the power to raise the dead to life.

(Chicago, June, 1984)

The living dead did not lack targets. Whites in general, Jews in particular. He insisted that he was not anti-Semitic, but when he ripped into Jews from the podium his flock would cheer and a smile would cross his face. His language was charged: Jews in the media were "demons"—the creation of Israel was "an outlaw act." Judaism itself was a "dirty" religion. In his kingdom Jews were castigated—and put on notice. "If you harm this brother [Jackson], I warn you in the name of Allah this will be the last one you harm," he proclaimed on February 25 in Chicago as Jesse Jackson stood beside him.

He saw himself as an American ayatollah Inspired, he pronounced judgments and promised vengeance, especially on those who had violated his own code and harmed his concept of black liberation. To Louis Farrakhan, *Washington Post* reporter Milton Coleman was not only "a no-good . . . filthy . . . dog." The reporter who first disclosed that Jackson had called Jews "Hymie" was also "a traitor . . . a Judas, Uncle Tom." An example must be made of Coleman, Farrakhan declared; Coleman must be banished. "From now on I'm going to try to get every church in Washington, D.C., to put him out. Put him out. Whenever he hits the door, tell him he's not wanted. If he brings his wife with him, tell his wife she can come in if she leaves him." And that is not all Coleman should suffer, Farrakhan said. "At this point, no physical harm," the prophet thundered, but "one day soon we will punish you with death." Later Farrakhan insisted that the words did not constitute a death threat, but the *Washington Post* was taking no chances. *Post* executives remembered that Black Muslim leader Malcolm X had been gunned down shortly after Farrakhan had said he was "worthy of death." *New York Times* reporter Paul Delaney remembered too. In 1972, after Farrakhan railed against articles Delaney had written about Muslim money problems and criminal activity, Delaney asked for and got police protection; patrol cars cruised by his Washington home. "You never know what someone who heard him might have thought," Delaney said later. So the *Post* would take no chances. Coleman would not cover Jackson again; guards would watch Coleman's house. "Hell yes, I was frightened," Coleman said months after the incident. "Some of the people who follow him are crazy enough to do anything."

What do you fear? I know what you fear. You fear the ideas that I represent because my ideas from God and Muhammad mean the end of your world. . . . It is an act of mercy to white people that we end your world.

(March, 1985, Chicago)

Many blacks laughed at his declarations. When Farrakhan threatened to "lead an army of black men and women to Washington . . . and negotiate for a separate state of our own," they chuckled or looked away. Carl Rowan, Vernon Jarrett, Bayard Rustin, Tony Brown, the Reverend Calvin Butts, Roger Wilkins rebuked him publicly. Newark, New Jersey, mayor Kenneth Gibson wrote a letter to Nathan Perlmutter of the Anti-Defamation League that Perlmutter delighted in passing around. "Black people are able to think for themselves, and the great majority of us do not subscribe to the negative ethnic, racial or religious references and speeches," Gibson wrote. "The implied threats by Muslim Minister Farrakhan," he continued, "do not represent the thinking of myself or other blacks who know the difference between righteousness and rhetoric." Farrakhan's statements offended many black ministers as well, and during the campaign they urged Jackson not to embrace Farrakhan. They're just as worked up as the Jews are, aide Gene Wheeler thought. "The Baptist ministry in this country was totally against that whole situation and Jackson lost, for a moment, many of the black Baptist ministers who supported him whole hog and sinker. They didn't attack him like the Jewish community attacked him. But their dislike for what his relationship was with Farrakhan was the same, absolutely the same . . . it was that intense . . . the ministers saw Jesse as bringing in an undesirable that he shouldn't bring in."

Jackson argued with them. You're wrong about this man. Give him a chance, he asked. "He is a man of great intellect . . . bright and humble whom I respect very much," he said. Surprisingly, no one saw trouble coming. Early on Jackson's advisors had anticipated problems he might encounter—foreign policy advisor Jack O'Dell's reported links with the Communist party, for instance—but Farrakhan was not one of them. "In any movement like this there's a certain naivete," the Reverend Bill Howard said months later. "We were guilty of being so clear about Minister Farrakhan and what the minister represented that we did not foresee any problem. . . . We just had not anticipated how unfamiliar the American public and their sons and daughters in the press would be, how little they would understand this."

They did know that Farrakhan struck a chord that even Jackson sometimes missed. "He articulates the vision and anger of people who feel they are suffering because of their mistreatment by whites," said Dr. James Turner of Cornell University.[48] Farrakhan knew how to ignite a crowd. Blacks "have always gotten a vicarious satisfaction and pleasure out of a black man giving white people hell," said psychiatrist Alvin Poussaint of the Harvard Medical School. And Farrakhan's version was pure, unadulterated—he dared say what many of them felt but could not afford to say. When Tuskegee, Alabama, mayor Johnny Ford introduced Farrakhan in Saint Louis (March, 1984) as "the concise conscience of Black America," 250 black mayors leaped to their feet and applauded for several minutes. Estimates of his organization's membership ranged from five to ten thousand, but thousands more came to hear him speak; after the Jackson campaign, the crowds were even larger: a reported five thousand people in

Houston, and in Philadelphia; six thousand in Detroit for an affair that one year earlier had attracted only a few hundred; in Atlanta, seven thousand reportedly packed a hall and an overflow crowd outside chanted his name. Explaining why she had come to hear him at a 1985, February, Chicago rally, the Reverend Willie T. Barrow, a longtime Jackson confidante, told the fifteen thousand assembled, "I'm here because number one, I love my brother, Minister Farrakhan. The devil don't like it, Chicago don't like it, the world don't like it—but we love it."[49] And the huge crowd roared.

There's one other black man in America that has power to raise the dead and that is myself. But you don't know Farrakhan.
(March 11, 1984, Chicago)

By 1984, Jackson and Farrakhan needed each other. The Muslim chieftain, whose membership had been lagging, needed to attract attention; Jackson needed Farrakhan to reach the black underclass that had turned its back on the system. For several years the two men had been friends, they had visited each other's homes, but now they became partners. On Thanksgiving night, 1983, Farrakhan visited him again, and at Jackson's dining room table the two put the finishing touches on their agreement. The partnership would be symbolic—and practical. Farrakhan, who provided Fruits of Islam bodyguards for Jackson until Secret Service agents were assigned, accompanied Jackson to Syria, where he impressed the Syrians with his fluent command of Arabic prayers. During the early days of his presidential campaign Jackson designated Farrakhan one of his "surrogates"; in that role the minister not only warmed up crowds before Jackson addressed them—he also spoke out vigorously for the campaign. At age 51, he registered to vote for the first time and urged his followers to do likewise. Jackson, standing nearby, hailed the moment as "historic . . . an important coming-together." For a while, Farrakhan was content to play the subordinate role; for the time being, that would best serve Jackson's interests—and his own. "You're not ready for Farrakhan," he told one Chicago audience, "but God is ready. So God gives you one that you like, that's closer to you. To start you jumping up out of your grave. My job takes off where Jesse's leaves off. That's why he and I are together."

But he never forgot his own agenda. Above all he was committed to that. And soon he would strike out again on his own, to the detriment of his patron. By then it was obvious that Jackson could never win—and that his campaign was gaining few white supporters. By then the possible benefits for the Nation of Islam had been gained too. So Farrakhan could reassert his own identity. Being someone else's surrogate, even Jesse Jackson's, had hobbled him too much. He could not be as outspoken. He had worked hard for Jackson, he had been restrained, but now he was chafing at the restrictions. So he became the Farrakhan of old, the firebrand. And when he did he became too great a liability and had to be jettisoned from the campaign. In a way he did not foresee, he was a catalyst: not only did he widen the rift between blacks and Jews—he also helped define the character of Jesse Jackson.

The Jews don't like Farrakhan so they call me Hitler. Well, that's a good name. Hitler was a very great man. He wasn't great for me as a black person. But he was a great German. Now I'm not proud of Hitler's evil against Jewish people, but that's a matter of record. He rose Germany up from nothing. Well, in a sense you could say there's a similarity in that we are rising our people up from nothing.

(March 11, 1984, Chicago)

Before Farrakhan, some Jews were still willing to give Jackson a chance. They had misgivings—Jackson was still on trial, and they were profoundly skeptical—but their minds were not yet closed. Farrakhan shut them—after this there could be no doubt. "Hymie" could have been a slip of the tongue; almost everybody uses slurs from time to time; even friends can disagree about the Middle East, they told themselves. But Farrakhan went beyond that. "Unspeakable stuff," one Jewish leader put it. How Jackson handled this radical black supporter, Jews agreed, would be the ultimate test. The question, as Harvard Law School's Alan Dershowitz put it, was this: "was he willing to rebuff ten thousand blacks by repudiating the racist dogma of a Farrakhan in order to reach out and potentially get the support of more whites? That for him was the litmus test. He failed it. He deliberately failed it. He said to America, 'I'm sticking to my own community. I am not gonna be a winner. I am not gonna be a national politician. I am not gonna endanger my small coalition to build a more fragile but much more broadly based community.' That was the test. And he made his decision."

The decision sent one message to Jews, another to blacks: that on this issue, Jackson would not be co-opted, that he was still one of them. Jews, on the other hand, were dismayed, even horrified. They felt that Mondale, Hart, and the rest of the Democratic party were too slow to anger, too unwilling to offend Jackson and black voters the party would need. They could accept the political fact that Jackson, by now a symbol of black aspirations, couldn't be bloodied too much. What they couldn't understand was what seemed to them to be the silence about Farrakhan. Why, they wondered, are the others so reticent? Al Vorspan, of the Union of American Hebrew Congregations, said:

> . . . what went beyond Farrakhan to me was an unwritten axiom of decency in American life which was usually observed. And that is if a bigot came down the pike spewing crap publicly, then he was the problem not just of the group he was kicking around and dumping on—but of all decent groups in society. . . . It was never "this is your problem, kid. I'm out of it."
>
> But in this one I had the feeling—and so did every Jew I know—that everybody was out to lunch. Nobody was around. That's what I think was profound. Where was everybody? Where was the National Conference of Christians and Jews? Or the National Council of Churches? Or individual Catholic bishops? Anybody? Not to mention black leadership. Also out to lunch. Political leadership in our country, mostly out to lunch

They're all paralyzed, Vorspan thought—this Farrakhan poison has infected more than a handful of black fanatics. Where, he and others wondered, would it end?

This I want the Jews to know and we want the world to know: that they are not the chosen people of God. . . . You hate us because we dare to say that we are the chosen people of God and can back it up. We are ready to do battle with you.

(June, 1984, Chicago)

Jackson repudiated the message—but not the messenger. His

people would understand the difference. "My sense of redemption," Jackson explained. "Jesus repudiated the politics of assassination, but he did not repudiate Judas," he said on one broadcast. On an April 24 flight to San Antonio he elaborated on the point: "I don't have the moral power to condemn a whore. The actions, yes. The person, no. . . . It's just not in my religion. That's something very absolute with me," he said firmly. He pointed out that critics had applauded him when he'd "reached out" to Orville Faubus (former Arkansas governor) and to George Wallace "even though people got killed because of him. Viola Liuzzo, hell she died because Wallace got things so worked up . . . I reached out to him . . . I've reached out to some of the lowest-down bastards you can imagine. . . . My whole life is about redemption; I can't change that now. . . . [South Carolina senator Ernest] Hollings was one mean son of a bitch when I was growing up, lots of people forget that, but I don't. People change, I know it, I've seen it."

Farrakhan can change too, he'd argue, if he's given a chance. Hell, he went on, the man has been an outcast for years—you've got to give him some room. "My purpose is to bring blacks into the system, not to drive them away," he said. Keep them outside and they'll throw bricks through windows. Isn't it better to bring them inside where we can at least talk to them, perhaps even change them? he continued. That was one of the few tenets he still believed after all the years. Let reporters snicker. This was how he saw himself, if few others did.

The wounds from "Hymie-Hymietown" still hadn't closed either. Now he felt the people who'd lambasted him in Manchester were demanding another pound of flesh. Again his mission was attacked, his ego shaken. Remembering how humiliating it had been to apologize once, he was in no hurry to bow and scrape for a surrogate's perceived misdeeds. Besides, what good had apologizing done in Manchester? His followers drew in close. "It's like they want him to issue a warrant for Farrakhan's arrest," said the historian John Hope Franklin.

"I felt very black at this point," Jackie Jackson recalled, bitterly. "White people were saying now, little children, you're not grown up. In order for you to function with us, this should be your behavior. I thought it was very arrogant of white people to ask us to explain Farrakhan, to ask us to disassociate ourselves from him. . . . We were treated very colored. . . . You don't ask white people to denounce, to disassociate themselves from the

Ku Klux Klan . . . Farrakhan has not gone around and burned crosses and killed people. And lynched them. He voiced his opinion. Jerry Falwell voices his. Nixon. Kennedy," the candidates wife said.

Everything was working against Jackson—timing, geography, ego, ideology. The controversy had caught the campaign off-guard; Jackson was barnstorming through Central America in June when Farrakhan labeled Judaism a "dirty" religion. The candidate was cut off from much of the outraged reaction and didn't initially appreciate the damage that had been done. Aides on the trip with him, equally out of touch, counseled him not to overreact. In addition, his instincts told him now was not the time to turn on Farrakhan. It just feels unnatural, he said. Back home campaign manager Arnold Pinkney knew "Jackson wasn't going to turn on a friend." And Pinkney worried about the political fallout if Jackson did. Recalling what had happened to black Los Angeles mayor Tom Bradley in 1982 when he ran for governor in California and slighted his basic constituency—causing a low turnout among blacks, a factor that contributed to his narrow defeat—Pinkney vowed "I wasn't going to let that happen here."

No one, though, had to tell Jackson that by turning on Farrakhan he risked more than offending the man himself. "He knows what his base is . . . to denounce Farrakhan would separate his own constituency," said aide Gene Wheeler. "Mr. Farrakhan expresses the outrage, the anger of a great many of Mr. Jackson's supporters," explained sociologist Harry Edwards, "and to renounce Mr. Farrakhan would be to renounce the credibility of that outrage, to renounce the credibility of that anger." Renouncing him was tantamount to political suicide; no campaign could be asked to do that, Jackson was told. "To repudiate Farrakhan would be a serious psychological problem for the black community. At this point, I think it is important that community have a sense of identity, even if white America does not understand it, and I told this to Jackson on numerous occasions," said the Reverend Bill Howard.

So as the criticism mounted, Jackson dug in. One day he would refuse to discuss the affair; the next day he would bristle: "Farrakhan is his own boss . . . I can't tell him what to do." From Havana he snapped at a television interviewer that "in America, people have freedom of speech to say what they want, about whom they want to. Don't keep putting me in the middle of this."

Of course, he was in the middle. In Washington Pinkney raced to cut the losses. The controversy over Farrakhan was threatening to drive Jackson's Cuban trip off the front pages and evening newscasts. "I thought it would all blow away, I really did," said Pinkney, but now he realized how wrong he'd been. Everything was focused on Farrakhan; even Pinkney's Jewish friends who hadn't complained to him about "Hymie" were calling now: how could you let him do this, Arnold?—this time your man has gone too far! Alarmed, Pinkney tried to move quickly. He would act before Jackson could stop him; together with Walter Fauntroy (congressman for the District of Columbia and Jackson advisor) and advisor Roger Wilkins he drafted a statement criticizing Farrakhan's remarks about Jews—"morally indefensible . . . reprehensible," it read in part—then telephoned Jackson in Cuba. Jackson's mind was on Castro then and little else; the deal he'd been promised before he left the mainland to release prisoners from Cuban jails seemed to be coming unstuck. The phone connection was terrible; the two parties could barely hear one another. Jackson didn't balk; Pinkney was surprised, he'd expected some resistance. If that's your thinking, I'll respect it, he said. They agreed to refine the statement and get back to him. Only there wasn't time, not if they wanted to make the network newscasts that night. The aides felt they had no choice: Jackson was coming back late that same evening, and they wanted the controversy over before he stepped on American soil. So late that afternoon Pinkney released the statement himself, and only later did he call Jackson and read it to him. No one called Farrakhan.

The statement helped quell part of the storm, but some of his critics felt that Jackson still hadn't gone far enough, that he'd traded hate and bigotry for political expediency. They called him weak. "You know what I think Farrakhan knows? I think he knows where Jackson's money has come from," barked New York mayor Ed Koch. "I think it comes from Libya."[50] Jackson denied the charge, but there were others. The slender man in the bow tie and tailor-made suit had become another albatross for Jackson, but this time he would not capitulate.

"As-salaam alaikum" (peace be with you), the Muslim leader would shout to the crowd.

"Wa-alaikum salaam" (and with you), the crowd would reply.

Standing nearby, Jesse Jackson would fold his arms and smile.

8.

BACK NORTH

March 18, 1984. Jackson timed it right. He swept into the Fellowship Missionary Baptist Church while there was still forty-five minutes left in Pastor Clay Evans' "Friendship Hour," a weekly live-from-the-pulpit broadcast designed to reach "everyone out there in radioland, in your homes, in your automobiles, behind bars."

Jackson knew the lure of the Friendship Hour better than most. He also knew the numbers: arrive during the broadcast and you multiply an audience of a couple of hundred Baptists fanning themselves inside one south-side Chicago church into several thousand potential black voters across a wide area of the city. It was two days before the Illinois primary, and things weren't going well.

That night Jackson had turned in a lackluster performance at the Illinois Democratic presidential debate—he had been less quick-witted than at the eight-man debate at Dartmouth in January, less aggressive than he would be in the three-man forum on March 28 in New York. He'd been more a face in the crowd than a standout in his home state. Mondale was looking stronger all the time. And in an earlier test of wills with Chicago mayor Harold Washington over who would control the state's convention delegates, the mayor had refused to yield and Jackson had been forced to back down. In his adopted hometown, the retreat had been embarrassing.

The black church would ensure him a crowd. The Friendship

Hour, 9 to 10 every Sunday night, would extend it. His ego needed a boost. It had worked before. Almost nineteen years earlier when he'd first heard the velvet-voiced Evans preaching and singing over the airwaves, Jackson was a nobody, just another ambitious young man up from the South driving down the Dan Ryan Expressway, almost broke, a young wife at home, three babies, studying for the ministry, thinking he was a born leader but with nothing to lead, with no way to reach the masses, a young man with dreams of greatness driving down a busy road in a town where no one knew his name and fearful that things would stay that way. Then Evans started singing "I Must Have Jesus" on Jackson's car radio. Evans was reaching thousands, moving people, getting through. Evans moved Jackson that day on the Dan Ryan. The 24-year-old divinity student turned his car around, headed for the Fellowship Missionary Baptist Church, and got there before the broadcast was over.

"He came right into my office and stretched out on the couch, feet up and all, I'll never forget that," Evans recalled. "I looked at him as if he was kind of strange, you know, taking over my office like that. A person doesn't usually act that way when they first come into your office. . . . Call it ego, call it pride . . . I looked at him slouched on the couch, and I felt like you do when you hold your baby for the first time in your arms; you have hope, but you don't know if they're going to use that personality and charisma for good."

Jackson became a Fellowship Missionary fixture. Michael Shaw, a church music director, remembered Jackson as "a shy kind of bird at first," standing in the church's foodline for free groceries to feed his family. "But once he got started, you could tell he was a leader." Jackson began working with the youth of the church, organizing retreats to Michigan and Wisconsin. He launched Operation Breadbasket from Fellowship Missionary, picketing white businesses for jobs and better service. Ultimately he became co-pastor, a title he still held in 1985. And Evans also began sharing the Fellowship Hour microphone with his rising protégé. In those early days of the civil rights movement, Jackson brought Martin Luther King, Jr., up from Atlanta. "When Martin couldn't get a pulpit in Chicago, he could get this pulpit," Jackson hollered at his audience that coming-home Sunday in March, 1984.

And the ovation was thunderous for their pastor-turned-presidential candidate. The 250-member Fellowship Missionary choir clapped and shouted in their shiny blue robes, rhythm building, voices rising, until they blurred into one undulating wave across the stage, and Jackson sang and raised his hands over his head and shut his eyes tight, a thousand hymns and Bible quotes away from Mondale and Hart and "Hymie" and Farrakhan and second primaries and disputed Defense Department cost overruns.

"Who you gonna vote for on Tuesday?" someone yelled.

"Jesse," came the shout.

"I don't hear so good," someone yelled again.

"Jesse," the scream went out.

Jackson let the adulation wash over him, standing tall and straight inside the tabernacle where he'd come nearly two decades earlier, where he'd mastered the magic he'd heard on the expressway. "If you want to be kept, God will keep you," the choir rang out each word as the congregation shouted and swayed.

The black church, Jackson said as he took the microphone, "is the only place where we can express ourselves—the only place where we can shout and sing . . . it's our form of free expression." Bosses, Jackson bellowed out to ensure his point, "they fire us without notice, they break our spirit, they break our hearts . . . some of us go along to get along . . . but if we can just make it to 'Fellowship' on Sunday. . . ."

What happened that July day in 1965, Clay Evans explained later, was a melding of two minds both bent on black power. "We saw something in each other . . . we took each other in." Fellowship Missionary Church had been his crucible, where his ego was forged with opportunity and a sense of power, Jackson suggested that March night in 1984. "To some of us this is the only platform we'll ever have . . . to some, it's a way out," he told the congregation. "That which I learned here, I've taken all around the world, and it's worked," Pastor Jackson boasted to his adoring flock.

Then, in an instant, he calmed. He was the cool, contained candidate again, watching with amusement as the crowd surged closer and closer to his tense government bodyguards. At one point, Jackson leaned down toward the press corps and giggled: "This is a Secret Serviceman's nightmare." But this was Jackson's safe port. He knew it.

Jackson would turn to the black church more and more as the

primaries continued and it became abundantly clear that his would be a mostly black campaign aimed at trying to build political leverage for himself and grass-roots black Americans. The black church—the traditional haven since slave days, where raids and boycotts and marches were planned and wounds were bound and the dead were mourned—would become Jackson's haven too, the source of some of his best crowds, the bulk of his money, much of his energy, many of his votes.

"This is home. I can't run any farther than here," Jackson told the Friendship Hour crowd.

April, 1984. He was back in the North. Campaigning in the old cities with the large black populations. The northern battlegrounds—Chicago, New York City, Philadelphia—would show whether the spark he had lit on Super Tuesday had spread beyond the South.

Jackson's spirits were high. Once again he had confounded some of his critics with his showing in caucuses held in Arkansas, Mississippi, and South Carolina on March 17. He had complained that the entire caucus system was unfair, "stacked" against long shots like him, "undemocratic." A factory worker who favored Jackson, he argued, would have to make his preference known as his boss, probably a staunch labor man who supported Mondale, looked on. "That's intimidating," Jackson argued; they vote that way in Soviet-bloc countries, not here. Caucuses might be good business for party bosses, he continued—caucuses were cheaper, attracted fewer people, and were easier to control—and good for an organization candidate, like Mondale. But they were not good, he said, for Jesse Jackson. Besides, he went on, many of his supporters were new to politics and unfamiliar with the process. In a caucus, where confusing rules could cause some to fall prey to savvy political operatives, Jackson saw danger for his followers.

There was only one recourse. The preacher would teach caucus strategy. In Mississippi, Arkansas, and Virginia (held over two days) he told them to think of the caucus as a church meeting. Remember those sessions where the minister is in trouble, he reminded them. First come the prayers, then singing, then testimonials. Then more singing "to make you feel good . . . then to wear you out." More singing. More prayers. Gradually, people start to leave. "Then when the crowd is thinned out, and only ten people are left, the agenda moves to reinstatement. And to salary hikes . . . it's like that at caucuses . . . when you start leaving, they start voting."

Be ready for the political tricks, he warned them. "Ministers, you take your congregations to the caucuses and then tarry there with your people . . . have your Saturday choir rehearsals at the site of the caucus. Give your free hamburgers away at the site of the caucus. . . . Go and stay until the vote comes out. . . . If we waited a lifetime, we can wait three hours . . . just sit right down and wait until your time comes." They're counting on our ignorance, he continued. Well, let's outsmart them. "Get up early on Saturday morning and get your visitin' out the way early . . . do your washing and ironing early that day . . . don't stop for no egg salad sandwich on the way . . . bring your lunch money and your Walkman. . . . You've waited this long, and you can wait a few more hours. It's been a long time since those slave ships landed and when you elect a president. . . . We've known agony and pain and death seeking the right to vote. . . . [Mississippi], your crying time is over. Dry your eyes. Make up your minds; your time has come. Saturday is show-up day and show-down time. Our time has come."

The sermons paid off. Flocks heeded the shepherd. As a result, Jackson did better on Super Saturday (March 17) than many observers thought he would. While he was clobbered in Michigan (Detroit mayor Coleman Young and the United Auto Workers delivered the state to Mondale), in Mississippi Jackson's turnout shocked some. When the results were tallied several weeks later, Jackson had nearly defeated Mondale.

In South Carolina, he did even better: only one other choice, "uncommitted," got more votes. With Senator Ernest Hollings now out of the race, Jackson hoped the Democratic state central committee would declare him its "favorite son" when it met in May.

But Jackson's success—and failure in the caucus system—came together most vividly in Arkansas. Jackson had spent little more than one full day campaigning in Arkansas. There had been virtually no money and no organization. Frank Watkins had worked the state for only two weeks, along with Ernie Green, a former undersecretary of labor in the Carter administration who'd helped integrate Little Rock high schools in the 1950s. Still, Jackson had finished a strong second with 34 percent of the vote to Mondale's 36 percent. Hart was third at 24 percent. Another 400 votes and we would have won, Jackson crowed, pointing out that Arkansas was only 16 percent black.

But the delegate count was infuriating: both Mondale and Hart ended up with more convention delegates—Mondale with 20, third-place finisher Hart with 9—and Jackson, who had nearly won, with only 6. "That's white-collar crime," he thundered. The fact was his vote had been concentrated in just a few isolated areas, while Mondale and Hart won in delegate-rich districts across the state. "Anything that tricky you cannot put much confidence in," Jackson scoffed.

Arkansas became a favorite illustration for Jackson. He cited it to show his potential appeal to white voters—and to show how the system was stacked against him. "There's something perverse about the rules," he would say. "When they made the rules, they didn't have me in mind—they had my kind in mind . . . they're designed to help the big shots and keep out the long shots. Who's a long shot? Well, a southerner is a long shot. A woman is a long shot. A black man." He vowed to continue his fight to get the party to change its delegate selection procedures: "we can't keep fattening frogs for snakes. . . . We must shift from client politics to peer politics . . . it's time for us to be peers, to be equal, not pears to be eaten."

It was in Illinois that the three Democratic finalists would meet head-on for the first time. Returning to his adopted home state, Jackson stepped up his attacks on both opponents for the March 20 vote. To the delight of crowds he gave Mondale the back of his political hand. "They say I'm in Mondale's way. Without Mondale, I'd have won Georgia, South Carolina, and Alabama. *I'd say that he's in my way.*" He criticized Mondale's failure to denounce second primaries and dual-registration in the South. Mondale, he said, is worried about ruffling the feathers of white politicians who need schemes like those to keep blacks from gaining power. "Mondale has caught lockjaw because he wants the votes of both the boll weevils and the cotton. . . . Well, you cannot run with the rabbits and hunt with the hounds," Jackson argued.

He chided Hart for giving two different birth dates—"whichever age he is, I'm still younger," he quipped—and for Hart's penchant for "new ideas." He'd tell audiences how he'd grown up in a house with no running water or electricity, just "a slop jar by the bed—we didn't need a new idea: we needed an indoor bathroom." Neither opponent measured up, he concluded. "Clearly their records are inadequate to make a difference. They must change directions. . . . These are not bad men, but they are not adequate for our times. . . . These are good men; I'm better."

He was asking Illinois blacks to rally round one of their own; he campaigned mostly in black areas, among black groups. And the Illinois black community responded. An estimated 79 percent of them voted for Jackson, helping him win nearly 350,000 votes, 21 percent of the primary total. Again he finished third.

The blackness of his vote was now becoming apparent. And an issue. In all primaries, no more than 9 percent of his total vote had been white.[51] When asked why so few whites voted for him, he quickly introduced the issue of racism. Whites rejected him, he said, not because of his politics—but because of his color. "It is not my fault whites have developed over history a lack of regard for the intelligence and hard work of black people," he told reporters on March 21 in Richmond, Virginia. Whites did so, he continued, "without even thinking," making his political task that much more difficult than either Mondale's or Hart's. Blacks voted for Mondale and Hart; whites did not vote in any numbers for Jackson. His complaint served another purpose. In the future, when he fell short of victory, the blame would rest not on something he had said or done—but on white Americans.

In New York's April 10 primary, Jackson continued to set himself apart. Not only did he court various minority groups—gays, women, Asians, Latinos—he started spending nights in the homes of poor families "to dramatize their poverty." He also stepped up his discussion of such controversial issues as a homeland for Palestinians and civil rights for homosexuals.

In Harlem, police cordoned off a street and residents hung out of tenement windows while Jackson rolled up his sleeves and helped shovel garbage. "When people are respected, garbage isn't left on the street . . . this shows profound disrespect for the poor," he complained. "If you're mad about the slums, vote about it," he hollered up at slum-dwellers. "If you want good medical care, then vote about it. . . . You can't be ignored any more. . . . Never again shall housing projects be left off the agenda. Or old folks or Medicare or welfare recipients. . . . Now there's a new agenda out because I'm running." He was trying to fashion himself as proconsul for the dispossessed. "We're tired of being laughed at, put down, and disregarded. . . . We're not just running for office—

we're running to get free. We shall be treated and respected as equals."

He was smarting that some in the media were treating him like a sideshow to the main event. He was livid over the *New York Times* account of the Chicago debate on March 18—". . . the debate . . . which also included Reverend Jesse Jackson. . . ." On April 1, during a three-way debate at WNBC-TV before the New York vote, Jackson bristled when Mondale and Hart seemed to be attacking one another—and ignoring him. "You haven't any right to go back to that topic and ignore me . . . the constituency I represent and the issues I raise won't go away," he said. Then he rebuked the two for a lack of statesmanship in their ongoing squabble over whether to move the U.S. embassy in Israel from Tel Aviv to Jerusalem. "While we posture about it, people could get hurt." And he came down hard for tougher sanctions against South Africa—and demanded that Mondale and Hart do likewise.

Ultimately he sought big black crowds at churches. Throughout New York City he preached his message of hope, telling them that what he had seen they too could see. "When some say the glass is half-empty, I say it is half-full. When I see a broken window, that's the slummy side. Train a youth to be a glazier. That's the sunny side."

The day before the primary he began reminding crowds that sixteen years earlier, to the very day, Dr. Martin Luther King, Jr., had been assassinated. "Tomorrow we have a chance to roll the stone away. Then there can be a resurrection. Just as there was a crucifixion sixteen years ago. . . . The day of crucifixion in 1968 will be the day of resurrection in 1984."

The fever from Super Tuesday had spread to New York. As Jackson walked down Lennox Avenue in Harlem to a polling place—accompanied by a choir from the Abyssinian Baptist church singing "Walking Up the King's Highway"—neighborhood residents and passersby fell in behind him. Before the day was over a staggering 87 percent of New York blacks had come out to vote for him in the primary. But even with 355,000 votes, 25.6 percent of the total, he again finished third in the delegate count. In New York City, he had outpolled Gary Hart by 100,000 votes. In statewide totals Hart had finished only one percentage point ahead of him—but Hart received almost half again as many convention delegates.

Still, Jackson's delegate total was climbing: now over 100, with the upcoming Pennsylvania primary on April 10 likely to boost that figure even more. He was running third in a three-man race, he told supporters, but he was by no means the odd man out. He would steal an idea from former heavyweight boxing champion Muhammad Ali and develop his own political "rope-a-dope" strategy: build support while Mondale and Hart flailed away at each other, wearing themselves out on the way to what Jackson hoped would be a deadlocked convention where he could hold the balance of power. And in the process, he told listeners, "we're winning our self-respect."

In Philadelphia, 53-year-old Frank Goode (no relation to the city's mayor) waited quietly for Pennsylvania's April 10 primary. He was planning to vote for Jesse Jackson. And against the past. The son of a Virginia sharecropper, Frank Goode still remembered a conversation he had with his parents' boss in 1948: "at that time I asked him why my parents couldn't go out and vote. And the lady that I was working for, she was a white lady, she told me that she didn't think black people had sense enough to vote."

Life had not gone the way Frank Goode had dreamed. In 1950, he had left Virginia—"I didn't want no part of farming"—and had come north. Hoping to become a mortician, he had enrolled in embalming school but had run out of money. He'd worked in a bakery after that, then as a brakeman for a railroad. Until March, 1984, he had worked in a slaughterhouse, at $7.85 an hour when the plant suddenly closed. No notice, no severance. "No sir, not one dime." Since then Frank Goode had worked part-time as a short-order cook; perhaps he'd try that again, maybe not. In the last six months, his wife had died; his two daughters and one son had moved out of the small house on the city's north side.

Frank Goode wasn't one to complain. Or to talk much about himself. But when the subject of Jesse Jackson was introduced, Goode's eyes sparkled and he grew animated. "I think he's dynamite . . . I'm a sleepy-headed man, but I stay up late for him on the news . . . he makes me proud." Is that, he was asked, reason enough to vote for Jackson—because he makes you feel good? Frank Goode pondered the question. He remembered a white woman in Virginia in 1948. Then he answered slowly. "I hate to say this, but that's what it's all about. Racial pride. . . . I'm voting for him because of racial pride."

Philadelphia attorney Obra Kernodle, 36, lived in a different world. Kernodle, a former Carter administration official in Washington, appreciated what Jesse Jackson was doing and wished him well. His wife, in fact, was an avid Jackson supporter and was running as a convention delegate pledged to Jackson. Kernodle wasn't so sure. You've got to be realistic, Kernodle kept saying. Mondale is going to get the nomination. We're going to have to do business with him, not Jesse. Mondale can beat Reagan. Jackson doesn't have a chance. Emotions had their place in politics, Kernodle said, but in the final analysis one had to use judgment, balance the choices, be calculating.

Sitting in his downtown office, Obra Kernodle paused and looked out the window. After all, Philadelphia's black mayor, Wilson Goode, had recommended Mondale. Then Kernodle spoke. "You know, once you get in that booth, it's gonna be mighty hard not to vote for Jesse."

In Pennsylvania's black neighborhoods, the Jackson juggernaut rolled on. Frank Goode and 75 percent of the state's blacks supported Jackson; despite the efforts of Mayor Wilson Goode, Jackson also carried Philadelphia. And he carried Homestead, Pennsylvania, population 5,092, near Pittsburgh, where he had spent one morning talking to unemployed steelworkers, most of them white. "We need someone like Jesse who speaks for poor whites . . . who's not afraid to stand up and give 'em hell," said Ron Weiser, president of steelworkers' local #1397. Jackson helped union leaders distribute free bags of groceries to unemployed workers' families. Overhead a banner read "The Truth Force for President." Overall in Pennsylvania, "The Truth Force" finished third again, with 16 percent of the vote.

After Chicago, New York City, and Philadelphia, no one could dispute Jackson's hold on much of black America. His movement now seemed to be attracting even the onetime doubters; and some of his critics grew silent. "My base is black America," the candidate said simply. If he was not yet its president, said Harvard Law School professor Alan Dershowitz, Jackson was certainly its "prime minister." The night of the Pennsylvania primary, sitting in his hotel room in the Bellevue Stratford Hotel, Jackson had sneered when told the labor vote was dividing between Mondale (the AFL-CIO's endorsed candidate) and Hart. "[AFL-CIO president Lane] Kirkland can't deliver his folks. I can," he said quietly. He was relishing the moment. "Does Jesse Jackson speak for all blacks?" he asked rhetorically, answering his own question. "No. But when you get 85 percent of the vote, you speak for a generous portion."

He was doing more than setting himself up as their spokesman; the movement had gone beyond that. "Jackson made it absolutely clear that the litmus test for your commitment to blackness was whether or not you supported, you endorsed and shared the enthusiasm that he had for his own candidacy," said California's black assembly speaker, Willie Brown. The way Jackson told it, how one voted was a new way to measure one's blackness, a new way to affirm membership in the black community. It was, said his critics, the "politics of race."[52]

Jackson used it like a sledgehammer: you have an obligation, if not to me, then to our people, our race, to your own identity; if I fail, we all step backward; if you're not with me, you're against all of us, you're lacking in allegiance to black interests, to blackness itself. So went the unspoken argument that spelled out the obligation, the duty. To a holy venture. Of running black.

While some grew angry at Jackson's new egotism, more and more black Americans throughout the country felt the pull. Unlike Richard Arrington and Joe Reed and Harvey Gantt earlier, many blacks were now unwilling—perhaps even unable—to resist.

Ken Spaulding's judgment said one thing. His self-esteem, his sense of community, told him another. He was trapped, and the price would be high. Spaulding, about to turn 40, had been careful all his life, and he would be careful now. An ambitious black attorney in Durham, North Carolina, he hoped for a career in politics, and after three terms in the North Carolina legislature he was running for Congress in the state's second congressional district, where two years earlier Mickey Michaux (see chapter 1) had lost a runoff election.

The race promised to be close. Only 37 percent of the district's voting-age public was black, but Spaulding had done his homework, had built a lot of bridges. His image, carefully cultivated, was sober, reasonable, nonthreatening. He had studied the district closely; with a little luck, and enough money, he had an outside chance to win. But he couldn't afford any mistakes. Nor could he ignore polls showing that Jesse Jackson frightened many white voters. His advisors warned him: keep your distance from Jackson.

Ken Spaulding knew the advice made sense. He also knew that Jackson was trying to open up the political system just the way Spaulding was trying to. Repudiating someone like that, Spaulding felt, would be hypocritical. Besides, he wondered, how could he spurn Jackson—then look his two children in the eye? Spaulding wrestled with the decision long and hard. His political future would hang in the balance. And when Jesse Jackson came to the area, there was Ken Spaulding at Jackson's side, at every stop. Spaulding had passed the "litmus test," but the price would be that his opponent capitalized on those joint appearances, publicized them throughout the district, especially where there were a lot of white voters. Ken Spaulding lost the primary contest. It was more than a Jackson backlash—the outcome wasn't even close. But afterward, Spaulding refused to complain about his decision. What he had done, he said, "I had to do."

But for every Ken Spaulding, there were legions of other Americans who shuddered when they were faced with Jackson's candidacy. For some, it was his support for Fidel Castro or an immediate withdrawal of the U.S. military presence in Central America or other parts of his program that some regarded as radical, even dangerous. To some it was Jackson's total lack of experience. "He's never held elective office. The American people are not about to put as president in the Oval Office a man who's never served in a state legislature or county commission or been on a school board," said columnist James Kilpatrick. For others it was the $150 handcrafted boots and three-piece suits, tailor-made by Dorman-Winthrop of Culver City, California, priced from $550 to $700, according to the aide who had ordered them. And the fancy turbo-prop plane once used by Dionne Warwick and Stevie Nicks, the one with the televisions and swivel seats and plush carpets that the minister-candidate had leased. Some balked at his rhyming, street-wise rhetoric.

And there was always his color.

In Tyler, Texas, K. D. Keelin sat in the driver's seat of the Rose City Cab company van—and talked about life. "Hell, I got blacks working for me. You know, it's like oil and water—one rises to the top. I got seventeen men, we keep six cabs running . . . I've seen 'em, I've worked with 'em. They're different. One of them with me got a wife and a girlfriend, you know what I mean." Keelin said he'd been around, had seen a thing or two in his fifty-four years. "I grew up in South Dakota, spent a lot of time in the service. Hell, far as I'm concerned, when 'old lady' Roosevelt let them in the service, we were in trouble. Face it, I'm what you might call prejudiced, that's right."

Jesse Jackson was inside, working a college crowd. Keelin listened for a few minutes—then continued. "He's running for a cabinet post, maybe secretary of state. He goes to the convention with those nuggets to sell, that's what it's all about. It's a known fact. Promise 'em everything—give 'em nothing: that's what all politicians do. He's a politician. . . . he's a carbon-copy of Martin Luther King. That man had the world right in the palm of his hand. This one could too. He's telling the poor people just what they want to hear."

K. D. Keelin said he considered Mondale "as much a Socialist as you can get." Keelin had no use for him, nor a kind word for any Democrat. Still, he thought Jackson might be onto something. "Tell you something. If they [the poor, blacks] stuck together, the way the Jews do, they'd walk this guy into office, you can bet on that." Then Keelin stopped, thought some more, and shook his head. One day in the future, and not too far away, he said, a black man will get himself elected president. "It's gonna come, there's no question about that. . . . And when it does, it's gonna be war. Black versus white. Just like Mississippi and Alabama. You know what King said about dogs in Birmingham: they don't know nothing about color."

"I think it's a matter of black pride to support Jesse Jackson. And I think that's what black people are doing and are gonna do. That's reason enough," said a 38-year-old black Philadelphia attorney, Ron Harper. Hundreds of miles away, a white state trooper was asked why he didn't go inside a Little Rock, Arkansas, church to hear the black presidential candidate. "It's not my denomination," the trooper said without a smile.

White racism. And black racism. For some people, Jackson's color was the only thing that mattered. "The country is just not ready for a black presidential candidate," said California assembly speaker Willie Brown. "To be honest, the majority of people who deny him deny him because he is black," the writer Maya Angelou said. "Of course, he didn't have a chance for many reasons. The most important of which was that he was black," said John Hope Franklin, long the country's foremost black historian. "Regrettably, the days of biasedness and bigotry are not over in many sections . . . Jesse never had a chance. Jesse never had a chance because, I'd have to say candidly, he's black—and the nation isn't ready for a black yet," said the Speaker of the U.S. House of Representatives, Thomas P. "Tip" O'Neill.

The number of death threats Jackson received was one measure of that sentiment. The Secret Service would not disclose how many people were arrested or questioned for allegedly threatening the candidate. Privately, however, agents admitted that there were more "serious threats" against Jackson than against all the other candidates combined. Nation of Islam minister Louis Farrakhan said that over 100 people were arrested; Jackson himself put the number at 14—but added that the number of "serious threats" exceeded 300.

Bigots would reject him outright, but other forms of bias were more subtle, sometimes harder to detect. Some people discounted him, never took him as seriously as they would a white candidate. As the black historian John Hope Franklin put it, many whites simply expected less of anything from a black, any black. Measuring that sentiment was virtually impossible. Racial slurs—calling his airplane "the jig's up," for example—were one sign, but often the bias went unspoken. Sometimes the words were not intended as a putdown by the whites who spoke them. Jackson, for instance, took offense when Walter Mondale was discussing black vice-presidential prospects: "You cannot expect those who have been excluded from certain opportunities in the past to have the same range of experience," Mondale had said. To Jackson the statement was condescending, at best. Its message, he thought, was clear: for whatever reason, "you cannot expect" blacks to be the same as whites—and that, said Jackson, was insulting, demeaning. John Hope Franklin, now 70, had run into that kind of attitude all his life. "When a black man can do something besides tap dance, people are surprised. You say, 'I was surprised that he, that he uh went to college.' But you don't say what you really mean: that you were surprised because he's black and went to college. You are surprised though. Because he's black. Just like you wouldn't expect a black man to run for the presidency. For you that is beyond the purview and the parameters which confine black activities," said Franklin. Those who fell into that category, who couldn't take the effort of a black candidate as seriously as they would take a white candidacy, were guilty, said *Harper's* editor Lewis Lapham, of treating Jackson's rhetoric as "a form of entertainment. Watching him play politics was like watching the Harlem Globetrotters play basketball."[53]

Racism, though, was a two-edged sword in this campaign. The fact of color—which made winning harder, if not impossible, for Jackson, which also put his life in danger and hobbled him at every turn—also made each political step possible, kept him on the stage, even kept him going. Because he was black, because he was in part a symbol, less was expected of him; to succeed, Jackson did not have to "win," as sociologist and sometimes Jackson advisor Harry Edwards conceded. "If Jackson were not black," said Edwards, "I question whether he would have been on the stage. . . . On the one hand, he is not taken seriously in terms of winning or ending up at the White House. On the other hand, the very fact that his campaign is symbolic of a lot of hopes and dreams of a lot of people in this country . . . I think that those kinds of considerations kept him on the stage when had he been a white candidate, given his financial situation and given his ranking in the primaries and so forth . . . I doubt very seriously if he would have been on that stage."

Jackson had been at this crossroads before; all his life racism had crippled—and propelled him. The question in the 1984 campaign was: would Jackson be exploited by racism—or would he exploit it? In columnist William Safire's phrase, would Jackson choose to be ". . . an American black, rather than a black American?"[54] Would he try to appeal to the best in black America, to its generosity and self-esteem—or would he prey on its fears? Would he shun white bigots—or meet them head-on? Goad them—or try to make them change? In short, would Jackson succumb to racism—or rise above it?

Some whites who considered themselves liberals, like Gil Kulick (see chapter 1), who were sympathetic to his cause, were disappointed as they watched Jackson wrestle with that basic question. They tried to understand what he was doing; at first they gave him the benefit of their doubt; some even tried to help. Ultimately, they pulled back, troubled by the way Jackson chose to run. Many concluded that the line between black pride and racism was dangerously thin—and that Jackson had crossed it.

Cuyahoga (Ohio) county commissioner Tim Hagen was a polical pro; a former Democratic county chairman, he was in the business of winning elections. Tim Hagen knew how to count votes, and he didn't waste much time with idealists out to save the world. "Babes in the woods," he called them. At first that's how he tended to think of the Jackson campaign: well-intentioned, but naive. But Jackson's kid-gloves treatment of Louis Farrakhan—and Jackson's statements about Jews—convinced Hagen that all Jackson cared about was black votes. Jackson, he concluded later, was little more than a racist. "You bet there was double standard," Hagen said. "Come on now. Of course there was. If it's a brother, he's excused. From making them adhere to a principle. Or measuring up to a standard. . . . He never talked about black racism, did you notice that? [Dr. Martin Luther] King, you remember, talked about both, how each demeaned an individual. But Jackson would embrace racism when it suited his purpose. . . . I think he's a real menace," Hagen went on.

Harvard Law School professor Alan Dershowitz knew Jesse Jackson too. On March 4, in Framingham, Massachusetts, Dershowitz sat on a panel that grilled Jackson; later that day on Jackson's invitation the professor climbed into the candidate's limousine and spent a couple of hours with him. Dershowitz was troubled by some things Jackson had said and done, but he came away from the private meeting impressed with Jackson's shrewdness, his quick wit. Later, though, Dershowitz became disillusioned. Jackson, he said, seemed unwilling "to broaden the base of his coalition at the expense of losing some votes within the black community." That, Dershowitz concluded, was the fundamental flaw of the campaign. It was also, he thought, the appeal of a racist. Running black *that way,* Dershowitz argued, became black racism. "I think you can be unabashedly black black and still want to build bridges" to whites, to Jews, to be serious about creating the so-called Rainbow Coalition, Dershowitz went on. But Jackson, he argued, had a different objective. "He's opted for a mixture which is destined to make him always a loser rather than a mixture which would've resulted in a loss this time but a potential win next time."

That, according to Dershowitz, made it "a flawed candidacy, a short-range candidacy. . . . It's very easy to finish third, if you're black in America, and you're a black candidate, seeking a black constituency. It's very easy to finish third. No trick. The hard thing to do is finish second and ultimately pave the way to finishing first. If you're content to finish third, if you're content to get your 20 percent, your 21 percent, your 22 percent, that's not very hard because you don't have to make any hard choices. You don't have to reject your own power base in an effort to reach out. But if he ever really wanted to try to finish second, then the true test would be before him. I don't know how he'd do at that test, but he wasn't put to that test. Because he limited his goals."

Finally, after working for Jesse Jackson for more than a year, Mary Summers decided that she too had had enough. Saddened and disgusted, she decided to walk away. That was not her style. Just over five feet tall, white, chunky, with a pixieish haircut and Coke bottle thick glasses, Mary Summers ordinarily radiated enthusiasm, good cheer. She liked to run every day to help release tension, she said. More likely to burn off all that energy, friends thought. She was a child of the Peace Movement; her natural habitat, it seemed, were the endless rallies against the war or armaments, long vigils, discussions about issues, tactics. At first she didn't know much about Jesse Jackson. Except that he seemed to share her fear of nuclear weapons. And her concern for the poor. Both wanted to redistribute the nation's wealth, to rearrange its priorities. He really cares, Mary Summers decided. He could be her vehicle.

She plunged headfirst into the campaign. Helping arrange his schedule, giving a hand with some speeches, gradually doing most of them and some of the important letters too. One letter (May 25, 1984), in which Jackson declined to attend a so-called unity dinner George McGovern was holding for all the candidates, was something of a classic: ". . . I will not be one more snake oil salesman . . . one more false prophet for my people," Jackson had written McGovern. The words were those of Mary Summers.

Even then she'd had some misgivings. In May, her husband, Bruce Allen, angrily left the campaign, charging that black officials running the Jackson effort in Ohio (Cleveland city council president George Forbes and state representative Michael White, in particular) were systematically excluding whites to further the black officials' own selfish interests, political and economic. "This campaign preached racial harmony; what it practiced was racial hostility," Allen concluded. Hot-tempered, idealistic, Allen complained to Jackson, but nothing changed. Be careful, Allen told Summers, "you're dealing with a bunch of people who have practiced race politics and contract politics all their lives."

But Summers had traipsed around the country with Jackson and after the convention had followed him back to Washington, D.C., to help him organize his national Rainbow Coalition. Typically, she worked sixteen, seventeen hours a day with few complaints. The crazy hours, the lack of food, and chaotic working conditions were almost an elixir, made her redouble her efforts.

Gradually, though, her enthusiasm began to wane. She had gotten to know both the public and the private man; while she still believed in Jackson's message, she was troubled by what she felt was his lack of discipline—"the ideas are great, but nothing is getting *done,*" she complained—his lack of follow-through. And by what she said was Jackson's "problem" with whites.

For Mary Summers the breaking point came in January, 1985. For three weeks most of the staff had not been paid. Now Jackson was flying back from a speaking tour in Europe on a Concorde jet with four of his children and several aides on the world's most expensive airline. Two thousand dollars per person. One way. Something in Mary Summers snapped. When Jackson returned to the office, she told him—respectfully, she felt—that his priorities were confused. That he'd better start doing things differently. Including, she said, the way he treated people.

Jackson stiffened. Lately he sensed that Mary Summers had become a malcontent, whining and griping. Perhaps she wanted more authority than he was prepared to give her, he said. Her notion of how to run an office—neat, orderly, like other offices—was not his way of organizing things. Sometimes, he felt, she was too zealous, even impractical; when they'd disagree over issues, she very rarely conceded anything. She was tireless, and sometimes that got on a person's nerves. "You're trying to sabotage my spirit," Jackson told her. And your comments, he added, are "racist."

Summers was stunned. She knew his shortcomings, but she felt this attack was unwarranted, almost savage. She had, she felt, proven her loyalty; she had earned the right to speak her mind. Now as Jackson continued to rebuke her, she thought back to earlier conversations when she'd listened as his close advisors, the Reverend Bill Howard and attorney Vic McTeer, both black, had sought to persuade Jackson that not all whites are bigots. They hadn't persuaded him, Summers concluded. Jackson really believed that; "that's his starting point," she said. Racism, she felt, motivated almost everything Jackson did. And she thought that he would not rise above it, that he could not. That the experiences he had known were too searing, the scars too deep for him to change. Several months after the incident, Mary Summers shook her head sadly. Yes, she said, his foundation is quicksand.

9.

JACKIE JACKSON

There had never been a contender for First Lady like her. Jackie Jackson always wanted you to know that. She was the oldest of five children whose mother picked beans for fifteen cents an hour. She never knew her father. She learned early to read the "Colored Only" signs and decided as a child "that was wrong." She was born in Fort Pierce, Florida, and raised in Newport News, Virginia, and at one point in her girlhood she said she considered becoming a nun. But she opted instead for a major in psychology and sociology at North Carolina Agricultural and Technological College in Greensboro, North Carolina. In 1961, she caught the eye of the student body president.

Jackson's chartered jet was bouncing around in strong headwinds somewhere south of Manchester, New Hampshire, and the candidate was having some difficulty trying to brace himself in an aisle and talk to a reporter at the same time.

It had been a twenty-hour day; still, Jackson was hammering out some point about Nicaragua, his eyes half-shut, leaning with both hands against the bulkhead. Suddenly, a figure appeared from a doorway in the dimly lit plane and nestled under Jackson's arm. The candidate took little notice, but Jackie Jackson only moved in closer, snuggling her head to her husband's chest. Finally she stretched both arms around his neck and interrupted: "Honey, come talk to me. I haven't seen you in so long." Jackson nodded to the reporter, and Jackie led her husband to the plane's private cabin and shut the door firmly.

Jackie Jackson had learned many roles since taking up with the going-places student leader at North Carolina A&T. Tonight she was the temptress, luring her husband from the media where fatigue could cause a misstep. A week later she'd be the prosecutor, arguing, demanding that he not apologize to Jews for calling them "Hymie," after the way they'd all but led him "to a crucifixion" because of his views on the Middle East.

Jacqueline Lavinia Brown Jackson—fiery orator; world traveler who'd been to thirty countries by 1985 and was adding more; a lover of fine perfume and expensive cognac, outlandish fashions, and her five children. Especially her five children. "They're silly, they're nice, they're political. . . . they've met so many great people in the world yet they're not pompous, they're basic kids, they ride the bus." One hour she might be admonishing reporters not to drink liquor on the campaign bus—"poor as the people are we're meeting, it doesn't seem necessary to do that"—the next she could be sipping a beer herself or sashaying down the aisle of the campaign plane—billowy dress flying, her arms and neck loaded with costume jewelry—and plop in the lap of a friendly writer or cameraman.

Jackie Jackson—concerned, complex; open, as outgoing a person as her husband was aloof; her speeches—often given without notes—were pro-women and anti-Reagan and dealt with problems of the young, such as drug abuse and alienation. She'd tell people everywhere she went that she'd make a "great First Lady" and she used to love to tweak Nancy Reagan. "I have no desire to be some pompous queen," she'd grin. "I'm not enamoured with things made by human beings . . . I don't want to do the evening gown bit and pick up flowers all over the United States. No, we're not that kind of people. I plant vegetables in my yard."

She said people who jump to quick conclusions ought not to about her. She was not the classical political appendage, she'd insist. She might have spent half her life looking up to and after the mercurial civil rights leader—"I think Jesse Jackson is the greatest human being alive today"—but she was no wife-on-the-scrap-heap, living vicariously off her husband's glare. She was adamant about that. Not Jackie Jackson.

She'd been married twenty-one years to a man she usually saw only a few days a month, whose life, as his good friend Gene Wheeler conceded, "ain't home, it's out here."

No big deal, she said. She had her own friends, her own causes, her own travels. She marched beside her husband in the early civil rights days and marched with the kids at her side when he was gone. Today, she went it mostly alone. She traveled to the Middle East to meet with Yasser Arafat before her husband did and became the first Jackson to rile American Jews with her gesture toward the PLO leader. She went to Lebanon and Central America, arguing against Reagan administration policies there. She still chuckled about the flap her Arafat visit caused. Not among the Jews—among the men on the board of her husband's Operation PUSH. "They said, 'We're not going to let you out of the country again,' that's what the PUSH men said to me, as if they had anything to do with me going in the first place [she had traveled with a group of women to observe the effects of war on civilians]. But I don't take them seriously . . . they go and talk about me behind my back, say I'm crazy, but it doesn't matter." Jackie said that she saw herself as "a mother of the world," responsible for the well-being of its poor and ravaged, not necessarily its male power-brokers.

The questions came up often during the campaign. "Where's Jackie?" "How come Jackie isn't with him?" "Is their marriage over?" One noticeable absence was the closing night of the Democratic National Convention in San Francisco in July. All the presidential candidates and their wives were on the podium. Jackson was there too but no Jackie. She said "no one really wanted" her up there.

"The straw that broke the camel's back was that Reverend Jackson and I were to stand on one side of all the other people so that it would not appear we were really part of that group—and I was told the things I could not wear on the podium, what colors not to wear, and I discovered that all the candidates' wives had worn the colors. . . . I had an insult level . . . I decided I would allow those who were interested in winning at all costs to prevail."

Jackie was vague about who told her what to wear and where to stand. She "was told," she said. But what was a problem for Jackie wasn't for Jackson, and he tried to persuade his wife, right up until the ceremonies began, that she should be with him that night in the spotlight, standing there next to him just as Mrs. Mondale was standing next to the former vice-president.

But Jackie refused. "We've disagreed before," she said. "I'm no robot." And if these kinds of episodes made people gossip about her marriage, let them. "My marriage is about five kids and a sameness of purpose and an understanding," she said. "I don't have to prove to anyone that I love my husband, that he loves me. And he doesn't have to prove it. We worked different parts of the cities and states because I could do that, and most women can't. Most women don't know enough about their husband's business . . . or have enough independence to be able to answer, when a reporter asks, 'are you speaking for your husband?' and you say, 'no, I'm speaking for myself. . . .' I don't pay any attention," she said. "*No* attention," she emphasized. The trouble was, Jackie went on, white people don't understand the relationship between black men and women. "We understand equality better. . . . I remember watching those old Clark Gable movies . . . the Caucasian woman would come up and they were so lovely . . . and they'd slap the man, and he'd just walk away. Well, we don't do that. You slap and you get slapped back. So the rule is, don't slap."

It was late in the afternoon the week before Christmas, and snow was threatening in Chicago. There was little sign of life around the cavernous turn-of-the-century house on the city's south side where the town's swells once lived. There were two half-decorated Christmas trees, one in the hall, with the lights unplugged; one in the living room, with no lights; a tinsel streamer had come untaped from the chandelier and was dragging on the hallway floor. Boxes of decorations sat waiting to be placed, red balls, silver ornaments.

Christmas was on hold here. Jackie was upstairs taking a nap. Jackie, Jr., and Santita, the Jackson's youngest and oldest daughters, were sick. Jackie should have been at a Rainbow Coalition conference at the airport—"my husband is going to fuss because I should know these things if I'm asked"—but she got up at 4:30 this morning to try to put together a trip to Ethiopia for a group of women peace activists and then took a nap.

Life seemed to be lived elsewhere than in this house on Constance Avenue. Everywhere there were knickknacks and souvenirs, remnants of one crusade or another, bric-a-brac from other countries, other places, not here—here there were empty chairs and empty rooms and unplayed pianos with dusty keys. Stacks of Jackson's portraits leaned against the walls; one large folder labeled "presidential portfolio" was stashed in a corner; a straw bowler had been tossed atop some copper mugs, the "Women's Network for Jackson" in bold letters on the band beginning to fade.

Jackie came downstairs and turned on the Christmas tree lights in the hallway. "Isn't it pretty?" she asked, pausing a moment to watch the tiny blue lights twinkling on the tall green tree. Four of the five children lived away now, at boarding school or college. Only Jackie, Jr., was still at home.

Jackie sat down at the dining room table and began to talk about life with Jackson and how independence and strong will and faith in God had set her apart from other candidates' wives in 1984. She explained how she had learned over the years to lead her own life and not to be concerned about Jackson's long absences.

"It's none of my business," she said. "I stick with my business . . . I would fight for his right to have his own business. . . . I did not marry my husband to imprison him," she went on. "Nor did he marry me to place me in a prison. . . . My husband is very involved, and I know that he would have very little time for recreation; and so I would feel that, you know, if he was relaxing, it would be like a day at the beach. . . . You see, I never look for trouble because my mother told me if you do you'll find it. And you'll dream it up. There'll be things you don't understand . . . and you'll stifle the individual you care so much about. And most relationships have been severed based on all of the suspicion. . . . Generally, women are insecure," Jackie said, as daylight left the drafty dining room and the tall cacti and banana leaf plants cast tangled shadows on the wall.

She didn't seem to notice that she and her visitor were sitting in darkness now. "I personally feel my husband is coming back whenever he goes out to work or wherever he goes. I'm secure enough to understand that he is coming back. . . . I think if I am running around inquiring about where, when, what, it has a way of nailing coffins, and severing relationships. . . . I'll give you an example. He loves basketball. It doesn't make me happy to go watch him play basketball. So therefore, I love to swim. I think life is as simple as agreeing that you play basketball and I swim, and that doesn't mean you have to sit with me by the pool." The only lights in the house now were coming from the hallway tree and the kitchen, where Jackie, Jr., sat on a stool eating potato chips and watching TV.

"The cutest thing happened with my husband once," Jackie said. "Finally, on my birthday, he mentioned to me, 'Now you get dressed because I'm coming to take you to dinner,' which was shocking to me."

Jackie didn't go out. "He doesn't like to take me out to dinner. He likes for me to cook. So what I did was, I cooked for him so he could eat and go to bed; and I went out with my girlfriends to celebrate . . . I thought about it and I said, 'Why should we sit there and roll eyes with each other over the dinner—and ruin my dinner? Him asking me, What does this taste like? Why would you eat that? Do you really like that?' Because he likes very plain foods." Jackie went on boasting of the birthday compromise as the shadows lengthened over the wide, cluttered dining room table, over the half-empty bag of oranges and the cereal boxes, over the figure of the woman of the house in a silken bathrobe, hands gesturing animatedly, talking on.

She talked about not prying and about being one's own person, about building a separate life. She never mentioned jealousy. She never mentioned how she was angered by Jackson's willingness to apologize for "Hymie," especially after "the Jews threatened my family and my home . . . they owe us an apology"; by his willingness to campaign for Walter Mondale during the fall of 1984 even though Mondale, she felt, had treated her husband shabbily at the convention and before. She never mentioned how she sat in the house and listened to Jackson on the telephone, making what she thought were unacceptable compromises—or how she'd say through gritted teeth, "I hate it; I just hate it," as an aide once overheard.

Jackie Jackson—coquettish, calculating, smart, angry; she turned 40 on the campaign trail and was so busy speechmaking she forgot to celebrate. A lot had happened since the pretty 19-year-old freshman turned the head of the student body president at North Carolina A&T, a lot of ups and downs, proud moments, babies, laughs, empty beds, many good-byes, many hellos, a lot of bending, a solidification of "understanding." One of the last people Jackson telephoned before he walked into the synagogue in Manchester to face the angry Jews was Jackie. She wouldn't go to the temple; she felt they didn't understand her pain, but Jackson would let her know he was going in now, and why.

Finally Jackie noticed the darkness in the house on the snow-threatening evening, a week before Christmas. She had trouble with one retina in bright light, she apologized. She got up, fixed coffee, looked at the clock, the lights flashed on, she hugged Jackie, Jr., the house came alive. "Fuss, fuss, fuss," Jackie chuckled. That's what Jackson would do when she came late to the Rainbow Coalition conference. "You're not leaving, are you?" she queried her visitor. "I'm enjoying this."

On October 8, 1984, Jackie went out to her garden and picked the last of the collard greens she'd grown that summer. Jackson was supposed to be home, it was his forty-third birthday, and she planned to cook him a meal. But something came up and he only stopped by the house for a couple of hours, no time for dinner. "He only came home for a short time," she explained, because there was fund-raising to do to get rid of the campaign debt, and the deadline was approaching.

But didn't that hurt, picking the greens, planning a meal, watching him go? Didn't some of it hurt? Sometimes? Jackie shrugged. She didn't speak for a moment, only smiled faintly and looked away, out past her visitor to some bygone place, to some simpler time. Then she caught herself, took another sip from the tall glass of Beck's beer, and answered square into her visitor's eyes. "You know, a little lady, who happened to be black, sang a song a long time ago. I think it was Dinah Washington. She sang: 'I don't hurt any more. All my tear drops are dry.'"

10. BACK SOUTH

April 27, 1984. The moment passed, and Avery Alexander didn't think that anyone had noticed. Jesse Jackson had stopped in Alexandria, Louisiana, to have lunch at the old Hotel Bentley. He'd walked up the front steps and had gone through the front door and Avery Alexander, now state representative Avery Alexander, had walked through with Jackson, arm in arm, smiling. Just like that. And with each step Alexander remembered those nights when he could not enter the Bentley. All those trips from New Orleans to Shreveport when he'd stopped, bone-weary, outside the hotel and had known it was pointless to ask because "I couldn't come in that front door unless I was going there as a servant." In those days he would keep moving across town to Third Street or over to Payson, to the black part of town where he'd find cheap food and lodgings.

As he walked through the Bentley, other memories came rushing back to Alexander. He remembered the frightened blacks cowering in church pews as white police on horseback crashed through the church doors. He remembered all those years when he'd taken, and failed to pass, the voter's literacy tests that local officials had devised so that no black could ever pass. He remembered how his grandfather had to humble himself to the young white overseer, Mr. Greenwich. And he remembered all those nights when the Bentley posted its invisible "For Whites Only" sign. Now he was walking up the front steps of the Bentley with Jesse Jackson. They passed through the lobby with Secret Service agents and aides and the herd of reporters trailing along behind. By the dining room the hotel manager asked quietly if he might have a word. Were the arrangements satisfactory, the manager wanted to know: "anything you need, Mr. Alexander, you just let us know."

Jimmy Jones, a 58-year-old white landscape architect, stood in the shade outside the polling place at Reed Ross High School in Fayetteville, North Carolina. Jones had no use for politicians, Democrat or Republican. "It's been a long time since I've seen a man who's a real politician, who's above the crowd. . . . Maybe we just don't grow them anymore. We don't have the Patton types, gross as he was." Jones was a Baptist, and a conservative. "A dyed-in-the-wool Democrat" who voted for Ronald Reagan in 1980—and who would probably, he said, vote for Reagan in 1984. But Jones was intrigued enough by Jesse Jackson to come hear the minister speak. Jones thought Jackson fancied himself another Dr. Martin Luther King, Jr., but Jones thought that Jackson fell short.

"He's grinding his own axe. He's an evangelist out to line his own pocket and feed his own ego. . . . He doesn't want to be president, he just wants to be a leader of his people. Now when people hear that they'll say it's just white scum talking. But I'm not saying it because of his color. But by his actions. His actions prove that he's out for himself." Jones listened some more. This fellow was certainly a good talker, he conceded. "If he was white, everybody would be for him . . . another James Jones, if you will. They can lead you to death if you don't watch it. . . ."

This was the final phase of Jackson's odyssey. More steamy gyms, more tenement slums, more crumbling tenant farmhouses. Eighteen- to twenty-hour days on a plane that kept breaking down and in motor homes driving through southern backwaters where Secret Service agents refused to let him switch on lights until the blinds had been drawn tight so that would-be snipers couldn't see in. Off through the foot-stomping adulation in ghetto halls and bayou churches, past icy stares of whites, beyond vicious threats from anonymous callers, both black and white. "You'd be surprised how many of them are black," said one agent. On through the hate and the chaos and the joy. "My road is long and it's hard to plow, but I wouldn't take anything for my journey now," he would holler, whipping one crowd after another into frenzy.

But as pride in black America swelled—"he's our modern-day Moses . . . come to lead us out of the wilderness," one minister solemnly intoned—Walter Mondale was moving closer to wrapping up the party's nomination, and a brokered convention was moving beyond Jackson's grasp. By comparison his campaign was becoming extraneous, a sideshow away from the main event. Like barnstorming black baseball players of the 1930s—the "Cool Papa" Bells and Josh Gibsons who could have excelled at the big time but who never got the chance. When tested, they'd dazzled white observers, much as Jackson had scintillated when permitted to join the other candidates in televised debates. Otherwise, like the old black all-stars, Jackson was left to spin in his own orbit. His political roadshow was richer, more vibrant than that of the other contenders. It alone set off sparks. But increasingly he was lighting up playing fields where the championship was never at stake. As the cheering there grew louder, so did the resentment of him in other parts of the country. As affection grew, the distancing process accelerated.

April 27, 1984. The night was warm and the crowd streaming into the civic center in Monroe, Louisiana, was boisterous. Prentice Hixon stood off to the side and watched. An electrical engineer, Hixon was also an officer in the reserve law association. He joined because he liked a well-run, orderly community, and he would do his part to keep Monroe that way. 'These people, these are our people," he said. "We live with them, work with them, we know them. They're black. Yes, but they're our people. We treat 'em fair. We don't take no guff. But we're fair. If we have to get rough, we will. And they know it. So we get along real good."

Hixon was 43, white, the father of four children ages 4 to 17. To supplement the family income, his wife drove a school bus. When he was younger, Hixon thought about leaving the area. But New Orleans seemed too big, too impersonal. So he came back home, where his roots were deep. "My folks are still here. Daddy is 80 now. They're both what you might call prejudiced. My momma's father was shot dead by an old slave nigger. Boy just went crazy and decided he had to kill someone."

Soon the civic center crowd was cheering wildly; tears streaked the faces of some. "Amen, brother . . . tell it to 'em, Jesse . . .

win, Jesse, win." Their chants rocked the arena. Prentice Hixon folded his arms and listened but showed little emotion. "I think Jackson's dreaming. It's not that the country isn't ready for a black man. I just don't think that it's ready for Jesse Jackson. . . . to me, the color of his skin don't matter. But he's a minister. He'd be the commandant of the armed forces. And when it comes to nutcracking time, I'm not sure that he'd pull the switch. He might say, Oh they're all the Lord's creatures. And in that few seconds, it would be too late. We'd all be dead, fried. So I'm not willing to have sitting in that Oval Office any preacher, black or white. That's my feeling, friend. Don't have nothing to do with color."

On May 5, a hot New Orleans morning, a panhandler approached Percy Walker, age 60, and asked him for twenty dollars. "If I got it, I got on somebody else's pants," Walker laughed, shooing the beggar away. Walker had a lit cigar in his hand, a package of cigarettes in his pocket, grey stubble on his black cheek, and the faint smell of whiskey on his breath. His tan pants and white shirt were wrinkled; a dirty straw hat sat on the back of his head. For twenty-seven years, Walker had worked in a concrete pipe company; but with high blood pressure, bronchial asthma, and arthritis in his left leg—"yes sir, you name it—and I got it"—Walker was now on disability and hadn't worked for the last nine years. "With the pneumonia I got from all that dust in the pipes . . . I thank God I made it—this far," he said.

He was a religious man, secretary of the trustee board at the Greater St. Peter's Baptist Church. "When I get up in the morning, I say my prayers. I ask the Lord to bless my children and relations. Bless the president and the mayor. I feel it's my duty, you know. I also said a special prayer for Jesse. I pray for him every day and every night. Just a few words. No, it don't take too long."

Percy Walker said he didn't know much about politics. But he did know the country wasn't ready yet for a black man as president. No sir, it certainly wasn't. Not much point in thinking otherwise, he said. Still, he'd voted in every election since 1948—"big or small"—and in 1984 he'd vote again. This time, for a black presidential candidate. "I get short-winded right now," he said, standing on the street corner. "I can't tote nothing. Can't walk too fast. But I'm on my way now to vote for Jesse. . . . if he got nerve enough to run, I got nerve enough to vote for him."

Jackson would not slow the pace, despite the odds. In earlier years he had pushed himself to the point of exhaustion, several times had even been hospitalized, and the future would be like the past. Partly it was stubbornness. Self-confidence. And faith. "Oh, there are a lot of facts around. But beyond the facts of the matter there's the faith of the matter." Critics wrote it off to ego, to pride, but Jackson would scoff: "They said walking up Calvary was impractical. That the tomb was the end. But the stone was rolled away. . . . the impractical became a fact. So we find ourselves in the homestretch of a campaign that was impractical from the start."

The way he and his followers measured things, he was *not* losing. That was another reason to keep going. "You've not lost the game when you're behind in the score—but when you give up," he preached again and again. Numbers were only one measurement, he told supporters. "We're not measured by whether or not we get there. Just whether we're going in the right direction," he said in a Palm Sunday sermon. "This is essentially a spiritual pilgrimage to save a dead people and revive a dying nation," he proclaimed one day late in April.

"Winning," he'd say, "is doing your best against the odds . . . in so many ways, we've already won this campaign. We've broken the shackles of doubt—and that's winning. We've removed the artificial clouds of inferiority. And that's winning." To hard-nosed political pros, arguments like those were just so much window dressing. Not so for Jackson's followers. "Even if he hasn't won, he hasn't lost . . . he has made America stand up and take note. In that sense he'll never lose," said Mrs. Ruth Hale, a Columbus, Ohio, supporter. The button on her lapel read "Now Is the Time." "It turns out he won't be the loser. Who would have dared to take a chance like this? He knows America isn't ready for blacks but someone had to take the step," she added.

In Nachitoches, Louisiana, Mrs. Hazel Batiste seconded the point. "You can't imagine what an inspiration this is to people of our race. So many of our kids feel trapped and hopeless. And helpless. It's good for them to have an example. We have so many kids who don't have fathers or heroes. We don't have heroes in America," she argued. As Jackson spoke to a half-empty arena at the Ohio State Fairgrounds, Hershel Craig held his 2-year-old son Jonathan on his knee. "My son can envision himself as being president now. He doesn't have to believe that he can't anymore. . . . he knows who Michael Jackson is. Now he knows who Jesse Jackson is, and that's a hell of a lot more important." At the University of North Carolina in Chapel Hill, child psychologist Valera Washington, 30, added her voice to the Jackson chorus: "all these possibilities that were unheard of when I was growing up. . . . We grew up with so many things that blacks couldn't do, and these kids are growing up thinking that they can do anything. Think about how much progress we made with the doors closed—and how much more they can make with them open. . . . I give him a lot of credit for energizing it. . . . there's only so much Martin Luther King you can push at these college kids. Every generation must have its own hero." In Knoxville, Tennessee, 12-year-old Athan Gibbs had memorized several of Jesse Jackson's speeches to recite in school and churches, wherever he was asked. "What do you want to be when you grow up?" Athan was asked. "The second black president of the United States," he replied.

There is an obligation, Jackson said, to take the campaign to all those places that had never seen a campaign before, to let people hear the sirens and see the flashing red lights and the white government agents bounding out to protect the black man whose background was so much like that of those who now looked on. "It is important that they see this," he said. "It's just as important as the voting." When he saw the power he had over crowds he knew, he said, that he was playing with dreams, even souls. It sobered him. He would not, he said gravely, abuse that trust.

At this stage in the campaign, every dollar he raised was matched by the federal government. In addition, for years he had crisscrossed the country making speeches, leading marches, attacking and counterattacking. That was second nature to him now; that was his life. He was exhausted. He was still terrified that someone would try to kill him. But he was also having the time of his life. He loved hearing himself introduced as "the only hope for this country . . . the son of thunder: six feet four inches of intellectual power, a bad black dude" then seeing the crowds go wild with delight. "I want to act presidential, but I want to holler too. Oh wow, ain't this fun," he bellowed one night in Newark, New Jersey, grinning broadly and rubbing his hands together.

Mud Fork, West Virginia. Jackson, who had spent the night in the home of Kernell Bryant, a disabled coal miner, was sitting around the morning breakfast table with Bryant and his wife and her 3-year-old son, Justin Daryl, while reporters and cameramen recorded the humble scene—the filigreed wedding certificate framed on one wall, the three-dimensional, multicolored replica of the Last Supper on another; the "Christ Knocking at Your Door" sheetmusic on the piano. In the framed picture atop the piano, the son in uniform wore two medals.

"My, these biscuits are wonderful," the candidate serenaded the woman of the house. A biscuit in one hand, a big bite in his mouth, Jackson bounced little Justin Daryl on his knee. "You're a real ham, Justin Daryl," he teased the 3-year-old.

"You're a ham too, Jesse Jackson," the 3-year-old replied.

Practical politicians figured that Pennsylvania would be Jackson's high-water mark. They conceded him Washington, D.C.—it was, after all, 70 percent black—but in none of the remaining states were the pockets of black voters big enough to hold out even the faint hope for a long-shot win. In those contests—Tennessee on May 1; North Carolina, Louisiana, and Texas on May 5; Indiana, Ohio, and Maryland on May 8; California, New Jersey, New Mexico, South Dakota, and West Virginia on June 5—he would (save in South Dakota, where his name was not on the ballot) be challenged by standards he had helped set in earlier primaries. In the South and Northeast, the turnout of black voters was substantially greater than in the 1980 presidential primaries: up, according to CBS News, by 19 percent in Illinois, 38 percent in Pennsylvania, 43 percent in Florida, 82 percent in Alabama, 103 percent in New York. He was able to mobilize blacks in tenements and in the southern Bible belt, but how would he do in those areas where the black vote was smaller—and more dispersed?

The Saturday before Palm Sunday the men in the Chattanooga, Tennessee, hotel bar got together the way they did every Saturday to watch whatever game was on television and to drink beer; it was their clubhouse, their private sanctuary. No wives, no bills, no pressure. A place to unwind at the end of a long week, to be themselves, by themselves.

Slowly this Saturday the lobby outside began to fill up with black men and women. The white men in the bar noticed and quickly exchanged glances; outsiders weren't welcome here, especially blacks, especially on Saturday. Then someone said that Jesse Jackson was coming to the hotel. "We don't want him around here," one of the men snarled. The mood turned ugly. Conversation stopped. The TV blared on, but no one paid much attention. All eyes were on the lobby and the government agents sweeping through. "Let's keep the lobby area open, OK, fellows?" the agents asked without waiting for an answer.

Cold eyes watched as blacks walked through the lobby. Bodies braced, became tense. The agents sensed danger, and when Jackson arrived they hustled him around to a side entrance. Later, when he was ready to leave, they took him out the same way, while the men in the bar protected their turf.

Later that night, during a speech in the city's Memorial Auditorium, a young black man lurched down the aisle, yelling at Jackson. Police moved to cut the man off, but the candidate admonished them: "Don't overreact. Don't overreact. . . . There's stress out there. The brother has something to say. The brother needs love."

The man calmed down after a while and was ushered away. "We must use our minds to resolve conflict," Jackson told the crowd, "not billy-clubs." He added, "If we can't reach out to him, what's the point?"

He took his campaign across the breadth of North Carolina, into the eastern corner of the state, "the forgotten part," as he called it. "The big cities will not be free until eastern North Carolina is free. When the slaves of eastern North Carolina rise up, they will free Charlotte, Raleigh-Durham," he told poor black farmers. In the heart of tobacco country, he called for the removal of federal price supports and again appealed to the small farmer: "If we can bail out the government in El Salvador, surely we can bail out small farmers at home . . . when you don't feed the feeder, the nation is in trouble."

Sometimes his approach was inspirational: "roll and run for office," he told a group of wheelchair-bound listeners in High Point. In Warrenton, he coaxed a member of the high school basketball team up to the microphone; gently Jackson began to interrogate him as the overflow gymnasium crowd watched the current—and former—high school stars. "You practice six days a week," Jackson began. "That's three hours a day, no TV, no radios. . . . When you get tired, you got to keep right on running. Right? . . . At the end of that, you get to be pretty good, huh?" The basketball player was still nervous, but the audience was starting to get the point. "Now let me ask you this," Jackson continued. "How many hours a night do you study?" Laughter filled the gym; a few students started clapping, nervously. "Have the TV on while you study?" Jackson kept asking. "Now you were very exact in how many hours you practice basketball, but a little shaky about studying." With a good-natured shove, he sent the ballplayer back into the stands. "Get the point? People are good at what they work at. You can slam-dunk a thought the same way you slam-dunk a basketball . . . if you work at it. If you're state champions, it's because you work at being state champions. You can be state champion in math, in accounting. . . . Use your minds, use your bodies, achieve against great odds . . . make up your mind you're going to be somebody—and you *can rise above your situation.*" And the students sprang to their feet cheering, the waves of applause now drowning Jackson out.

Throughout the state he also demanded that whites start supporting black candidates the same way that blacks had supported whites. "The divine law of reciprocity," he called it. Blacks are tired of being treated like Democratic party "concubines," he said. "This ain't no part-time love affair. We're grown people. We want to get married. Now."

Typically, he was running two or three hours late for every appearance, but huge crowds waited and smothered him with love. "Not only do we offer you our church, not only do we offer you our percentages, we offer you ourselves," said the Reverend Leonard Macon in High Point, North Carolina. One who came out to see Jackson in Charlotte was Robert Faulkner, a former roommate—and football teammate—at North Carolina A&T.

"Ever think you'd see him running for president?" Faulkner was asked. The old linemen chuckled. "Listen, after some of the stuff we done, I'm still getting used to him being a minister," Faulkner replied.

Near Pembroke, North Carolina, state highway patrol officer K. K. Daniel watched as Jesse Jackson fed biscuits to chickens and helped slop some hogs. "Soo-eee, soo-eee," the candidate yelled as the cameras recorded every dip and coo. K. K. Daniel turned away laughing.

The candidate had just spent the night with a family of Lumbee Indians who rented a tumbledown house just off Pembroke's Chicken Road. Its porch sagged, the rocking chairs hadn't been painted, and plastic was stretched tight over where windows had been. Inside, however, there was a large color television set—and a cordless telephone. "This has been an area of great oppression, violence, and exploitation," Jackson told reporters as K. K. Daniel listened.

K. K. ("little kids, knee high on up, call me 'Mr. K. K.' Everybody here calls me K. K. It's for Kenneth Kearns. But don't tell no one . . .") Daniel had been on the state force for thirty-three years, and in that time he had seen a lot of campaigning politicians come and go.

"Hell, they pick the most miserable house they can find. LBJ, few years back, went into one up there in Halifax County, sat down and fell right through, damn near busted his ass." K. K. Daniel laughed at the memory and continued guarding this year's candidate.

In the final round Jackson cleared the first hurdle. In Tennessee, only 17 percent black, he put together a coalition of environmentalists, "peace-activists," and college professors to help run his local campaign—and with its help he not only carried the city of Knoxville, he also picked up 25.3 percent of the primary vote and 14 of the state's 76 convention delegates. The same day he scored his first clear-cut win over Mondale and Hart. In Washington, D.C., Jackson amassed a crushing two-thirds of the vote (Mondale got 25 percent and Hart, with 7 percent, came in third). Washington gave him 8 more delegates. The primary turnout in the city, 108,000 people, also set a new record. "Tonight is a victory for boats stuck on the bottom," Jackson told fifteen people gathered to celebrate his win. He spoke to them only for ten minutes, however; it was late, and the next day he had to leave for Dallas and a debate with Mondale and Hart. He almost didn't make it.

Before touching down in Texas, his chartered turbo-prop Electra flew through an area where thirty tornados were reported; most of them—the plane's terrified passengers figured—taking direct hits on the plane. Time and again the aircraft pitched to the side, sometimes plunging hundreds of feet downward through the sky. "Hailstones rubbing against the fuselage sounded eerily like skeletons shaking in the wind," UPI's Matthew C. Quinn wrote later. Inside the plane camera equipment, food, and hand luggage tumbled from overhead bins and flew about the cabin; a 250-pound cameraman, sitting on the floor at one point, was lifted almost to the ceiling. Some passengers screamed and cried; a stewardess got sick. Former State Department spokesman Hodding Carter, on board to prepare a report on Jackson for public television, said, "it was the most frightened I've been on a trip, and in twenty years I've flown thousands of miles with the secretary of state." When Jackson reached Dallas, he fell to his knees and pretended to kiss the ground. And his emotions weren't contrived. "That flight was too much for me; my anxiety level hit the breaking point," he told his shaken aides. The next day Jackson switched to a Learjet.

He darted from the center of Texas to the Gulf Coast, then swooped down into the Rio Grande Valley, a private air force of other Learjets rented by the television networks chasing him at every stop. In the blistering noonday heat at McAllen, he departed his luxury aircraft long enough to tell a crowd of dirt-poor farm workers: "you picked the fruit that made America strong. Now you must eat the fruit and grow strong yourselves. . . . If you want a decent minimum wage, vote about it." We share a common background, we have both been victims, he told Mexican Americans. "I wonder if a president could survive off a butter and cheese diet. . . . We need meat and bread, but men and women cannot live by bread alone. We also need our self-respect."

At 2:15 A.M. Jackson's motorcade screeched to a halt outside a small house in San Antonio; the candidate spent what was left of the night at the home of Hortencia Zabaera, mother of fourteen. In the Southwest, as in Baltimore and New Haven, he attempted to "focus attention on the plight of the poor." Despite the hour, excited neighbors crowded around the celebrity as a mariachi band from a local restaurant serenaded the assemblage with "Guadalajara." "The El Barrios," Jackson kept calling the locales, even after being admonished that "the" and "el" meant the same thing. But the bulk of his time in Texas was spent in familiar surroundings. "WELCOME REVEREND JACKSON. THANKS FOR LETTING OUR VOICES BE HEARD." The sign outside the St. Agnes Baptist church in Sunnyside, Texas, was printed in bold capitals; in Texas, as in Selma and Harlem before, he went back to the black church. "There's no house like the Lord's house. Here we can come and lay our burdens down. Here we can find joy. And acceptance."

In Sunnyside, and across the state, he would thank them for coming this night, for their prayers and support, for their love. Gently at first, then with his voice rising, he would list what had to be done. "We must study war no more. Stop mining the harbors of Nicaragua. Bring the boys home from Lebanon. . . . we must feed the hungry, clothe the naked, protect the needy."

The air was warm. Cardboard fans provided by a local funeral home waved back and forth in the pews. "You tell 'em, Jesse; tell 'em good," one worshiper shouted. The Reverend was sweating fiercely now. "There is nothing that pains me more than to see our children in darkness. They are faced with utter darkness. Rather than face the ugliness or the uncertainty of the darkness, they try to escape. Into TV. Into alcohol. They reach for the only thrill they know: they make babies. . . . Someone must broaden the base of their thrill syndrome: having breakfast in the morning is a thrill. Graduating is a *thrill. Holding a job is a thrill.* . . . All of life is a thrill."

It is not too late, it is never too late, he told them. God is redemptive—He keeps on giving us chances. "You may have missed Birmingham, but God keeps giving you another chance. You may not have gone to Selma. You should have, but maybe you didn't. Now God is giving you another chance. . . . Dry your eyes. Come alive, May 5. You get another chance. . . . You too have been oppressed; you've had that heavy foot on your neck."

"For four hundred years, Jesse," cried a voice in the back. In the background, with no cue given, the choir now began to sing softly. "Come by here, oh Lord, come by here. Somebody needs you, Lord. . . ." The Reverend was finishing up now. "We paid our dues for democracy, paid our wages and died in war without getting our vote; now we've come home for democracy." Exhausted, his face gleaming with sweat, his clothes soaked, Jackson stepped back from the lectern and stared off into the background. "Oh come by here, oh Lord, come by here," the choir sang, repeating the stanzas over and over: ". . . oh, oh come by here. . . ."

His other appeal in Texas was more earthy. The Texas caucus system, he argued, was designed to confuse, exhaust, discourage: Texans first had to vote—then they were required to return in the evening to transact caucus business. It was tedious and time-consuming. And sometimes costly for those who had to travel long distances. Don't let that slow you down, Jackson preached from the pulpit of the Friendship Baptist Church in San Antonio. "Come back Saturday night. It's really just a matter of attitude. . . . Take your congregations to the caucus—and have a prayer. If you don't understand it, just sit there till they call your name: Jesse Jackson." It was the same sermon he had used in Louisiana earlier, adapted to local circumstance. "Come alive, May 5. Vote twice to make it right. To do it right, you got to come back at night. . . . There. They put all that in their regulations, and it took up ten pages, but we've just said it in a few words. . . . Talk to me now. *Come alive, May 5. Come back at night to do it right. Vote twice, to make it nice.*"

In Texas Jackson won 17 percent of the vote on May 5; in North Carolina he finished third, with 25.4 percent of the vote. Louisiana gave him the sweetest prize of the day. Taking their lead from Governor Edwin Edwards, many Louisiana Democrats stayed home to protest a federal court order requiring the state to hold a primary. With the white boycott, Jackson's supporters swept their man into first place with 42.9 percent of the vote. The Louisiana vote was not counted until late on the night of the 5th, and Jackson's victory in a state where blacks were still asking courts to enforce voting rights was largely overlooked by the media. Louisiana was not crucial; Mondale's big win over Hart in Texas was.

Jackson was angry about news coverage but more so about the disproportionate distribution of delegates. "We're being robbed," he complained. Mondale, he pointed out, was getting about 40 percent of the primary vote—but was winning about 51 percent of the delegates. Jackson, on the other hand, was getting about 19 percent of the vote—but barely 8 percent of the delegates. "Mondale has 11 percent more than he earned, about 200 delegates more—and I have 11 percent less . . . something wrong with that," Jackson said.

His problem was that his vote was largely concentrated in just a few districts; there a massive turnout would not offset scant turnouts in other districts. His favorite illustration was Fort Worth. At one caucus session, almost 600 people had shown up: 21 of them wanted Hart, 60 wanted Mondale—and the rest, more than 500, wanted Jackson. The overflow guaranteed Jackson that particular caucus, but he could just as easily have done that with the first 250 voters. The other 250, he argued, "were wasted." The principle of one man, one vote was violated, he maintained: "if your vote does not count, you are disenfranchised . . . any time the rules are such that the one that gets the most votes doesn't get the delegates, something's wrong with the system, not the candidate."

It wasn't just Texas, he pointed out. In the caucus state of Virginia, the same pattern applied. There he had come in first in the popular vote. But Mondale had received more delegates. Once again Jackson's strength had been limited to a few areas; in some places he ran up huge totals, but Mondale's strength was spread more evenly throughout the state. As a result, Jackson finished third in the delegate count, 26 percent to Mondale's 30 percent, with 28 percent uncommitted. "This is white-collar crime," Jackson insisted. (It was not the first time he had made the argument. In Vermont, he received 15 percent of the vote—and zero convention delegates; in Connecticut, 12 percent of the vote—and only one delegate. In Arizona, he would get 13 percent of the vote—and again, only one delegate. None of those states, he pointed out, was exactly a black bastion. Each showed, he argued, his appeal to nonblacks. But the system, he went on, was stacked against him.)

Not everyone accepted Jackson's arithmetic. After making its own study, the *Washington Post* concluded that the rules had not hurt Jackson as much as the candidate claimed. The threshold rule in the primaries, the paper found, had cost Jackson only 50 delegates; coming up with a figure from various caucuses was much harder. Still, the *Post* concluded, there was "a good-faith basis" for each rule Jackson complained about. DNC chairman Charles Manatt pointed out that the system both helped and hurt other candidates as well when their strength was as localized as Jackson's was. In a sense, some of their votes at caucuses were also "wasted." No, said Manatt, there would not be any change in party rules or procedures, not this late in the game. Not in this election. Jackson kept pressing his demands. If the party does not pledge itself to change, he threatened, blacks won't feel much like supporting the party in November.

11.
FRANK WATKINS

Spring, 1968. Driving back to Indiana, the Reverend Frank Watkins and his wife were happy. The previous morning he had taught a Sunday school class and preached two sermons in the Blacksburg, Virginia, church; she had sung in the choir, and afterward some church members had invited them to a local pizza parlor. "Everyone got along fine . . . everything went very well," he recalled.

Blacksburg seemed different. Five times he had tried to get churches in other cities to hire him, and each time he had failed. The churches did not have to explain why, so he could only guess. Maybe it's my theology, maybe they're uncomfortable around someone who marched against the war in Viet Nam and for civil rights, he surmised. Board members in one Chicago church seemed very interested—until his wife told them her first priority was graduate school, not church business. The board members stiffened, he remembered; they wanted only docile wives who always promised to put the church first. At the time none of that seemed too important, so he kept sending out letters, presenting his credentials. There was a church available in Montana, twelve miles from the Canadian border; "the hunting up there is excellent," one of his seminary friends told him, and Frank Watkins, who had never hunted, had laughed. But the rejections had wounded him, and he was starting to wonder if he would ever fit in.

That's why Blacksburg was so important to him. This time

all the pieces seemed to fit. "Without meaning to sound boastful, they were very impressed with me," he said quietly. "If I don't miss my guess, we'll soon be calling this home," Watkins told his wife as they drove back to Indiana to wait for the decision. "If we don't get invited here, then I don't know anything about human nature," he added.

Years later he could not remember whether the church had called or had written to say it would be hiring someone else. He did remember how he felt. Years later it still hurt. "I was really brokenhearted. I remember I cried. So did my wife." Something had broken that would never fully heal. He would not expose himself like that again. "I kind of concluded I needed to go another way. I didn't need any more rejection, or humiliation."

Later, in 1969, he came to Chicago; helping community groups organize in the city's near north-side hillbilly ghetto, he saw Jesse Jackson lead a march against hunger—and he was impressed. In 1971, he joined Jackson's staff. The relationship, he insisted, was strictly "professional . . . I knew where I was going . . . and I saw Jackson as a vehicle for getting there."

Roughly the same age, they were a terrible mismatch—Jackson so flamboyant, Watkins so plain—but somehow the combination worked. They would share their dreams, and Watkins would weave them into speeches; he would pack the firebrand's traveling bags and arrange his trips and schedule his news conferences. Over the years, some others working for Jackson either walked away or quit in disgust. But Frank Watkins stayed on. In the lean years he was sometimes Jackson's only aide; gradually he became the most trusted, the most loyal. He even bought a house two blocks away from Jackson's, to be close by. At times he'd go months without being paid, but he rarely complained. What's with this guy, some Jackson supporters sneered—doesn't Watkins know he's white? "Mighty Whitey," Jackson called him, usually with a smile, sometimes not.

Criticism didn't hobble Frank Watkins because he had been an outsider too long. "I was the first rejected stone of the Rainbow Coalition," he'd joke much later. His parents, poor and uneducated, were devoutly religious; their son could not "go to the show, or even dance . . . one day they came to school and told my teachers I couldn't even square dance. I was very embarrassed." Telling the story later he still cringed.

Eventually he rebelled. By the eighth grade he had learned how to outswear, outsmoke, and outdrink all the others. Like a young Jackson in South Carolina, Watkins found relief on the playing fields. He was the only white starter on the basketball team at his Saint Louis high school; in baseball he was good enough to become the city's all-star centerfielder and catch the eye of pro scouts. Major league baseball was his dream then—"that's all I ever wanted to be," he sighed.

He enrolled in tiny Anderson College in Anderson, Indiana. Not because it was a Church of God school—but "because of Carl Erskine," he said, with a broad smile. Erskine, the college baseball coach, the onetime Brooklyn Dodger pitcher who'd set a World Series record in 1956 by striking out fourteen New York Yankees—"including Mickey Mantle, three times"—Erskine was one of Frank Watkin's heroes. Watkins loved sitting in the dugout listening to the old Dodger reminisce about the mighty Campanella and Newcombe and Snider; he loved the lore of the game, its excitement and comradeship. Almost twenty years later, the crack of the bat was still fresh. With Anderson trailing Hiram College eleven to nothing in the bottom of the ninth, Watkins had tripled with the bases loaded—not once, but twice—and had then stolen home to tie the score." Erskine still remembers those triples," he added.

Several years after that glorious afternoon Watkins introduced Erskine and Jackson at the funeral of Dodger star Jackie Robinson; Erskine was a pallbearer, and Jackson gave the eulogy. Several months later, as a result of that introduction, the town-fathers in Anderson asked Erskine to meet with Jackson to prevent racial turmoil in the town. The meeting had been a success; there was no trouble, and Frank Watkins was not surprised: he had seen Jackson help defuse other situations, had watched him win over skeptical, even hostile whites. Jackson, he knew, could disarm or inspire a crowd in a way that Frank Watkins never would be able to.

That's one reason why Watkins stayed on. Besides, how else would he ever get to attend Jackie Robinson's funeral? Or enter the White House itself? "I have opportunities with Jackson that I would not have dreamt about on my own," he conceded. "I'm at least in proximity to something that is changing American politics and is changing American history and world history. That's cracking the four-minute mile to me; that makes all the sweat and agony worth it."

Close, but never quite there: somehow that seemed to sum up Frank Watkins. He always seemed to be out of sync. He was either way ahead or hopelessly behind, and sometimes it wasn't easy to tell which. A shy person who felt things deeply, he was divorced; other than his fire-engine red sports car—"the driver's seat has eight different positions," he said sheepishly—Jesse Jackson was his whole life. "Reverend," he called him, even in private. "He's the toughest, the smartest man I've ever known," he'd tell friends, ignoring some of Jackson's shortcomings, rationalizing others. While the Reverend danced in the limelight, Watkins worked offstage in dingy offices where repair bills went unpaid and broken Xerox machines lined the walls.

No one applauded Frank Watkins. Sometimes Jackson included him in the cutthroat basketball games that Jackson loved, but Watkins would also find himself shunted aside. You gotta stay out of sight because blacks might not understand a white being up here, Jackson once berated him; while Watkins understood, the separation hurt. There had been other putdowns—Jackson could be a tyrannical, impossible boss; Watkins had considered quitting more than once. But he would not. The dreams and the brokenness were still there, so Frank Watkins accepted the outrageous working conditions and the abuse. "If you can't be used, you're not useful," he insisted. A bar of soap left on the shelf benefits no one, he'd argue. Blacksburg and five other churches might not have wanted him, but here at least he could make an impact. "I have something I can contribute, and I've been able to contribute to Jackson . . . I'd rather be the tail of something than the head of nothing," he added.

He was an idealist still trying to come to terms with his age. The idealism would be tempered, but it would not disappear. Subjugating himself, he dared great things for Jackson. On June 2, 1982, he sat for nearly four hours with a word processor in the basement of Operation PUSH and explained how Jackson could run for president.

"We must do to the left what George Wallace and Ronald Reagan did to the right, that is, build a political constituency that must be taken into account. Politicians have a limited education. They don't know how to read or write very well, they only know how to count," Watkins wrote. In the PUSH basement the objective was limited. "[Jackson] should not run as a 'realistic' candidate with a chance to win. My own judgment is that he could not be nominated or elected president in 1984. . . ." Gradually Watkins began to think it all was possible; look, it could have worked, he'd argue later, still carrying the original memo with him. If we had gone into Iowa early and worked the state and done better there, then we could have gone into New Hampshire with some momentum; then we could have won Georgia. And Alabama. Mondale would have been forced to drop out. Appealing to the have-nots, we could have won the nomination . . . his listeners would smile and nod their heads. They would not take his memo seriously. But he could wait. He could wait for all of them. "That's one reason I survive," he said later. "I have a long-range perspective. I'm not talking ten or twenty years. I'm talking about something I've given my life to."

The goal mattered more to him than the moment. One he could handle; the other kept slipping away. One afternoon as it rained in Indianapolis, Watkins stood in a hotel lobby patiently sorting out pages of a Jackson speech. Don't you get tired of this? he was asked.

Sure, he replied. But nothing worth getting comes easy, he went on. Look at major league ballplayers—they're always bouncing from one city to another. Just like us, he brightened. Slowly the hotel lobby faded away, and he drifted back to the green fields where the sun was always shining. "Could I have made it? . . . Well, I didn't have outstanding talent. I would have had to work on my hitting. . . . but I always felt that if I'd been brought up through the minors. . . ." Outside it was raining harder, but Frank Watkins never even noticed. "If I had had the coaching, I could have . . . I was always able to rise to the occasion, to handle the challenge. . . . I think I could have."

12. RIVER JORDAN

At an Indianapolis fund-raiser in May, a stunning young woman in a skintight silvery gown slithered to the stage and presented Jackson with a contribution for $1,000. "Wow-eee," the candidate purred. "That's a $500 dress." As she slinked off the stage to whistles, Jackson's eyes followed. "And a $10,000 walk."

For his campaign though, there wasn't much to laugh about in Indiana. Or Ohio either. In the Hoosier State, Jackson banked on a big turnout in mostly black Gary, whose mayor, Richard Hatcher, was co-chairman of Jackson's national campaign. In Ohio he counted upon the political muscle of Cleveland city council president George Forbes. And possibly some assistance from Ohio governor Richard Celeste. "There's a chance we can get this guy," Arnold Pinkney told Jackson; Pinkney had known Celeste for years, and the governor had not yet committed himself publicly to anyone. At the eleventh hour, Jackson flew late at night from North Carolina to Columbus, Ohio, to plead his case. "Reciprocity is real to me. I hope it's real to him," Jackson said en route. Reminded that the Carter-Mondale administration had appointed Celeste director of the Peace Corps, Jackson countered that Celeste wouldn't have been elected without black votes. "Mondale gave him a job; we gave him a position." The candidate was buoyant, almost belligerent. Celeste listened to him politely but was noncommittal. The day after Jackson left Ohio, however, Celeste announced his preference: Mondale.

Indiana was conservative—far too conservative to be offset by the black vote in Gary and Indianapolis, Hatcher thought—but Jackson would still try to light a fire there. Returning to Indianapolis, he described himself as "the urban candidate," calling for restoration of $10 billion in social programs cut by the Reagan administration; "the administration has no urban policy. Its cuts have devastated social and economic programs for millions of people in our cities." He proposed radical steps to wipe out the nation's budget deficit: not just the 20 percent reduction in military spending he'd been proposing, but also an emergency surtax of 1 to 10 percent on all income over $25,000. "Tough medicine is needed for tough times," he pleaded.

In Maryland, he was forced to play catch-up. Mondale had already sewed up most of the state's Democratic leaders. In Baltimore, Jackson tried to go over the heads of the party bosses and appeal directly to the city's 200,000 black voters. "Chicago's time came. New York's time came. Philadelphia's time came. Baltimore, your time has come."

Citing the high unemployment rate of blacks nationally, and particularly in Maryland, Jackson launched into a favorite illustration. "You know, they make you think you got to read nine thousand volumes on industrial policy to understand the industrial collapse. That ain't so," he told them. The honey bee, he said, holding up a flower for a prop, "the honey bee gets high off pollen, that's what gives it its buzz." Big corporations were like honey bees, he continued. Corporations get their pollen from the nation's inner cities, from inner city people. But unlike the wise bee, he argued, the corporations don't replenish what they use. "These plants close without notice, then they sow their pollen in South Africa, Taiwan, and Korea . . . they're taking our nectar then sowing their pollen in slave labor markets abroad . . . they're killing the flower."

Complaining that the other candidates were ignoring Maryland, he went from Prince George's County to Maryland's Eastern Shore. Then back across the Chesapeake Bay. I'm not going to abandon people the way the Reagan administration has, he insisted. "The fact is that Jesus would be in *real trouble* under the Reagan administration. . . . Under Reagan, Jesus' family would not have had the manger weatherized; Jesus would have probably caught pneumonia." And when the president found out that the three wise men were coming, said Jackson, "he'd take tax money to start a Star Wars to stop them."

The time devoted to Maryland paid off. He again finished third but with an impressive 25.5 percent of the Democratic primary vote; he also carried Baltimore. Ohio and Indiana, however, were disappointments; the turnout in Gary was less than he had hoped, and in Ohio George Forbes proved no match for the Celeste-Mondale team. In Ohio, Jackson got only 16.4 percent of the Democratic vote; in conservative Indiana, a dismal 13.7 percent. The candidate didn't linger in the Rust Bucket; he was already heading east, to New Jersey. And then west, to California.

May 17, 1984. "This is indeed an *occasion*," said Mrs. Francis Harris, 79, standing in the brilliant California sunshine. She had come to hear Jesse Jackson speak outside the Japanese American Cultural and Community Center in the Los Angeles Little Tokyo area, and for the occasion Mrs. Harris wore her Sunday best, a bright yellow blouse with a fancy purple corsage. Jackson, she said, "makes me excited. When you're feeling low, he always perks you up. He's got that old time religion."

She was also afraid, she said, for Jackson. Born in Montgomery, Texas, she had come west in 1941 to work in the airplane plants, and she had learned from experience how generous—and how mean—the country could be. "Anybody trying to stand up for the poor, something always happens to them. They kill them. I'm afraid of what will happen to him. Before they let him be president, they'll do away with him. Still a lot of prejudice here."

Jackson's faith had helped preserve him, she went on; in this campaign Mrs. Harris saw the hand of Providence. She paused and gave her interviewer a hard look; she somehow sensed he didn't understand what she was trying to say. "Do you know the saying—'before the end of time, the bottom will be on top'?" she asked. "That means we will be on top. We've come from slavery, you know. It's the Lord at work," she said very firmly.

There were only two weeks left in the campaign. But his "organization" was still misfiring, still making mistakes. The candidate knew it; and while he would sometimes complain, nothing changed. Late one May afternoon, Jackson sat slumped in a chair in a Holiday Inn room near the Holland Tunnel. For half an hour he tried to find a plane to fly him, his staff, and reporters to Mexico City. The trip was essential, he said, to help "spotlight the growing U.S. military involvement in the region." But his aides had not been able to secure a plane. The television networks, long annoyed by all the campaign snafus, had resorted to chartering their own plane. For the Mexico City flight Jackson wanted everyone together.

"Reverend, can't you leave this chore of finding a plane to someone else?" he was asked.

"Been burned too often doing that," he replied. "No, I'll handle it myself," he said, turning away to dial another call.

Accompanied by Kenneth Gibson, Newark's black mayor and co-chairman of the state campaign, Jackson blitzed New Jersey. In the state capital he spoke out against what he called "the evils of the international debt crisis. . . . bankruptcy forces austerity which makes life even harder for those who already don't have enough." At a housing project in Trenton he also played a spirited game of basketball with housing project residents barely half his age; after catching his breath, he then counseled them "to develop both your cognitive—and your motor skills." To striking workers outside a Merck Pharmaceutical Company plant, he presented himself as a hard-core unionist: "We should never use Taft-Hartley. We should repeal it. Give workers a chance," he shouted. In Newark, before a festive crowd waiting for a giant city parade, Jackson gave what he called a major address—on the subject of Africa. "Africa, your time has come. Africa, you've climbed the rough side of the mountain. But trouble don't last forever." Throughout the state, his political barnstorming seemed a curious grabbag of political fact and fancy, but the mostly black audiences were large and supportive. Late one night he wrapped up a campaign swing at Newark's Symphony Hall. "I don't know what the future holds, but I'm secure in the fact of who holds the future. . . . Against great odds, we express an unshakable joy because of an unshakable faith. . . . Like a raging pent-up wind, I was here. Years ago when you needed me. Now I come back asking you to co-venture with me."

As Jackson left for the Southwest, reporters cornered him coming out of a Newark hotel and gave him a T-shirt. "I Love Hymie Town," it read in bold letters. Jackson scanned it, glanced around, tossed the shirt into a waiting bank of cameras so the lettering wouldn't show—and walked off, laughing.

En route to Phoenix, he decided to make a dash across Arizona—to Window Rock, seventy-five minutes away, by helicopter—to address the Navajo Tribal Council. The gesture gave his schedulers, and Secret Service agents, mild apoplexy, but the Navajos loved him. They showered him with blankets and jewelry, and the largest Indian newspaper in the country endorsed him for president.

"You're a great nation," he told them. "You've been banished to the reservations to die, but you live anyhow. . . . You are a blessed people. How the nation has treated you is a source of shame and disgrace. How the nation treats the Indian is the moral test of our nation," he went on, calling for the abolition of the Bureau of Indian Affairs and the creation of a new cabinet-level department for Native Americans. To the Hopi council, his message was much the same. Coal leases executed on behalf of Indians with large mining companies were "exploitation," he insisted, and must be scrapped. "You've endured the worst our nation has to offer," he consoled them.

We're accustomed to begging to the Great White Father in Washington, one Indian leader told him. "When you're elected, what shall we call you?" Jackson beamed. "No more Great White Father, that's for sure. . . . And no more 'Yassa boss' either," he replied, wrapping his questioner in a giant bear hug.

May 21, 1984. The day that had begun in Texas and spilled over into New Mexico finally ended in Oakland about twenty-one hours later. At the hotel desk, the clerk was slow and surly. For several minutes he couldn't find a room key for the two Secret Service agents. It was nearly 1:45 A.M. The next day's schedule was supposed to begin in less than five hours. "It's gotten worse. It wasn't possible, but it keeps getting worse," one of the agents grumbled. Finally the clerk found the keys. "Will there be anything else, sir?" said the clerk, trying to feign interest. The agent gave him a weary look. "Yes, just one thing. Don't mind the loud noise. It'll just be my service revolver exploding into my head," he said walking off toward the elevator.

Inside the McKinley Baptist Church in Los Angeles, the Reverend F. R. Higgins compared Jesse Jackson to other pioneers honored by the black congregation. "Jesse Jackson is opening up doors that were shut in our face. The Lord is using him in a marvelous way. White people, some of them still dread the idea that a black man is the candidate for the presidency of the U.S. But it's a veiled mercy. That's right, it is the veiled mercy of the Lord. . . . Some dreaded the day Jackie Robinson came. But he elevated baseball. Lifted it by his very presence. We find that Jesse Jackson, in a political sense, is doing the same thing. . . . I say run, Jesse, run. I say don't you get weary. Because there's a great camp meeting in the White House." Jackson had not yet arrived, and the church was only half-full. When he appeared, the sanctuary filled quickly, including eight white motorcycle riders who had been waiting outside the church for the last hour. Just before Jackson spoke, the bikers slipped into the last pew.

In California, Jackson again tried to attract outsiders who had shunned—or had been shunned by—the political process. In San Francisco, he appeared at a rally sponsored by gays. From San Diego he darted into Tijuana, Mexico—"we see our goal as global"—to complain that illegal farm workers were being made into scapegoats for the problems of U.S. agriculture. In Los Angeles he told Japanese Americans that U.S. immigration policies were "racist"—and that auto workers in Japan were being used as "whipping boys" to cover up the mistakes of auto executives in Detroit. In Pasadena, he appeared at a rally for Armenians—"we must get the Armenians and the Turks to talk to each other." At Hollywood Park (racetrack), he led a procession of aides and reporters and bodyguards to shabby racetrack workers' housing behind the horse barns to show that racetracks spend more on horses than on those who groom the animals. "You got to go to the backstretch to see how life really is. The profits get greater, the horses run faster . . . but the boats on the bottom still don't rise," he proclaimed.

In Berkeley, he marched grandly through city streets with paraplegics, telling those who accused him of "exploiting" the disabled that "my brothers and sisters in wheelchairs say that chrome belongs in the Rainbow Coalition." In Watts, he assailed the administration's proposal to pay teenagers less than the minimum wage to stimulate teenage employment. "Our appetites aren't sub-minimum; we can't buy clothes at sub-minimum prices," he argued. In Los Angeles, his motorcade flashed down Figuero Street past a rooming house with a faded sign that read "This Hotel Welcomes Anyone. Absolutely No Prostitutes." As the caravan's red lights washed over the scene, two derelicts struggled to their feet and waved at him long after the candidate had swept by.

June 5, 1984. He had delivered a thousand sermons by now, grabbed tens of thousands of hands. Gnarled fingers had reached out to touch his finely tailored suits and had been held up like blessed icons before their owners' eyes. He'd grown hoarse and surly; silly and sullen; proud and desperate. He'd lied. He'd apologized. He'd compared himself to Jesus so many times he was dubbed "our black Messiah." He had amassed over 3½ million votes and would take over 400 delegates to the Democratic convention. But no real power, no leverage: to Democratic chieftains, he was everything from a nuisance to a pariah to a political joke.

It was 7:30 A.M. The last day of the primary season. One last project. There was no crowd. "Come out and see the next president of the United States. I don't care if you are in your bathrobes," a campaign worker yelled into the still morning. Twenty people grew to thirty to forty or fifty.

"One thing that excites me about getting up so early to vote is that not too long ago we were getting up early to pick cotton," Jackson told the small knot of people. But the line was lost on his sleepy onlookers, and Jackson's mind seemed elsewhere. "This is the end of a long campaign . . . designed to bring you up, wake you up, shake you up, shake the very foundation of our nation," he said. The rhyme was there but not the spirit. Jackson walked from the center of the project to a polling place, down 10th Street, pausing under a spreading tree. Brenda Ingram stood at the edge of the crowd. "Just the fact that he made it this far makes us proud," she said. "We'll probably never see it again." One more testament from one more project-dweller; one more pair of blazing eyes and a newfound hope with an uncertain half-life.

No matter how much a parent loves a child, there "comes a time when a child must go on his own," Jackson said, this last day of the campaign, as if bracing himself. "I must move on to other places now," he called out. "I brought you as far as I can bring you. You must shoulder the burden and responsibilities and go across the chilly Jordan. Each one has to swim for his or herself," Jackson said, speaking, it seemed, more to himself than to the small crowd gathered under the tree.

They listened, the women in their faded housecoats, the toddlers with bare feet, the middle-aged man in the "Free Huey" T-shirt. But Jackson seemed to have an audience of one, and his message was one of innocence lost and opportunity missed and power eluded. It was like no other speech in the campaign. "There comes a point when leaders can't take you any farther," he lamented under the tree. "And you must go it on your own. Go it on your own," he said solemnly, standing in the bright California sun, the last morning of the last day, while elsewhere other leaders with better credentials were lining up to take his place as the next black contender for president. You're on your own, he told the people in the projects, while across the Bay, at San Francisco's Moscone Center, Democratic National Convention planners already had lined up his in-hall trailer and computerized communications system and walkie-talkies that would have symbolism but no substance when the session opened next month.

"You must go it on your own," Jackson told his followers, playing out the final scene with the certainty of someone who had known it was going to end this way all along.

13. SOUTH OF THE BORDER

May 28, 1984. The Camino Real Hotel, Mexico City. As Jesse Jackson completed a news conference, he announced that he'd be returning to Central America soon. "Possibly even to Cuba," he told a room full of newspeople and supporters. Startled reporters exchanged glances and stopped writing; a few shook their heads, even started to chuckle. One walked to the back of the room where Secret Service agent Jim Dotson was sitting. Dotson was neither shocked nor amused. "I have it on good authority," the reporter said to the agent, "that just before Christmas, Jackson is planning to visit the North Pole—to free Santa's workers."

"Don't worry about a thing," the agent deadpanned in return. "We've had an advance team there for the last week." Dotson forced a thin smile and then shook his head.

Ordinarily, presidential hopefuls—especially those still in search of a nomination—content themselves with campaigning within the boundaries of the continental United States. Where most voters lived, where the primaries are held. Not Jesse Jackson. "Our Rainbow Coalition must function beyond conventional politics," he said, and an expanded itinerary was, he felt, part of that expanded mission. Using the same rationale, in May, 1985, Jackson traveled to Biburg, West Germany, where President Ronald Reagan met with West German chancellor Helmut Kohl; in November, Jackson went to Geneva for the Reagan-Gorbachev summit. There, in an extraordinary 45 minute session, Jackson not only presented the Russian leader with 1 million signatures calling for a ban on nuclear testing, but also, according to the *New York Times*, "held his ground and speaking in measured, respectful tones" pressed Gorbachev about the condition of Russian Jews. "There is a great anxiety among the American people about the plight of Soviet Jews," Jackson told Gorbachev, after which he branded Gorbachev's response "unacceptable."[55] Later, even Jackson's most outspoken critic was impressed. "We commend him for his persistence . . . and his eloquence . . . ," said a statement released by the American Jewish Congress. For Jesse Jackson, then, functioning "beyond conventional politics" was normal behavior. So on May 27, 1984, nine days before the California primary, he jetted into Mexico City for a whirlwind 24-hour visit. "I go to Mexico first and foremost because I want to stop war in Central America," he said when asked why he was leaving the United States. War in Central America, he insisted, was "imminent." And American soldiers would probably be sent in to fight, he went on. If so, the ensuing debate at home would tear the country apart even more than the rancorous debate over Viet Nam, he continued. We must "give peace a chance . . . choose dialogue over deployment . . . there is more power in cease-fire than in more fire," he said.

The one-country foray would also let him spotlight differences he had with Reagan administration policies for the region. "We can't resolve our problems . . . by gunboat diplomacy and by military advisors. Our no-talk foreign policy has been an ineffective foreign policy," he said. While in Mexico he said he would also look for ways to end the international debt crisis. To critics, Jackson's visiting Mexico City was just one more grandstanding stunt. Jackson wasted little time on the criticism: remember those who scoffed at the Syrian mission—and who laughed last, he countered.

The Mexico City pilgrimage started off well enough. The Mexican Senate's Committee on Foreign Relations gave him a respectful hearing. "Militarizing the region is not the way to go," he testified, assailing the U.S. policy of providing Honduras, Guatemala, and El Salvador with military advisors. Several committee members disagreed with Washington's policies too, and Jackson listened attentively as they criticized the administration. "You're suggesting that we think before we shoot . . . I get the point," Jackson replied when one member finished, adding that U.S. budget deficits and interest rates should be slashed to ease international debt problems. Again, Mexican legislators concurred.

Mexico's foreign minister Bernardo Sepùlveda Amor gave Jackson a courteous hearing as well. His government also had reservations about some Reagan administration policies and had along with Panama, Colombia, Venezuela (the so-called Contadora countries) urged the resolution of armed conflict by negotiations. Sepulveda and Jackson agreed that the source of Central America's woes were poverty and disease, not Communism. Ronald Reagan has it all wrong, Jackson told reporters after his 30-minute session with the Mexican envoy. "His [Reagan's] basic approach is that of the premise of manifest destiny and gunboat diplomacy and big-stick diplomacy, as opposed to negotiations. . . ."

Still, the trip seemed contrived, artificial, incomplete. Jackson had proclaimed that he would be meeting with the Contadora leadership, but a meeting never did take place. Bad planning, and a driving rainstorm, forced the cancellation of what aides described as a major rally at the University of Mexico City. The candidate was left with time to kill, dead time, hardly the sign of a successful mission. Still, "we leave Mexico with our spirits lifted," he told the farewell news conference; he not only said that he'd be returning to the region—but also announced plans for the Fourth of July: thousands of students would, he said, be mobilized along the U.S.-Mexican border to link hands in friendship. The effort, Jackson modestly noted, was not without parallel: "Gandhi marched to the sea. Martin Luther King marched to Washington. Jesus marched to Jerusalem. We must march to our common border. We must promise to heal each other and not kill each other."

Although the trip to Mexico City brought mixed results, the activity did generate publicity for Jackson that would be welcome in two states with large Hispanic populations (California and New Mexico) that were holding primaries June 5. The trip also convinced him that other trips in the future might be useful. Such as right before the Democratic National Convention.

Crammed with sixty-three reporters and technicians, nearly thirty Secret Service agents, and a dozen aides—including one speechwriter, a translator, an analyst from something called the Council of Hemispheric Affairs in Washington, D.C., and Jackson's three sons—Jackson's chartered plane lifted off from Chicago late June 22 and arrived in Panama City at 7 the next morning. For the first time within memory, Jackson was early. "Hermano [brother] Jesse" read one hastily draped banner that sagged overhead in the muggy heat. For forty-five minutes, the candidate waited aboard for Panama City's mayor to show up and welcome him. The mayor never did appear, but Jackson was not dismayed. Wearing a crisp blue safari suit, he bounded out of the plane and onto the Tarmac, where a group of Panamanian children waited to greet him with dances and songs. At a news conference inside the airport terminal, Jackson said he'd come to the region because Central America was teetering on the brink of war, and "this summer may be our last chance to work for peace before the fall offensive." He also denounced administration policies for the area. He did not, however, criticize Cuba, the Sandinista government of Nicaragua, or the guerrillas fighting the government of El Salvador, each a scheduled stop on his whirlwind journey. Aren't the Cubans trying to overthrow the government of El Salvador? he was asked. "It would not be appropriate to answer that," he replied, changing the subject.

A few hours later, Jackson's swollen motorcade wound its way through Panama City's narrow streets to the presidential palace overlooking the Pacific Ocean. Jackson walked through a lobby of strutting peacocks to the office of Panama's president, Jorge Illueca. "The visit of Mr. Jackson is very important to the region," the president told reporters. "He has been successful in getting representatives of the U.S. mass media to come to Panama and Central America to see firsthand the situation," Illueca said, smiling at the room full of cameras and reporters.

That night, as a hundred people picketed outside denouncing Panama's recent elections as rigged, Jackson greeted Panamanians inside the steamy Don Bosco Cathedral. A Salvation Army band played "Jacob's Ladder," and a black choir sang "Elijah, Rock." Soon Jackson was leading the Spanish-speaking congregation in a broken-English version of "I Am Somebody. . . ."

The next morning his presidential-style entourage pulled up near the tomb of former Panamanian president Omar Torijjos, "the late great Torijjos," as Jackson called the onetime Panamanian strongman. "When it's all totaled up, Torijjos was a winner," he added, standing in the warm sun next to a golf course, under a mango tree sagging with fruit. At one point, Jackson looked up and saw two dates on Torijjos' tomb, the late leader's birth and death dates separated by a dash. "We don't know when we're going to be born. And we generally don't know the date of our expiration, when we're going to die. Two dates. And in between, the dash of life. When we have to make choices and judgments," he extemporized.

Then it was on to the Panama Canal. One judgment the United States made was clearly wrong, Jackson argued, and that was the Canal. He called it "a badge of disgrace," which he said had helped "dehumanize" the Panamanian people. It showed "the worst dimension of American segregation and South African apartheid," he added. "Shame, hurt, pain, denial, disgrace, and economic exploitation"—all that, he said, is what the Canal represents. All that misery, however, did not prevent Jackson from leading his retinue to the Miraflores locks, where he scampered up a flight of steps and presided over the opening of one lock for the cameras.

Most of the next day Jackson was closeted in room 516 of the Panama Hilton with rebel leaders from El Salvador opposed to the government of that country. He was trying to promote a cease-fire between the rebels and the government of Salvadoran president José Napoleon Duarte. "We must develop a radical passion for negotiation," he said after the meeting, telling reporters that the rebels were now willing to go to El Salvador to negotiate for peace. It was, Jackson trumpeted, a real "breakthrough." Later, rebel spokesman Ruben Zamora conceded that the rebels still had not agreed to lay down their arms, which Duarte had insisted was necessary before any talks could begin. Zamora also made it clear that the rebels in their talks with Jackson had done little more than reiterate their previous positions. But Jackson put a better face on the situation. "Both groups are armed and fighting; someone must break the cycle . . . take the risk and give peace a chance," Jackson told reporters, announcing that he was taking what he called the rebels' "moral appeal" to San Salvador and would personally deliver it to the government there. As Jackson was concluding the session with the rebels in the Panama Hilton, Nation of Islam leader Louis Farrakhan was going on the radio in Chicago. In that broadcast Farrakhan called Judaism "a dirty religion" and the creation of Israel "an outlaw act."

Monday, June 25. As the candidate's plane descended into El Salvador, a network cameraman danced in the aisles and chortled to his fellow passengers. "I want you all to remember this. That we're all Americans. That we're all in this together. That if one gets a scoop, everyone gets it. That if someone gets hurt, leave 'em." The passengers laughed. But no one knew quite what to make of the occasion—or how to proceed. "If there is a pay phone, what do you put in it?" One reporter asked on arrival. The confusion hardly pleased Jackson's bodyguards; in the chaos of El Salvador's civil war, the unsmiling agents were worried about the threat of violence against Jackson. "This guy is a prime target for the rebels . . . meat on the rack," said one agent. Under their tropical shirts they slipped on white bullet-proof vests. "Give us plenty of room when we land," one yelled. A military helicopter hovered overhead as Jackson's plane landed; the candidate was hustled into the airport terminal, then into a waiting four-wheel Chevy van, with bullet-proof windows; as it raced into the capital city, the armed helicopter followed overhead.

President Duarte received Jackson at the gleaming presidential palace, and afterward both men stood on the palace steps and answered questions from reporters. Our talks, Jackson said, "were long and extensive and fruitful." Duarte was gracious. "There is nothing new here," he said of Jackson's proposal. But since it was what Duarte called "a moral appeal," and not a tactical demand of the rebels, the government would consider it, he said, and would also present it to the people for their consideration. Many reporters listening to the president felt that the entire performance was comic; rather than embarrass Jackson by stiff-arming his message, Duarte was using diplomatic mumbo jumbo, double-speak that meant absolutely nothing. Jackson, however, seized upon Duarte's words to claim more progress. "This is a wise move," he said of Duarte's action, "a step in the right direction . . . our challenge is to break the cycle of pain and give peace a chance. . . ."

Thanking Duarte, Jackson then headed for a jail outside the capital to meet with imprisoned labor leader Hector Orsinos. Earlier Orsinos' family had begged Jackson to meet with the prisoner, but Jackson's Secret Service detail had said no. One member of the advance team who'd visited the prison a week earlier said he'd been made physically ill by what he'd seen: "guys with their tongues cut out . . . some pretty terrible stuff, let me tell you," he had said. But squeamishness was not the cause of the agents' reservations. Going to the jail was too dangerous, they concluded; roads to the compound could not be adequately secured, safety could not be guaranteed. Annoyed with their reasoning, Jackson discussed the situation with Duarte, who told him the agents' concerns were exaggerated. I'll even send along my personal secretary, Duarte assured the candidate. Jackson called in the Secret Service detail chief and introduced him to Duarte. "Now you tell him, Mr. President, what you just told me," Jackson instructed his host. Duarte repeated what he'd said—the trip would be perfectly safe. The agent was furious—he could hardly contradict the president of the country where he and the candidate were guests. And certainly the agent could not do so to the president's face, as Jackson also knew. The agent asked the president if he might have a word with Jackson. "The least you can do, Reverend," he snapped, "is to leave your sons behind. That is, unless you want them to be targets too." The sons stayed, but Jackson went. (Duarte's secretary didn't go either; when the caravan departed, the secretary couldn't be located.) The venture was uneventful.

Returning to the airport outside San Salvador, Jackson learned that many reporters were ridiculing his talks with Duarte, that most stories filed had said the stalemate in El Salvador continued—in short, that there had not been the breakthrough Jackson had claimed. "We got them to agree to talk about talking," Jackson snorted. "That's more than anybody else has done." Three days later, despite all the good fellowship in room 516 and the proclamations thereafter, rebel guns boomed in El Salvador again. In one bloody battle, rebels stormed and seized the country's most important hydroelectric dam, and in the fight to get it back 123 people were killed.

The trip to the San Salvador jail slowed Jackson's schedule. By the time he arrived at his next stop in Havana, he was three hours late. It was dark by then, but Cuban premier Fidel Castro waited for Jackson as the candidate got off the plane. "He honors us with his visit," Castro said. Hundreds of Cubans lined the rooftop of the terminal building at José Martí airport to watch the two men, but there was no applause or cheering as the two men drove off in a Soviet-made Chaika limousine, only silence.

At the fancy guest house where the Cuban government housed its guest, Jackson and Castro sat together by a swimming pool, a table nearby literally sagging under food and drink and sweets. Jackson aide Frank Watkins used the occasion to get Castro to autograph a three-peso Cuban note. Jackson told his host that the time had now come for the two countries to normalize relations, but Castro was noncommittal, his cigar making small clouds of smoke as he listened and watched. Soon he escorted Jackson to a song and dance extravaganza staged for Jackson at the National Theatre of Cuba. After a few minutes, Castro left, but Jackson stayed until the end, telling reporters that he thought he had detected strains of Stevie Wonder's music in the Cuban entertainment.

The next morning Jackson appeared on the CBS Morning News from Havana and was asked about Farrakhan's statements. The candidate bristled. "I don't understand what he said. I don't understand the context of it. I feel no obligation to respond to it. I think it's absurd that you are trying to get a reaction from me on this." After the interview, he was sullen and angry. "Find out right away what he said. All of it!" he barked to one aide. Then he was off for a tourist's view of the capital—off to the Cuban Museum of History, where he asked about slaves brought to Cuba from Africa; off to a modern hospital, where he peppered officials with questions about the country's free health care: How much are doctors paid? Do illegitimate kids get the same care as other children? On the way out he signed the hospital's guest book: "Health is wealth. Health is for everyone. Peace. Jesse Jackson."

Jackson met Castro that afternoon at the nondescript Palace of the Revolution, and in that grim, squat building the two men talked from four P.M. until nearly midnight, accompanied by their staffs. At one point, Jackson's youngest son, Youssef, then 13, sat in at the conference table. "Thank you, Reverend Castro," Jackson said to his host after one long monologue by the Cuban leader. When the marathon session ended, Castro announced that he was releasing from Cuban jails twenty-two Americans, most of them serving time for drug-related offenses. Jackson hailed the gesture: "if this release from Castro is another sign of him wanting to normalize relations, then this release could set the two nations free."

As the two men talked, nearly three hundred reporters waited in a nearby auditorium. Then they waited another thirty minutes as Jackson read the ten-point statement he and Castro had signed. Jackson said the document was historic: the Cuban government would consider letting some of the so-called Cuban boat-people who had illegally emigrated to the United States—and who were now sitting in Florida jails—come back to Cuba; it would consider exchanging ambassadors with Washington.

But the first question to Jackson was not about any of that. "Reverend Jackson, it has been forty-eight hours now since Louis Farrakhan called Judaism a gutter religion. . . . Do you finally have a reaction to that? And do you repudiate those remarks?" The question seemed to surprise Castro, who chewed on a cigar as Jackson waited for the questioner to finish. Then, his voice not concealing his anger, Jackson replied: "I shouldn't respond to that . . . I'm going to focus on this agenda [the ten-point program] . . . that can save the lives of thousands of people in this hemisphere."

The next day Jackson was off on another frantic trip: this time to schools Castro had established on the Isle of Youth. "Indoctrination centers," Castro critics called them, but Jackson was enthusiastic about what he found. When he returned to Havana, Castro greeted him at the University of Havana, where Jackson got a standing ovation. "Long live Cuba. Long live the U.S. Long live Castro. Long live Martin Luther King. Long live Ché Guevara. Long live our cry of freedom. Our time has come," Jackson said to thunderous applause. The two men then went to a Cuban church, where they sang "We Shall Overcome" with another overflow crowd. Cuban officials hastily noted that this was the first time Castro had been in a church since the revolution.

The trip, however, was not getting the rave reviews back in the United States that it was drawing in Havana. The Farrakhan controversy (see chapter 7) had drawn much of the attention away from the prisoner release, and some Americans were openly complaining about getting back convicted drug-dealers and smugglers, some of whom faced immediate arrest upon their return. Before leaving for Managua on June 27, Jackson told Castro the release gesture was not being treated as much of a breakthrough, at least in the U.S. media. The wily Castro understood perfectly. As Jackson's plane lifted off for Nicaragua, Jackson used the intercom to announce that Castro had decided to release another twenty-six prisoners: this time, all of them Cuban—and each a so-called political prisoner, jailed for actions the Castro government had once deemed "injurious to the nation."

Jackson spent only a few hours in Managua, but that was enough time to ruffle more feathers back home. Standing alongside a swimming pool at the government residence called Protocol House, Jackson praised the Sandinista government "for putting Nicaragua back on the road to democracy, peace, and reconciliation." Contra guerrillas fighting the government, he said, are not "a legitimate political force" and should immediately lay down their arms and surrender. Have the Sandinistas been faithful to the principles of the revolution that overthrew the hated Somoza regime? Jackson was asked. "We had a revolution of our own. . . . It was thirteen years from General Washington to President Washington. It has been only five years in Nicaragua," he replied.

Heading back to the United States, Jackson swooped down in Havana to pick up the prisoners. "Don't you get caught in any bad behavior between now and when I get back," he'd told them in prison, as his aides in Washington were releasing a statement that called Farrakhan's recent statements about Judaism "morally indefensible."

Jackson and Castro met one time at José Martí airport. "Fidel, Jackson—Fidel, Jackson," the airport crowd, noisy this time, chanted time and again as the two men walked, like seasoned campaigners, toward the terminal building, stopping to shake hands in the tumult. Inside, Castro gave Jackson a cigar. "A peace pipe," the candidate quipped, promptly stuffing the wrong end in his mouth before Castro rescued the nonsmoker by lighting the cigar and returning it to his guest. Wreathed in billowing clouds of smoke, the two men beamed at one another. Later, Castro said he'd never met anyone quite like Jackson.

Like Syrian president Hafez al-Assad earlier, Castro had found reasons to do business with Jesse Jackson. Holding the American prisoners longer wouldn't do the Cuban leader any particular good; releasing them—and some Cuban political prisoners—might win him a few points as a humanitarian and at the same time discomfit an administration in Washington that persisted in depicting Castro as a tyrant.

Jackson's critics complained that Castro had turned the candidate into a stooge, that Jackson had been used. The truth, however, is that the prisoner release benefited both men. Castro got rid of some people he didn't need in return for some declarations that couldn't be enforced; Jackson not only got publicity, he turned what some called a grandstand stunt into another successful rescue mission. Without the trip, he pointed out, nearly fifty people would still be sitting in Cuban jails.

Returning home, Jackson described his mission as a great success: "the moral offensive that President Castro and I launched is the catalyst to realize those dreams of peace and progress of the western hemisphere as a war-free zone." But Jackson's opinion was far from unanimous. Publicly, the State Department dismissed the trip as insignificant. "We don't think it reflects any basic change in Cuban policy . . . we see the release of these prisoners as essentially a humanitarian accomplishment by Reverend Jackson rather than as a politically significant event," said State Department spokesman Alan Romberg. Both the president and secretary of state rejected appeals by Jackson that he meet with them to discuss his impressions of Castro. Privately, officials let it be known that Secretary of State Shultz considered the whole trip "scandalous." President Reagan even suggested that Jackson might have violated the Logan Act by going, although the president later conceded that Jackson probably hadn't broken any law.

Other Jackson critics were indignant at what he'd said. Criticizing the U.S. government at home was one thing—but to do so abroad was quite another. Some couldn't follow his arguments: how one guerrilla force (in El Salvador) was legitimate but another (in Nicaragua) was not. "What is the man doing?" James Reston asked in a column, then answered his own question: ". . . playing buddy with Fidel Castro in Cuba goes beyond the normal bounds of political and personal arrogance. . . . he is interfering with the constitutional rights of the president and Congress to conduct foreign policy. . . ."[56]

All the controversy notwithstanding, Jackson had managed to stay in the headlines and on the evening news broadcasts. In the week before the Democratic National Convention, when even the party's front-runner and his closest challenger were all but ignored by the news media, no other candidate could make that claim.

And the trip had proved something else. At home, Jackson could get lost in a crowd of political opponents; in Central America, he was the crowd. In the United States, he could not arrange a three-way meeting with Mondale and Hart; in Central America, he was greeted by presidents and given welcomes generally reserved for heads of state. At home the mainstream could sweep him aside; abroad, he could still negotiate prisoners out of a jail cell. Speeding around Panama City with sirens blaring and a herd of reporters in tow, he was important. A moment was being seized. As Janis Joplin sang—freedom was just another word for nothing left to lose.

14. THE SWIMMING POOL

In California, he finished a distant third, with just under 20 percent of the vote. New Jersey was better; coming in third there, he received almost 24 percent of the vote, and his margin of victory in the state's largest county (Essex) showed that he had done more than simply attract the support of black voters in Newark, East Orange, and Montclair.

All told, he had lasted longer—and done better—than any black presidential aspirant ever had. He had received over 3½ million votes, had finished first outright in two primaries (Louisiana and Washington, D.C.), had gotten more of the popular vote than the others in two more states (South Carolina and Virginia). In the process he carried 41 congressional districts and 7 major American cities. He would go to the San Francisco convention with 384 delegates pledged to him.

June 6, 1984. Meeting reporters in a Los Angeles hotel the day after the last primary, he'd been asked what he'd learned from the campaign and he answered by remembering how naive he'd once been—and humble. Once in this hotel, he chuckled, he'd been invited to a free continental breakfast. So he had passed up the "sizzling western steak" dinner he really wanted. "Who would eat a big steak at night if they were going to have a continental breakfast the next morning?" he asked. But when the free meal came and it was only rolls and juice, the kid from Greenville couldn't understand. "I associated the continental with the car—and it really was Volkswagen breakfast," he said, poking fun at a rare target—himself.

But he'd learned about more than breakfast menus here. In 1972 George McGovern, then the party's nominee, had been staying in the same hotel. McGovern had dispatched Jackson on an errand downtown to help round up the black vote; on the way back, Jackson had walked by the hotel's swimming pool. There, he said, he'd seen the candidate's advisors sitting with "the pundits . . . the Mary McGrorys, and Teddy Whites, and Frank Mankiewicz's," all of them sitting around that pool, "strategizing, cogitating, philosophizing," he said. He too had wanted to stay, had wanted to be close to the action, but he had been shooed away, the black youth still tending to chores for the white man. "Twelve years later, we're back," Jackson said, proudly. "And this time, we're sitting around that pool."

15. IMPACT

July 12, 1984. Geraldine Ferraro's image on the small television screen flickered against the snowy background. The portable black-and-white set, plopped down on Jackson's dining room table, was vying for space with a bottle of corn syrup, its top gone, a large white bowl filled with lemons, and a giant cookie jar, a long-ago gift from the Georgia Coalition of Black Women. On the TV set, Ferraro was being introduced in Saint Paul, Minnesota, by the party's soon-to-be nominee, Walter Mondale. A national television audience watched as she smiled and the Saint Paul audience drowned her in applause.

The Jackson family had been campaigning, and there had been no time to clean the messy house on Constance Avenue in Chicago. The candidate sat amid the clutter. Mondale had not called to tell him of the vice-presidential choice. Jackson got the word from reporters, secondhand.

"America is about doors being opened," Ferraro said on the television set. In the dining room, where he sat alone, Jackson watched the door slam shut on his dreams. For the rest of this campaign, she would be the party's novelty, its fresh face, its future. Ferraro talked on. Jackson sat and listened, one hand on top of the other, left leg draped over the right, and said nothing as the tiny black-and-white figures on the screen waved once more to the cheering crowd and then disappeared.

All the hand-wringing amused him. The delegates had been

seated, the nomination of Walter Mondale was assured, the platform had been drafted—but even now, just a few hours before he would address the convention, almost no one knew what he was going to say. Everything was set—except for him. He was the only wild card, and that was what he wanted. Let the others wonder; let them worry. It wasn't exactly power, but it was as close as he could get.

His forces had been outnumbered and outmaneuvered. And they had accomplished very little. Language on affirmative action: that was all the Mondale camp had conceded. The rest—abolition of second primaries, a 25 percent cut in military spending, no first-use of nuclear weapons—all those proposals had been rejected. No one had consulted him about the party's vice-presidential selection. Or about the new chairman of the Democratic National Committee. And a few delegates, incensed by his earlier refusal to repudiate Louis Farrakhan, still wanted to deny him the right to speak to the convention. "We're more visible now than ever before—but we have less power," he grumbled. He wanted to be a political force the party would have to respect, but this time he would have to settle for being humored and then rebuffed. He wanted history to judge him important, but at this convention he was not the main event.

He knew that. And he knew the speech might be his last, best chance. For attention. For input. For the last several days he'd worked patiently on the message, writing nearly all of it himself, jotting notes in between meetings, scribbling notes in his limousine. Mondale's people had provided information about the Reagan administration record and about economics. But they didn't know what, if any, Jackson would use. Mondale aide Bob Beckel tried to get Jackson to tip his hand as the two men stood on the balcony of Jackson's hotel and looked out over the city. Jackson wasn't saying. "Tomorrow, Beckel, you'll either be a chump, a chimp—or a champ," he twitted the Mondale emissary who had courted and tried to negotiate with him the last few months.

Jackson's staff didn't know what he would do either. Only two or three of them had seen parts of the text; to prevent leaks, they had been kept in the dark. Would he let the world know how angry, how hurt, they were at the way they'd been treated by the party, they wondered? Or would he play the role of statesman? Would he lash out at the party? Or embrace it? The staff, the delegates, even the pundits speculated. ". . . he can disrupt the convention and trigger a bigger national backlash against himself and the party than he has caused—or he can lend his eloquence and his anger to mobilize that party for the immense challenge that Ronald Reagan and Reaganism present," David Broder wrote.[57] Which would it be?

Jackson alone knew. Long ago he had made up his mind. In a quiet conversation one April morning while flying from Chicago to Memphis, he'd assessed the situation: "Everybody is waiting for the monkey show. 'Will he walk out? Won't he?' Just waiting for the monkey show to happen. Hell, I never had any intention of walking out. I've invested too much to do that now."

His eye was on the future, and he would do nothing to jeopardize the place he felt he had secured. But publicly he could not tip his hand; unpredictability had always been his greatest strength, and he'd be strongest now if the others didn't know what he would do. So for the last two weeks he had resorted to the kind of political broken-field running that had brought him this far: maddeningly inconsistent feints and spurts from one statement to another. We need unity in the party, he would proclaim—but there must be justice too. We want Reagan removed—but don't threaten us to make us fall in line, he'd quickly add. In Raleigh, North Carolina, he sent a message to party leaders: we want to win badly, but don't twist our arms. Don't tell us that if we don't play by your rules we'll get four more years of Reagan—our self-respect counts for more than this election. "Don't be stampeded," he told followers in New Orleans. "Never be playing cards and let somebody scare the joker out of your hand. Use it when you need to use it." Would he support a nominee who did not denounce second primaries and dual-registration, as Mondale did not? "I would not," he replied firmly in Atlanta. Some days he seemed to mean it. Other times he'd relent.

In Los Angeles two days before the convention opened, he said he was sorry if he had said or done anything in the campaign that caused anyone pain. Otherwise, he stayed on the offensive. Everyone had to be kept guessing. That way the suspense would build, the impact would be greater. It was also safer that way. Many of his closest aides, enraged that the party had given the campaign so little, would have erupted, perhaps even rebelled if they'd known how conciliatory he was prepared to be. Especially the apology. That would stick in their throats. The battle over apologizing before the Manchester speech had been bitter, and this would be even worse. He knew it: "he wouldn't let nobody read his speech. Anybody would have read it before that night . . . would have discouraged it," said longtime confidante Willie Barrow, shaking her head. Most around him were hurting, and they had no intention of licking their wounds. What they wanted was blood.

There is a proper season for everything. There is a time to sow and a time to reap. There is a time to compete, and a time to cooperate. I ask for your vote on the first ballot as a vote for a new direction for this party. . . . But I will be proud to support the nominee of this convention for the Presidency of the United States of America.

(Jackson's convention speech)

Victor McTeer was ready to walk out of the convention. A black lawyer from Greenville, Mississippi, he had learned to be patient, but his patience was gone. McTeer knew what it was like to lose—"hell, I been banging my head against walls all my life," he once joked—but this time, McTeer felt that the Democratic party was toying with all of them: that the past, the months of emotion and pride and hard work, counted for nothing. They're not giving us a damn thing, he muttered. They're pushing our face in the mud. "You all mad because you came out here and the women got vice-president, and the South got Bert Lance, and Manatt got the DNC—and you ain't got nothing. You upset because you don't have anything," Jackson told a group of black delegates, and when he said that he was talking about Vic McTeer.

Throughout this campaign, I've tried to offer leadership to the Democratic party and the nation. If in my high moments, I have done some good, offered some service, shed some light, healed some wounds, rekindled some hope, or stirred someone from apathy and indifference, or in any way along the way helped somebody, then this campaign has not been in vain.

(Jackson's convention speech)

Vic McTeer had spent much of his life taking on the system—and winning. A big man, proud and intense, he was the first American-born black to graduate from Western Maryland College, the first to win All-America football honors at the Westminster, Maryland, school; later, in the courtroom, he had won verdicts and settlements few thought possible.

Learning how to win had also taught him how to lose, and Vic McTeer could accept defeat. If . . . if, there was a chance to win. At this convention he felt there was none. Two hours before Jackson addressed the delegates, McTeer spoke to them too and argued for the abolition of state laws requiring a second or runoff election when no one candidate received a majority of the primary vote. He had prepared carefully, as if at trial; now, as then, he was precise but also forceful, even passionate. But he had gotten nowhere. The convention delegates' vote against his position had been overwhelming. It's worse than 1964, he sighed. These people have learned nothing. Nothing's changed. "There was a lot of anger there . . . at that point, as far as I'm concerned, my whole position was—let's split. Leave the party. We create the Mississippi Freedom Democratic party all over again, and we'll go our separate way. . . . We had lost the vote. We had decided that we were going to leave the floor, and the hell with it. . . . Remember, I'm from Mississippi. We step out of the party if we don't like what they do."

"Wait a minute, Vic. If you leave now, you'll miss Jesse's speech," Willie Barrow warned him.

Steaming mad, McTeer sat back down. Maybe, he hoped, Jesse will let them have it. Forty feet away from the podium he found himself urging Jackson to "castigate the whole Democratic party . . . and say to them, you've done to us exactly what you did to Fannie Lou Hamer [Mississippi Freedom Democratic party vice-chairman, expelled from the convention] in 1964."

If in my low moments, in word, deed, or attitude, through some error of temper, taste, or tone, I have caused anyone discomfort, created pain, or revived someone's fears, that was not my truest self. If there were occasions when my grape turned into a raisin and my joy bell lost its resonance, please forgive me. Charge it to my head and not to my heart. . . . As I develop and serve, be patient. God is not finished with me yet.

(Jackson's convention speech)

McTeer exploded silently when he heard the apology. "When he said to the Jewish community, forgive me—my reaction was:

for what? . . . he did not have to apologize for anything he had done. . . . I questioned that apology. I questioned it like hell. . . . There were a lot of supporters who'd been upset with a conciliatory speech at that moment."

When the speech ended, McTeer applauded politely.

"Man, that's a great speech," said the delegate standing alongside him, Jackson State University professor Leslie McLemore.

"I thought it was bullshit, Les. We're going nowhere," McTeer replied. But all around him now there was laughter and cheering. There were even tears. McTeer was confused. "Gradually I'm realizing that white people around me are crying. I mean the men. I'm not talking about no lightweight little white girls. I'm talking about we're-going-to-fight-you-nigger-till-you-gone white folks. They were sitting there in tears . . . and this white lady, who I don't remember, she grabbed my hand. . . . I'm standing there next to this white lady from Mississippi who's there in tears on my shoulder. I realized 'My God, I'm part of something very important.'"

As the delegates around him celebrated, McTeer's anger slowly gave way. "I don't think any of us were prepared for the reaction that we would see from white people to that speech. I don't think any of us were prepared to sit there and watch those white men and women from Mississippi sit there, in tears. I mean, we don't touch each other. For that lady, that white lady to sit over there and put her arm in mine and say, 'Oh, wasn't it wonderful?' well goddamn, I thought, where am I?"

He was smiling now. And proud. "This time I felt the guy [Jackson] is rising above himself. . . . He is really talking to the American people. He realizes this is his cathedral. . . . Jesse Jackson held church in the Democratic National Convention. He appealed to white folk in the same manner that he appealed to black folk, and white folk were moved the same way that black folk were moved. . . . It was a remarkable performance."

We are co-partners in a long and rich religious history—the Judeo-Christian traditions. Many blacks and Jews have a shared passion for social justice at home and peace abroad. We must seek a revival of the spirit, inspired by a new vision and new possibilities.

(Jackson's convention speech)

What is going on here? the candidate's wife wondered. She and her five children were sitting behind Jackson on the stage, and they couldn't hear most of what he said. "We would glance at the monitor because we couldn't see his face. You know, when you're sitting on the stage, you miss most of the presentation." But in front of her, white Americans were crying, and Jacqueline Jackson couldn't understand why.

She wasn't in the best mood that night. She felt her husband had been treated unfairly by reporters and badly by the party, and she thought that she had been given second-class treatment too. "We were not really wanted. And I think the thing that broke, the straw that broke the camel's back was that we were . . . to stand on one side of all the other people so that it would not appear that we were really part of the group." Irked, and unable to see or hear much, she found herself thinking of other things, of other places. Trivial, everyday things like packing her two sons off to college in a few weeks. Or buying trunks and pressing clothes and "is the dog all right? And who's gonna take care of the house when I got to take the kids to school?"

We are bound by shared blood and shared sacrifices. We are much too intelligent; much too bound by our Judeo-Christian heritage; much too victimized by racism, sexism, militarism, and anti-Semitism; much too threatened as historical scapegoats to go on divided one from another.

(Jackson's convention speech)

She applauded some parts of the speech: "when he said, Oh America, you ought to be ashamed of yourself—oh my goodness, I wanted to just jump up and run out of there. I felt so good." But the apology dismayed her. There is no need for this, she thought. "If we had intentionally gone before the American people to deceive them, if that is the case, and I had been discovered then, then I would apologize. If my purpose has always been for the good of the American people, then I think I owe no apology." We're the ones who've been deceived and cheated, she felt: "as a person living in America, I have been lied to when I was told that I was separate but unequal." If anyone deserves an apology, she concluded, we do.

Sitting there bathed in lights and applause, Jackie Jackson

tried to comprehend what was taking place. Why, she thought, why must we always be the ones to apologize? Why do whites always want that? "It's strange that America always seems to rejoice when we're in an apologetic role . . . why is it that I have to hear from white people that black folks need to apologize?" Is that why this audience seems so happy? Because once again we're asking for mercy?

We must turn from finger-pointing to clasped hands. We must share our burdens and our joys with each other once again. We must turn to each other and not on each other and choose higher ground.

(Jackson's convention speech)

The applause surged forward again and again. Jackie Jackson could see more smiles now, see them nodding their heads, hugging one another, beaming. What is wrong with them? she found herself thinking. Why are they so relieved? Why were they so fearful? Especially of us? "I saw tears and we were confused . . . I said, 'Well, what did he say to upset them this way?' . . . It was a strange kind of fear that was present. . . . The fear confused me, that people were so extremely fearful. It was like—what are you expecting us to do? The things that we're capable of doing?— . . . I was just very floored with the fear. The white fear of us . . . I felt like an Indian in a tent on a reservation saying what, why are they so worried about us, those who have worked the land and who gave corn to help a nation survive through the winter. What is this fear?"

Our flag is red, white, and blue, but our nation is a rainbow—red, yellow, brown, black, and white—we're all precious in God's sight. America is not like a blanket—one piece of unbroken cloth, the same color, the same texture, the same size. America is more like a quilt—many patches, many pieces, many colors, many sizes, all woven and held together by a common thread.

(Jackson's convention speech)

Lotte Arnold was too busy tending bar that night in Chugger's Lounge at the Holiday Inn in Jackson, Tennessee, to pay much attention to Jesse Jackson's speech. "I saw part of it, not much, mind you. I was working that night. . . . The TV was on; it was the night our piano player was there. Roger Hatch—he's not with us any more—he was playing. So the TV was on down low. I was waiting on customers. Frankly, I didn't pay it no mind at all, because I didn't really care what he said. My mind was already made up."

Pouring drinks at Chugger's three nights a week was Lotte Arnold's second job; for the last twenty-two years she had worked full-time as secretary in the Jackson County Sheriff's Department. "I get 'em drunk at night, sober 'em up by day," she chuckled. But Lotte Arnold wasn't laughing about Jesse Jackson the day in April when he attracted a large crowd near the Jackson courthouse, and she stood off to the side to watch. "I wouldn't vote for him so I wouldn't even waste the time listening to him," she explained then.

Jackson didn't worry her, she insisted. But she was bothered by what she felt was happening to the country. Things have simply gotten out of hand, she said. And Jackson only seems to be making things worse. "Now take those blacks over there listening to him," she gestured. "They got nowhere else to go. They don't work. Just as long as they get that welfare—that's all they care about. You know it's true," she continued.

Now 50, divorced, Lotte Arnold was accustomed to speaking her mind. Folks in Jackson don't much beat around the bush, she said. "I remember a joke going round these parts when they were debating whether to give [Dr. Martin Luther] King a holiday or not. And someone here said, hell, let's shoot four more—and we'll get the whole week off." She laughed again.

Aren't you afraid, she was asked, that if blacks get in office they might do to you—and to your children—what whites have been doing to blacks for years?

No, she scoffed. Not really. Then she paused. Well, maybe, she added. "Now don't get me wrong. When a black is qualified, they deserve to get the job. But not just because they're black. The ways things are now, the deck is stacked. . . . Now, nine times out of ten, a black will get the choice over a white when they're applying for the same thing. I don't think that's right." She went on: "The blacks are the ones who get everything. The whites nowadays don't have any say-so. The blacks don't have to do anything. The whites are being slowed down. With a black president, it would be a black country. . . . It wouldn't be the America we know."

The speech, all the attention Jesse Jackson got, everything he did—all that, said Lotte Arnold—should tell you something. "He brought to light that something like that is possible. And if we're not careful, it could happen again. . . . Somebody is gonna have to do something . . . the ones that are on our side, you know what I mean, they're gonna have to do something." No, said Lotte Arnold, there wasn't much talk about the speech that night in Chugger's Lounge.

Even in our fractured state, all of us count and all of us fit somewhere. We have proven that we can survive without each other. But we have not proven that we can win and progress without each other. We must come together.

(Jackson's convention speech)

Willie Barrow sat in the Illinois delegation and smiled. "I never cried, not once. I don't cry often. I'm not a crying, teary person. I release my joy by smiling. Or I was doing my little Jackson banner up in the air. It was going up and down, up and down. That's the way I was." She had been with Jackson for eighteen years and had, she said, "heard him make greater speeches," but she had never been prouder of him.

Willie Barrow had come a long way from that dusty road in Texas forty years ago where she and some of her classmates piled up rocks and tree branches so the schoolbus carrying the white children would be forced to stop for the black children who had to walk the fifteen miles to school. "That was my first test, my real emancipation," said Barrow, who went on to become a Church of God minister and who, thirty years later, was still organizing, still protesting, traveling as far as Paris and Hungary, even Hanoi, to "help stop our boys from being killed."

Wearing bright mascara and billowing, rainbow-colored dresses, the Reverend Willie Tappin Barrow, D.D., was easy to spot, impossible to ignore. "Hell, she's twice the speaker Jesse is," one Chicago politico said admiringly. Over the years she had learned her way around the city's south-side politics, but a national campaign was foreign turf. She wasn't quite sure how to proceed, so she did what she'd always done—she plunged in furiously, joyfully. "We ain't never been this way before," she told a Newark, New Jersey, audience. "We work eighteen, nineteen hours a day. And when I go to sleep, I sleep fast. Because I want to see what the end is going to be. . . . This is the first time we got together . . . I tell you, this country will never be the same."

It was all uphill—and she loved it. Despite the obstacles, whatever the odds. Nothing would slow Willie Barrow down. "See, we never had nothing. We always bit off more than we could chew. We never had enough money. But it worked. God has always blessed us at the right time." Yes, she conceded, we had hoped to do better at this convention, but she would not despair. "Before, we used to just try to come to the convention and hope we'd be asked for advice on black issues. Before we used to pass notes to whites in the trailers. . . . We've never even been in a trailer. Now we have our own command post, our own whips, our own floor leaders. Blacks in the trailer," she repeated, her eyes flashing. Winning to blacks sometimes looks like losing to others, Willie Barrow said.

When I see a missing door, that's the slummy side. Train some youth to become a carpenter, that's the sunny side. When I see the vulgar words and hieroglyphics of destitution on the walls, that's the slummy side. Train some youth to be a painter and artist, that's the sunny side. We leave this place looking for the sunny side because there's a brighter side somewhere.

(Jackson's convention speech)

The granddaughter of slaves watched another descendant of slaves speaking on the podium, and she knew that progress had been great. But Willie Barrow also knew something was still wrong. And she didn't have to remember back to some Texas country road to know what it was. So much more could have been done, she found herself thinking; we could have done so much more. Beneath her smile, there was bitterness. Much had changed, but too much had not.

"The only thing that I was saying was—this is the president. Only reason he's not is because he's not white . . . the only thing that got me was just because he's black, he is not the candidate. Just because of that. . . . and here are these same people that say 'I curse you, Jesse'—why this time they're crying, they're saying 'I can't resist you, Jesse.' But because of your face, 'Because of the way I was taught, I got to reject you'—inside I feel you . . . outside, I got to cry out that I don't want you."

I just want young America to do me one favor: exercise the right to dream. You must face reality, that which is. But then dream of a reality that ought to be, that must be. Live beyond the pain of reality with the dream of a bright tomorrow. Use hope and imagination as weapons of survival and progress.
(Jackson's convention speech)

Al Vorspan didn't know what to expect when he sat down in the den of his Long Island, New York, home to watch Jesse Jackson's speech. The vice-president and director of Social Action for the Union of American Hebrew Congregations hoped the candidate would make some sign of contrition. But Vorspan wasn't very optimistic. "I was afraid he'd take the opposite tack. Or ignore the thing altogether." He had worked with Jackson years before, had admired and then been disillusioned with him. With this guy you can never be sure, Vorspan thought.

Al Vorspan watched the entire speech and was impressed. "I said, 'Holy Cow, in his own way he's trying to address our problem—and make a kind of apology' . . . I thought he handled it with relative grace," he said. Still, Vorspan was skeptical. "I thought in these conventions, talk is cheap. That he's got to do more than just mouth words. I had, well yes, a lingering suspicion that things were not what they seemed. And as the speech went on, my reservations got sharper and I said to myself: we were right. We were right all along. We were right to condemn anti-Semitism—and treat him the way we did. And we'd be wrong now to fall on our knees and kiss this guy's ring. You know, that's what I was afraid of: that some people in Jewish circles might do that, that we would forget all that had happened." He added: "I remember thinking . . . watch it: I like what he's saying, but he's on a high wire, he's on a roll. It's passionate, it's rhetorical—but what does it mean?"

Sitting there in the den Vorspan remembered the times he'd worked with Jackson. He'd seen such promise then. And just as quickly he thought of the pain, the anguish Jackson had caused him and other Jews. In San Francisco the delegates were dancing and hugging one another, but Al Vorspan wasn't ready to join in. "I found myself thinking that it's a real shame. He's smart, he's so smart, such a quick learner, he's outclassed all the others . . . but it's really sad that it was so flawed. It really was a tragedy . . . he did come to symbolize black aspirations. And they're legitimate, God knows. But sometimes he isn't. All that investment by the black community in so talented a guy who's so tainted . . . with all that brilliance, if he'd been like [Dr. Martin Luther] King, this speech, this campaign could have been transforming."

It had not been, Vorspan concluded sitting there in the Long Island darkness long after the television set had been switched off. And the more he thought about Jackson, the sadder he got. "What a waste," he found himself thinking. "What a squandered opportunity."

Our time has come. Our faith, hope, and dreams have prevailed. Our time has come. Weeping has endured for nights, but that joy cometh in the morning. Our time has come. No grave can hold our body down. Our time has come. No lie can live forever. Our time has come. We must leave the racial battle ground and come to the economic common ground and the moral higher ground. America, our time has come.

(Jackson's convention speech)

Some found Jackson's speech ominous, even menacing, and turned away in disgust; but never again in this campaign would he reach so many. For fifty minutes, alone—with no one to edit him, no one to interfere—he spoke to a nation. Lotte Arnold and her customers in Chugger's Lounge might not have paid attention to the speech, but much of America did: more people watched that address than any other part of the convention, an estimated 33 million saw him. Other blacks had addressed other conventions, but the circumstances here were unique: history, entertainment, suspense—combined. CBS News anchorman Dan Rather, given an advance text, even encouraged parents to sit their children in front of a set for what he called "this extraordinary moment." And the longer Jackson spoke, the bigger the television audience grew, the higher the ratings climbed. Television executives weren't accustomed to that. "People tuned in to see him, and stayed . . . you'd have to say that Jesse Jackson's speech was *the* audience event in terms of ratings . . . the largest draw of the convention," one network vice-president said.[58]

The speech was the campaign in miniature. By the time he

finished, he had once again ignited the emotions that had propelled him to San Francisco: hope—and hate. Once again they would determine the imprint he'd make in the months and years ahead.

Impact. Legacy. Backlash. Jackson may have cornered the nation's attention for fifty minutes that cool July evening in San Francisco, but the speech was more an underlining, an exclamation point in a story that had begun years earlier, written by thousands of anonymous Americans, black and white, on picket lines, in courtrooms, at lunch counters in the South. The impact he had on American politics was theirs as well. "Jackson did not start the energy for black action in 1984, but rather responded to energy that was already there," said Dr. Brian Sherman of the Voter Registration Project. Bigotry and the seeds of hatred were also there, and Jackson rekindled those flames too.

How many people did Jackson influence? To get involved? To run? To win—or to lose? It may never be possible to pinpoint. Election experts will gather the data from hundreds, perhaps thousands of individual races, and even that will yield only part of the answer.

"It's wrong to look at now, or a year from now even, to measure his impact," said Ann Lewis of the Democratic National Committee, who points out that the antiwar protests of the sixties didn't have a full impact on the party until 1972. "The real test was not 1984. But it will be 1986 and 1988 . . . the real test of whether Jesse Jackson is a movement is when these state legislatures and city council seats come up," said Timothy F. Maloney, a liberal white Maryland state representative. And maybe not even then, said conservative columnist James Kilpatrick: "the most significant result or aspect of the Jackson factor is not going to be found in the presidential election in November of 1984. It is going to be found in the state and local elections over the next ten, fifteen years . . . in your school board elections, in your county commissioners, your vote for sheriff." John Lewis, a black city councilman in Atlanta, agreed: "the real impact, some of it cannot be measured but will be witnessed for some time to come." California's shrewd black political leader Willie Brown, no fan of Jackson, nonetheless dubbed him the "Jackie Robinson of American politics who . . . will spawn a whole lot of little leaguers in many cities and counties that you and I will never hear about." The impact might be hard to see at first, said Maya

Angelou, but it could last for generations: "the effort does not fall away any more than the ripples of a quiet pool actually have to cease and have no effect on the distant shore. That pool, when it is disturbed by the stone, reacts and has effect on the distant shore."

Mabel Thomas, sitting in the Georgia delegation at the convention, thought it was "the best speech I ever heard in my life. It was overwhelming. I was overjoyed." Mabel Thomas was also practical. She tape-recorded the speech, brought it back to Atlanta, and played it for the volunteers who were helping her try to unseat the first black woman elected to the Georgia state legislature. "It lifted their spirits. They were so uplifted by his vision that they had no choice but to work hard. . . . It motivated them to work for the person . . . who is willing to speak out for the people," she said.

Mabel—"they call me Able Mabel"—fancied herself as that kind of person. When Jackson announced his candidacy, she was a graduate student in public administration at Georgia State University. She had interned in the Georgia state senate and had dreams of holding office but no hopes of realizing them. Then she heard Jesse Jackson. "He projected so much insight, so much hope, so much vision . . . he was the driving and motivating force behind my decision to run . . . he said things about how it is time for new leadership. He said to grass-roots people, you can come forward now. You don't have to settle for just trying to influence your state representative—you can be a state representative," she said in a slow, deep voice reminiscent of a young Barbara Jordan.

She was only 26. Her opponent, though forty-five years older and dubbed "Uncle Thomasina" by some in the district, still had all the advantages of incumbency and was, after all, the pioneer. So "Able Mabel" had to do more than play a tape recorder for some volunteers. Capitalizing on the attention she'd received working statewide for Jackson, she campaigned throughout the district, going to every senior citizens' center, every meeting she could find. I believe in Jesse Jackson, she told them. And my opponent does not, she would add.

The election wasn't even close. "Able Mabel" won in a landslide. In January, 1985, she became the youngest member of the state legislature.

"Able Mabel" wasn't the only one. In other parts of the country, the "Jackson factor" was more than just noise and some dreams. In Vermont, 21-year-old Micque Glitman, a University of Vermont junior, upset a two-term state legislator. Jackson's stand on arms control and foreign policy had motivated her. "It was his notion that anyone can which inspired me to run," she said. (In Vermont, with the smallest black population in the country, Jackson supporters won seven other seats in the statehouse as well—along with the post of Democratic national committeewoman, the Democratic nomination for Congress, and several local party offices.) "Able Mabel," Micque Glitman, Jackie Walker in Dallas County, Alabama, who had run for—and won—the assessor's post (see chapter 5). And there were others.

Two days before Mississippi's August 3 primary, someone set fire to the Pleasant Hill Baptist Church in Louise. Next door was the filling station and convenience store owned by Arvell Bullock, who was trying to become the first black supervisor in Humphries County. Later, investigators would conclude that the fire had been set by a local resident who'd been squabbling with his wife; but the day after the church burned no one in Louise knew that, and many black residents were terrified. "Setting fires is one way the white power structure sends us messages," said one lifelong Mississippi native. The panic spread quickly. But the next day Jesse Jackson came to town. At the burned church he led a prayer service, then the singing of the old civil rights song "Ain't Nobody Going to Turn Us Around." After that, the fear seemed to subside; self-confidence returned. Black voters vowed not to be intimidated. And Arvell Bullock—"I support Jackson, yes sir, I support him 100 percent"—Arvell Bullock squeaked into office by a handful of votes.

The spark also caught fire in Prince George's County, Maryland. "Jesse gave us an idea, and we took the idea and turned it into reality," said one of his organizers there after Jackson's Rainbow Coalition increased both the turnout of black voters and its own influence. Likewise in Hinds County, Mississippi, where Jackson supporters stunned long-entrenched white party officials by winning twenty-three of thirty seats on the party's executive board. The pattern repeated itself in other parts of the state. It was not just new blood—something else had changed. "It is different here. . . . The kind of blacks that were there before were the kind who would not speak out, who'd check with the power structure, ask do you approve of what we say or of doing this here. But the kind of blacks on it now are more vocal kinds of blacks and will speak out without checking. They will sort of speak their own mind," said Evan Doss, the black tax assessor of Claiborne County.

January, 1984. The candidate had just led an estimated fifteen hundred people from the Jackson State University campus to the steps of the Hinds County Courthouse. They marched through the rain to register to vote; some residents called it the biggest march in Jackson for years. While several sour-looking courthouse workers agreed to stay overtime to register the crowd, 18-year-old Martha Jones stood on the courthouse steps. She was crying.

"I'm so proud, I'm so proud," she kept repeating, sobbing as she spoke. "We have a black man running for president. In my heart I think he can win, but if he doesn't I'm not gonna be sad. At least he gave it a try. You never know nothing less you give it a try." Rain poured down, and the young girl stood on the steps watching the long line of new registrants pick up their forms from the tight-lipped county workers.

Black registration soared. Up over an estimated 1.2 million blacks in eleven southern states alone. Nearly 5.5 million registered there by the election of 1984, compared to the 4.3 million registered in 1980. The increase since 1982, nearly 30 percent, was nearly thirty times greater than the increase of two years earlier. In eleven southern states, blacks registered at a higher rate than whites; in nine of the eleven, the rate was more than double.[59] "Their presence changes the political possibilities of this country," said James Baldwin. (NBC News found that in the Georgia and Florida primaries, 20 percent of the black voters had registered within the previous six months. And a CBS News/*New York Times* survey found that from 4 to 11 percent of all black voters were voting for the first time. In some speeches, Jackson claimed that figure was actually closer to 25 percent.) Typically, Jackson claimed credit for most of the increase—and was quickly challenged by those who had been working the turf longer. Jackson's effort, Joe Madison of the NAACP sputtered, "was the least productive of any registration drive in the country." The opposition to Ronald Reagan and his programs, Madison insisted, is "what kicked off this phenomenon, and Jesse Jackson came along and put his foot on the accelerator."

It wasn't just registration. In 1984, more blacks voted, more blacks took part in the primary system than had ever done so before. In all six southern states holding primaries, the percentage of blacks voting exceeded the percentage of whites who went to the polls. After Super Tuesday (March 13), the margin increased. In North Carolina, 46 percent of all registered blacks voted in the primary compared to just 29 percent of the whites who were registered. In Tennessee, the difference was more than two to one (22 percent black turnout compared to 10 percent of whites). And in Louisiana it was greater still (29 percent to 8 percent). Elsewhere participation by blacks climbed sharply too: up 36 percent compared to 1980 in one black area in Ohio, up 82 percent in a largely black district in New Jersey, up 87 percent in part of Alabama—up a whopping 127 percent in part of New York City.

Some of the enthusiasm he generated spilled over into the general election as well: in November, 1984, an estimated 740,000 more blacks voted than in 1980. In Mississippi, 48,000 more blacks went to the polls than had done so four years earlier, an increase of 24 percent. In Virginia, the increase was 27 percent; 43 percent more blacks voted in Arkansas; 50 percent more in Georgia.[60]

Several factors sparked the record turnout. In black America dislike and distrust of the Reagan administration were intense; some blacks also felt a loyalty to Walter Mondale. Jackson boosters, however, credited him for most of the surge in both registration and turnout. Barbara Jordan described what she saw in Texas, and the same held true in Virginia and other southern caucus states:

> I have seen people who don't know what a precinct convention meant and that was just a big question and certainly had never attended one—I have seen these people excited about something. . . . To see those people who have just never known before that such a meeting took place, to see them come and participate, that was a very positive thing. And it was Jesse Jackson's candidacy

> which did it. . . . In Jackson's campaign we saw the involvement of new people, new black people, the transformation of the disenchanted and the person who did not feel the political process offered anything in terms of involvement. That person was turned around.

In Norfolk, Virginia, 80-year-old "Nannie" Lewis waited several hours to get her name on the right forms for her first party caucus. She was doing it, she said, because of Jesse Jackson—and Henry Jones, her grandfather, born a slave. "They called him a free-issue because he was brought up in the master's house and learned to read and write and figure. He was very smart and very active and very religious, and he wanted his children to prosper in life, not to come up as he did but to live better. He used to tell us when we were little kids what it meant for him to be free," she said. "I'm here for my grandfather's right." Another first-timer, Veronica Tutwiler, mother of two, considered it an honor too. "Proudest moment of my life," she said shortly before casting her vote for Jesse Jackson.

Jackson was not the only reason for the enthusiasm and the turnout, but some nonpartisan observers agreed that his role was critical. Jackson "had a major influence," said the respected Committee for the Study of the American Electorate (CSAE).[61] Even conservative sociologist Nathan Glazer found that Jackson "did reach out to and galvanize one very important part of the electorate . . . he had an enormous impact . . . getting people to vote." And after the biggest one-year increase of elected black mayors recorded since 1970 (to 286, or 31 more than in the previous election year),[62] a Joint Center for Political Studies publication (Washington, D.C., 1984, p. 10) concluded that one reason so many new mayors were elected was "Jesse Jackson's coattails."

(Several months later not everyone thought that Jackson's coattails were long enough; in Virginia, one black politician even asked Jackson to stay away. Virginia state senator L. Douglas Wilder was running an uphill campaign to become the first black to win a major state office in the South since Reconstruction; Wilder knew that if he wanted to win in a state where 80 percent of the voters were white, he would have to play down, not emphasize, his blackness. So the 54-year-old Richmond attorney moved carefully. He would curb any rhetoric and would court white, not black groups; to affirm his mainstream candidacy, he would secure an endorsement from the mostly white Fraternal Order of Police; in this campaign there would not be any noisy, emotional appeals to mobilize the black vote. And when Jesse Jackson, an old friend and fraternity brother, called and volunteered to campaign in Virginia for Wilder, Jackson was told—politely, but firmly—to keep his distance. Jackson, as well as other nationally known black figures, did not appear for Wilder in the state, and the strategy paid off: on November 5, 1985, Wilder received 44 percent of the white vote and won over his white Republican opposition by nearly 50,000 votes.)

Easier to pin down than his effect on voter registration and turnout was his impact on the issues in the campaign. He cornered a few the other candidates couldn't afford to touch: trade with South Africa, the rights of Palestinians, an "evenhanded" policy in the Middle East, famine in Africa. Repeatedly he brought them onto the agenda. On South Africa he challenged Mondale directly, admonished him for being on the board of directors of a company, Control Data, that conducted business with the apartheid nation and forced Mondale to propose tougher sanctions against South Africa than he had suggested before. Getting issues aired was one thing; getting them included in the Democratic party platform was something else. Most of Jackson's proposals were soundly rejected in San Francisco.

But there were other yardsticks. While his seat-of-the-pants campaign may have been the most disorganized in American political history, it nonetheless helped give birth to a new black political network. Many of the staff that traveled with him, the lawyers and teachers and businesspeople who enlisted in the field to help him, began as political amateurs; for many of them a national campaign was new. The lessons they learned from 1984 could be used later. "This may turn out to be Jesse Jackson's major legacy, the involvement of the black professional in the political process," said Tom Cavanaugh of the Joint Center for Political Studies. "The card files and mailing lists that came into being are not going to go away," he added.

Jackson's impact went beyond those volunteers. In Mississippi, Lew Armstrong saw the way Jackson had touched Armstrong's two young sons. "I saw them move from doing mediocre in school. Now their performance indicates the pride they have in themselves and in being black. Something just clicked for them.

They met him! That's what it was." A black sociologist on the other side of the country had not met Lew Armstrong's kids, but he had seen his own 3-year-old recognize a Jackson who wasn't Michael on the television screen; that's crucial, said Harry Edwards, "that's particularly important in black America given the dearth of creditable role models that we have. What we're really looking at here is as much a training-ground and image-development process, a role-model development process, as we are looking at a presidential campaign. Some young black male or female or Chicano model or female or Asian male or female is sitting out there perhaps in high school, perhaps as an undergraduate at some college looking at this and getting ideas, beginning right now to nurture notions about what is possible and what is impossible in the political arena in this country."

It is reaching beyond black America, said Maya Angelou: "young white boys and middle-aged women and old black men and teenage Hispanics can think a little larger now than they have thought before." In North Carolina, lawyer Mickey Michaux saw one set of values being junked for another: "black kids were in a complacent situation: go out there and get me a job, get me a couple of bucks, stand on the block and play my big box! But when Jesse comes, even the drunks on the corner recognize that there's something there." That awareness is historic, said Alvin Poussaint of the Harvard Medical School. A psychiatrist, Poussaint felt that he was seeing "a true move further away from a slave mentality for black Americans . . . many black youth who feel inadequate and inferior, it's going to give them quite a boost. It's also going to give a boost to those blacks in the middle class who, with a little bit more assertiveness, can be much more effective in whatever they do. I think the Reverend Jackson took the movement a giant step in terms of its psychological uplift or its momentum. I think he's moved a lot of black people from feeling passive, intimidated, and afraid to feeling that well, yes I can. That I should assert myself. That's very important."

Jackson has started something that cannot be stopped, said James Baldwin. "Nothing will ever again be what it was before. . . . It changes the way the boy in the street and the boy on Death Row and his mother and his father and his sweetheart and his sister think about themselves. It indicates that one is not entirely at the mercy of the assumptions of this Republic, to what they have said you are, that this is not necessarily who and what you are. And no one will forget this moment, no matter what happens now," Baldwin concluded.

There was a price to pay. He was running against the past, the old ways, the fear. And the past, threatened, turned like some wounded beast to attack its hunters. Although trapped, it knew the terrain, could plunge into the underbrush, hide—then burst suddenly upon them. Bleeding and enraged, it was still cunning.

Sometimes their weapons wouldn't be enough. In the quiet of the cheap, wooden homes the delta farmers rented and could not afford to lose, in their mind-numbing jobs that could easily be given to someone else, there the hunters could be reasoned with. There the truth would seem much different. Let Jackson holler in the town halls, in the crowded churches. Outside, in dark corners, the past would be sharpening its claws, and hope and inspiration would not be enough.

"Well, I figured if I could beat that man, I might be able to show that there could be law and order in Quitman County." Fred Robinzine had good reason to think that. More than half the Mississippi county's residents were black like him, and many were enraged with "that man," county sheriff Jack Harrison, who'd been indicted for beating a black prisoner in the county jail. The prisoner said Harrison had also threatened to castrate him with a penknife. Twice Harrison was tried and twice he was acquitted, each time by an all-white jury. Black Quitman County was not surprised. Justice here, they felt, sometimes took strange detours or got lost altogether. But this time they could do something about it. This time they could register, they could vote—and they could rid themselves of the white sheriff many had come to hate.

This time too they had Jesse Jackson on their side. He had come to the county during 45-year-old Fred Robinzine's primary fight against four whites. Until then many blacks in the area hadn't given the Head Start worker much of a chance. Jackson's coming changed them. "After he got there and gave his speech, it seemed to uplift the blacks . . . and it sure encouraged me. I got out there a little more, and I tried harder to win," said Robinzine.

Robinzine tried hard, and he had ideas no one had even considered before. "I could have talked to the Board of Supervisors about providing recreation facilities for the teenagers so that maybe they'd burn up some of that energy and stay out of jail. Nobody is trying to do these things now," he lamented. He talked about visiting schools and getting rid of dope, and for a time winning seemed possible. In the primary Robinzine trailed Harrison by about ten percentage points.

Then, he said, the intimidation began. "Large plantation owners started threatening those who lived on their places. And they were afraid to say anything because they said if they did, they'd have to move. One lady was working for our campaign, and her husband was a field hand. They told her if she supported Jackson she'd have to move. Other places they told renters the same thing, they'd have to move if blacks won. They told the old people it wasn't time for blacks to be in these positions yet." Simple, sincere Fred Robinzine didn't give up. He kept remembering Jackson's message. And his spirit: "he gave us a lot of hope. We figured, if Jackson can do it in the country, maybe we can do it here in Marks, Mississippi." They figured wrong. Despite the numbers, despite the past—perhaps because of the past—when the votes were counted, the white sheriff defeated his black challenger. The vote wasn't even close.

John McGlennon also thought the "Jackson factor" could help him into office—and he too was wrong. A white political science professor at William and Mary College in Williamsburg, Virginia, McGlennon was running for Congress in Virginia's First Congressional District against incumbent Herbert R. Bateman. Two years earlier Bateman had defeated McGlennon 54 percent to 44 percent.

This time McGlennon was more optimistic. Bateman wasn't that well known in the district, and a lot had happened since the first election: mostly Jesse Jackson. In Virginia's presidential caucus meetings, he had outdistanced the rest of the field, had easily swamped everyone in Bateman's home city of Newport News. Black voter registration rolls had swelled. Of the thirty-two congressional districts Jackson won in 1984, only four were represented by conservative white Republicans, like Bateman; and of the four, election experts considered Bateman the most vulnerable. This would be a laboratory test of the "Jackson factor." Would the enthusiasm last? Could it be transferred?

The moderate McGlennon was no dreamer, and he knew it

wouldn't be easy. Blacks in the area were excited by Jackson—but they were plainly not excited about John McGlennon; a few had even tried—and had nearly succeeded—in dumping McGlennon and replacing him with a black candidate. There's a bigger problem, McGlennon thought. Jackson's campaign had inspired blacks—but it had alarmed many of the district's white voters; to McGlennon some of them seemed genuinely frightened. They're starting to abandon the party, he feared. The town of Hampton, for example, was about 60 percent white, but McGlennon worried because Hampton sent almost no white delegates to the state convention. The message whites here are getting, he said, is that the Jackson movement is by, for, and about blacks—no whites need apply. "The phenomenon reinforced the notion among southern white voters that this was a party of blacks," he complained.

Earnest and straightforward, McGlennon sought both black and white support. He tried to harness the energy Jackson had unleashed. "When our progressive white allies win, blacks win too." Jackson had said that, and John McGlennon tried to make the same point. "We can change the face of Congress," Jackson had boasted. But not here. The movement that crested in the Virginia primary seemed to ebb by the November election. This time when the votes were counted, John McGlennon lost by an even bigger margin than in 1982.

Backlash.

That too was Jackson's impact, part of his legacy. What happened to John McGlennon and Fred Robinzine didn't happen only in a congressional district in Virginia or a sheriff's race in Mississippi. And it was more than what conservative writer William Rusher called "the historical tendency . . . of blacks to vote for blacks, and whites to support whites." Rusher's description was far too neat, too bloodless. The reality was more deeply felt, more emotional, sometimes ugly, even violent. Mississippi's former governor and 1984 senatorial candidate William Winter spoke for many: "whites feel they don't have a home in the party." He was speaking of Hinds County, Mississippi, where Jackson supporters had swept aside twenty-three of thirty whites on the county's Democratic central committee. But he could just as easily have been talking about Howard County, Maryland. "There's been a lot more polarization around the issues," said

Maryland state representative Timothy Maloney. "The litmus test now is the color of a person's skin . . . we are not witnessing a shift in ideology but a shift in skin color . . . we're farther away from color-blind voting than we've ever been. The message is vote black, vote black. Which is just as nefarious to me as vote white." Polarization: that was the favored word of public opinion experts, and one of them put the matter bluntly: "Jackson is a poisonous influence to the Democratic Party. He turns an awful lot of whites off—and not necessarily because they're racist," said William Schneider of the American Enterprise Institute.[63]

The political reality was felt beyond Douglas Wilder and John McGlennon's Virginia. It was perhaps illustrated best in the most unlikely place: Selma, Alabama, which Jackson once called "the cradle of our democracy." Almost twenty years earlier, a 1965 march in Selma had aroused a nation and helped galvanize a Congress. Twenty years later, whites in Selma were aroused another way. This time they formed an organization to get whites to register and vote. Selma Area Voting Encouragement, they called it. SAVE, for short. To save them from one thing: black power, the threat represented by Jesse Jackson. Jackson was not the immediate target. The mayor's office in Selma was. Joe Smitherman, a six-term incumbent, versus F. D. Reese, a former city councilman. A white businessman versus a minister who wanted to become Selma's first black mayor.

Jackson visited Selma several times to help the Reese campaign, and the onetime associate of Dr. Martin Luther King, Jr., was grateful. Even though the city was 53 percent black, whites outnumbered blacks on the voter registration rolls. But Reese felt that Jackson was helping cut into that margin: an estimated 2,000 blacks had registered in Selma for the first time. And by election day blacks had a slight edge. "I think Jackson's coming certainly helped to inspire people who heretofore had not registered . . . it certainly helped people to get involved in the political process. It was quite an inspirational experience," said Reese.

The inspiration, however, cut both ways. Across town, whites saw what was happening. They heard Jackson. And they acted. "Normally whites don't fool around much with registration," Smitherman said later. But this time they worked furiously. Not just because they "feared the idea of a black mayor," he said—but also because they feared Jesse Jackson. "Jackson helped me with the turnout because he inflamed whites. . . . he helped me raise funds, and he got the whites registered. The way Jesse Jackson went around screaming about the Jews got me support from the Jewish community, which is influential in business here. . . . It had a backlash effect. It was counterproductive. Jesse Jackson made people so mad he turned them off with his radical ideas. For every black vote he got, the Republicans and independents registered two whites—that was true all over the country."

Each side dug in. Would the town of 27,000 that earlier had been a symbol of white resistance now become a symbol of black empowerment? To shouts of "freedom now, freedom now," Reese addressed a packed congregation: "there are rumors that when I am elected mayor, I am going to fire all the white folks. I am not going to do that. Now some white folks have to go . . . what we need is justice." Smitherman, who had appointed blacks to several city boards and who had many friends in the black community, thought that the Jackson-Reese crusade was shortsighted. Appealing to race here isn't enough, he felt. "They were saying they marched to get the right to vote. That's what they were singing about. But people around here, they want to know who's gonna to pave my street. Who's going to put in my sidewalk and who's gonna get me a job. They're not going to vote for a black just to say they've got a black mayor. They had no burning issue except changing a black face for a white face," he argued.

Smitherman knew his city. In the runoff election, Reese got very few white votes; and while the black turnout was high, it was not as high as he had hoped. Many of the newly registered blacks voted, but many who had been registered for years stayed home. Smitherman coasted to an easy victory. "They thought with all these new deputy registrars they could get the numbers. They had them going up and down the streets signing people up, and they thought they could get the numbers, but they just couldn't do it," he said later.

The mayor and his challenger agreed: new black registrants had made the race closer. But each knew that was only part of the political equation in Selma, that the white response had been the critical difference. Yes, Reese concluded, Jackson's coming to town might have tipped the balance—in the incumbent's favor. "When you have an outcry, a crisis—save the white community—they're gonna come out. They're gonna try to save their ship from sinking. Whatever the cost may be." Smitherman, settling in for his seventh term, had no misgivings about Jackson. "I loved to see him coming in here. Any time he wants to come here—he's welcome."

The cabbie in Chattanooga, Tennessee, wanted to know what was going on at the Memorial Auditorium. Jesse Jackson is in town, he was told. "Jesse who?" he said.

"Jesse Jackson, he's running for president, you know," said the passenger.

"Never heard of no Jesse Jackson," the cab driver answered. "Just heard of some nigger running around making a lot of noise." When the cabbie found the passenger was a reporter, he said "How 'bout mentioning something good about Chattanooga. Like it's the home of Little Debbie's Snack Cakes. That it has the largest military park in the world. Not about some nigger coming to town."

The bitterness, the fear, the digging-in: backlash wasn't found only in a Chattanooga cab; it went beyond Selma, even beyond what William Manchester called "hard-bitten men with brushfire eyes."[64] The feeling spread to many places: that somehow in this campaign, blacks had gone too far, pushed too hard, been too loud—and that the Democratic party had gone too far, even bent over backward, to accommodate them. That was the crux of the problem—that was the perception.

For many, Jackson was the chief antagonist. Why embrace a party that included an unbridled egotist, a black racist, out to line his own political pocket, as some viewed him—someone satisfied to ". . . court all-black constituencies with more militant-than-thou appeals," as *Washington Post* editorial writer Michael Barone later (February 17, 1985) put it. As southern whites grumbled, the party wants "them"—not us.

John Kingsbury wanted to believe that Jackson wasn't one of those "militants." And for some time he did believe it. Working in Illinois in the late sixties, the white Church of Christ minister applauded Jackson. "I was an admirer of him in the early days. He came on as one who wholly supported civil rights. I felt blacks needed help and support at that time if they were to ever get out of the ghetto. Jackson was encouraging youth to take on the responsibility of their own lives, to lift themselves up, to take some control of their own destiny."

Despite occasional doubts and misgivings, Kingsbury remained an "admirer" for several years until he went to hear Jackson address a council of churches conference in Columbus, Ohio. That day in the late 1970s, John Kingsbury's attitude changed. "I was prepared to be enamoured by his personal approach. But he left me cold. He was speaking to a white audience, and all he was doing was attacking us. The funny thing was, if he ever had a group of strong supporters, it would have been that group of ministers who were by and large sympathetic to the black cause. But instead, he lashed out at us for a variety of reasons. I just felt he was disenchanted with the white culture in general. . . . I was expecting a lot more out of the man, and he was totally anti-white."

When the 1984 campaign came along, his three college-age children each supported a different candidate—one for Mondale, one for Hart, one for Jackson—so Kingsbury had good reason to follow the campaign closely, to see if he'd been wrong about Jackson, to see if the candidate had changed. That's what he was looking for. But nothing he saw or heard altered his earlier conclusion. Kingsbury found that he was still suspicious about Jackson, still uneasy. He still felt "left out." Jackson, he thought, was not interested in finding an antidote for the way he'd affected some people; he's just interested in pressing ahead with his own agenda, with the interests of black, not white America, Kingsbury thought. One Sunday in Columbus, Ohio, he would go out of his way to get a glimpse of the candidate. Yes, he admitted, if he'd known earlier about the appearance that day he might even have paid money to hear Jackson speak. Even now, in 1984, John Kingsbury would like to have seen Jackson change. And Jesse Jackson, he felt, hadn't.

John Kingsbury wasn't alone. In August, Gil Kulick—the bright, articulate State Department diplomat who'd stood hollering "run, Jesse, run" at the Lincoln Memorial—was ignited by the budding campaign. Ten months later, in a California polling booth, he gave Jackson one final thought, then "with absolutely no enthusiasm" punched his ballot—for Walter Mondale. Jackson had failed him, Kulick came to believe. The promise had been abused.

In a Washington restaurant late in 1985, Kulick tried to explain his disillusionment. There was no one episode, he said, no single statement by Jackson that had soured him. Instead, the disappointment came gradually. There were the little things at first, certain telltale signs. Slowly, Kulick began to see what he felt was a "meanness" in the candidate—a "nastiness" aimed at whites. Sadly, Kulick concluded, he'd been drawn into a campaign laced with racism. "What disappointed me overall was his unwillingness to broaden his campaign, the very narrow focus that he maintained on black issues. I mean he made the obligatory references to arms control and foreign policy, but there was no question he was focusing very narrowly on the black vote."

There was the "Hymie-Hymietown" incident. Kulick was "bothered," he said, that Jackson "would feel comfortable enough . . . that he didn't feel he really had to conceal that kind of thought." Sure, Kulick argued, many whites and blacks slur each other in private, "but I remember thinking, would Martin Luther King have said something like that?" Kulick tried to rationalize Jackson's attitude. "I think there is a level of endemic anti-Semitism among blacks that it would be almost impossible for him [Jackson] to have escaped . . . [so] I accept a certain natural tension between blacks and Jews." Yet when Jackson was forced to apologize for the remarks, Kulick heard only hollow words. It was a bogus performance that night in the Manchester synagogue, Kulick felt: "totally insincere, purely expedient . . . it didn't ring true."

And there was Jackson's rhetoric about the Rainbow Coalition, which Kulick came to believe was just empty noise. "There was a lot of cognitive dissonance between his talk of the Rainbow Coalition and the content of the issues he addressed most of the time." Jackson was talking "rainbow," but more and more he was embracing just one color—black. Kulick was beginning to feel left out. As a young diplomat working in foreign countries, Kulick had spent long hours studying politicians, had learned what pressures they responded to, what they could and could not ignore. Kulick understood Jackson's responsibility to court the "locked out," the disenfranchised, to consolidate the black vote. But Kulick heard no overtures to him, to Gil Kulick, white

American voter. "I didn't think he was . . . making any effort to reach me . . . if he reached me as a sort of by-product of his main appeal, that was fine with him—he'd be happy to have my vote—but he wasn't making any concessions. . . . He didn't seem to be making any effort to take my concerns into account—not my concerns as a white person, but my concerns as a non-black person."

Kulick was not naive about Jackson's purpose. From that day in front of the Lincoln Memorial, "I never really had any doubt that . . . all this was to establish himself as the de facto leader of black America." But Kulick had not bargained for the exclusion. Thoughtfully, carefully, in the Washington restaurant, Kulick picked his words. Forget, for a moment, "Hymie" and "Hymietown," he said. Forget Louis Farrakhan's attacks on Jews—the Black Muslim leader's venom was "no big issue with me," Kulick said, and he felt that it didn't prove that Jackson was anti-Semitic. Forget the flashes of temper during the campaign when Kulick saw his candidate fail "to show grace under pressure."

Those factors alone, Kulick said, would not have caused him to desert the one contender he believed "was clearly making more of a statement" than the rest of the Democratic field. Kulick was sensing something more ominous. "When Jackson was talking to blacks"—and more and more, Jackson was choosing only black audiences—"he could have done more to reassure the whites who were overhearing him that he was not blaming all of the blacks' problems on whites. I got the sense that without openly courting the hostility that blacks feel toward whites, he implicitly tried to exploit it and take advantage of it . . . he clearly intended to exploit racist sentiments that may have already been there."

Kulick heard whites being made scapegoats. "Frankly, you almost—I hate to say this—but you almost had to be a self-hater, a self-hating white to vote for Jesse Jackson." And, Kulick came to believe, Jackson "would probably have a certain amount of contempt for whites who did vote for him." Kulick began to sense hostility—a sense of apartness, the need for a target—in this case, white America. "I just detected a kind of meanness" toward whites, Kulick suggested. "It's hard to specify it more than that. I just sensed the kind of meanness I didn't like."

Kulick believed Jackson had squandered an opportunity to unite those whites who'd long rebelled against discrimination and the exploitation of blacks, those who understood black resentment and felt it was justified. Like John Kingsbury, Kulick felt that Jackson had gone too far and that he had come dangerously close to inflaming black hostility, not redirecting it. So, in the end, Kulick turned away because he felt he had been turned away. "I'm not black, you know. And I don't respond to the same appeals that black voters do. I can sympathize with it, I can support the idea of a serious black candidate. But it wasn't where I was . . . it didn't draw me in."

Months after the campaign was over, Kulick found himself using the same phrase John Kingsbury had used in another part of the country. "I felt left out," Kulick repeated. "I didn't think Jackson was talking to me, that he was making any effort to reach me. And I wanted him to. I felt that he had let me down and I bet there are an awful lot of liberal whites who felt the same way, a lot . . . who were open to being persuaded, who wanted to be persuaded. I would have been happy to have been able, with a clear conscience, to cast my vote for Jesse Jackson. I didn't. I was disappointed that in the end I couldn't do that. I felt that he did not want my vote."

The backlash, the resistance, was as much a part of Jackson's impact as the hopes that he raised. Cold water from one would douse the flames of the other. To be sure, he affected the white vote—in July, 20 percent of all whites queried in a Gallup Poll said they'd probably vote in November, because of Jackson.[65] But not for him. In fact, few white voters did support him. "Jackson never received more than 9 percent of white votes in any state for which exit polls are available," said Tom Cavanaugh of the Joint Center for Political Studies. And the Rainbow Coalition was growing steadily blacker. As the campaign progressed, "although Jackson's share of the black vote went up . . . his share of the white vote appears to have declined." Jackson tried to turn that pattern to his own advantage. On March 21, in Richmond, Virginia, he complained that while blacks often vote for whites, whites tend to regard blacks as inferiors and withhold their support from black candidates. Politically, the argument was ingenious: it would not be his fault if he lost elections—it would be theirs, white America's. Don't blame him or what he had said and done—blame racism. Once again he would be the victim.

Even the positive numbers, Jackson was learning, had a gloomy underside. Selma's election was not an isolated incident. Republicans, conservative whites, even evangelical Christian groups had seen what was happening and were mounting their own drives. Partly—probably largely—because of him, they had redoubled their efforts. The result, according to the Committee for the Study of the American Electorate, was that, although the number of blacks registering to vote had climbed, registration overall benefited Republicans more than Democrats: while Democrats improved their advantage over the GOP in four states, Republicans had net registration gains over Democrats in ten states. In five southern states alone (Louisiana, North and South Carolina, Florida, and Kentucky) over 400,000 blacks had been added to the rolls—but white registration there had climbed more than 1.2 million. In Louisiana, where black registration increased 18.2 percent in the last two years, the increase of newly registered Republicans was three times greater (56.3 percent); the increase of newly registered blacks in Florida (18 percent) was more than offset by a surge of 26.4 percent in Republican rolls.[66]

Even in areas where blacks registered at a higher rate than whites, the white total stayed higher. In Georgia, for instance, black registration climbed 15.6 percent from August, 1983, to August, 1984—while the rate of increase for white registration increased only 9.7 percent. Still, in raw numbers, that meant more than 170,000 new white voters, but only 75,000 more blacks. Likewise in Louisiana. The black registration rate there of 11.4 percent was almost twice the white rate of 6.6 percent. But the number of new white voters (99,169) was far greater than the number of new black voters (55,169).[67]

When measuring Jackson's impact, backlash and the downside of registration numbers weren't the only negatives. He failed to get the party to change its election rules and procedures. The nine southern states and Oklahoma still required runoff or second primaries (which Jackson continued to insist violated the Voting Rights Act of 1965, but which many party leaders felt helped blacks win elective office). Mississippi kept its dual-registration system, which worked hardships on the rural poor. State legislatures still had power to gerrymander voting districts; local government bodies could annex white areas to help dilute the black vote. He had fought against all those things. Party officials did agree to set up a Fairness Commission as he'd requested. But that in itself was no big achievement—after all, there had been a fairness commission four years earlier. And while this one did accept Jackson's request to lower the so-called threshold (percentage of the vote a candidate had to get in presidential caucuses and primaries to qualify for a share of the state's delegates in that election) from 20 to 15 percent, the commission also decided to increase—by more than 200—the number of party leaders and elected officials who automatically got convention seats, the so-called super delegates. Small wonder, then, that after the commission's decision in October, 1985, Jackson complained that the changes actually made the situation worse—that the lowering of the threshold was more than offset by the increase in the number of super delegates. "What you are doing is creating a national gerrymandering process stacked against independents and minorities," he complained to the party's new national chairman, Paul Kirk. Kirk didn't bother to respond; privately, however, party officials said that when the commission met for its crucial vote, neither Jackson nor anyone representing him bothered to show up. In short, one of the "concessions" granted Jackson—one of his presumed achievements—had, by Jackson's own admission, blown up in his face.

Scrutinized closely, the gains looked meager. Not only had some of his achievements been offset, not only had his forces been "song and danced" at the Democratic convention as one supporter angrily put it,[68] not only would a black candidate spurn his offer of help in Virginia and pundit George Will refer to him as "a comet hitting the earth's atmosphere, burning brightly but fatally and soon to be a small cinder,"[69] but further examination would also suggest that Jackson's own role had been exaggerated, his personal claims—such as registering 2 million blacks—wildly inflated, his political contribution suspect. Months after the election, the NAACP's Joseph Madison was still fuming over what Jackson had said—and what he had done:

> He provided the symbolism and the incentive. But the bulk of the work was done by the traditional organizations (NAACP, Urban League, Voter Education Project). . . . ABC, CBS, NBC, hey, they should be ashamed of themselves for reporting that Jackson registered all those voters. How do you think that makes my volunteers feel? Goddamnit, you see Jackson there with about

> one hundred people marching them up to register, then by the time the evening news comes on it's way up to one thousand; and Jackson's getting on that ragged plane of his, flying off somewhere to make another speech. Goddamnit, no one hears about the two thousand registered by little old grandmothers and college students and church women and old people in senior citizens' centers.

There were also signs that some of the "gains" might be short-lived. "Flukes"—that's what veteran Mississippi lawmaker Henry Kirksey called them. A black state senator who'd been flattened by the state's political establishment for decades, Kirksey felt that Jackson supporters had ousted whites from party posts mostly because the whites had been caught napping. Hell, he muttered, "if the whites had any idea that Jackson would be able to mobilize blacks as he did, they would have been out there in force. That was a onetime deal where you catch folks off-guard. It's not going to happen again. These people are not that dumb. They will intend to prevail, and they're going to do whatever is necessary." Kirksey, and others who'd worked with Jackson, doubted whether Jackson was disciplined enough to take the steps necessary to repel the likely counteroffensive.

In some places it had already begun. In November, 1984, Dallas County, Alabama, had elected Jackie Walker (see chapter 5) its first black assessor in one hundred years; but when she was killed in a February, 1985, car crash before taking office, the all-white Dallas County Commission appointed a white man, chief clerk Tommy Powell, to take her place. Walker had beaten Powell twice—in the primary and in the general election, where Powell had run a write-in campaign—and outraged Walker supporters denounced the commissioners' action. "It's a slap in the face," said one. "Blacks aren't even second-class citizens in Dallas County—they're more like third-class," said another. But Tommy Powell became assessor.[70]

It wasn't just that the gains might be temporary. Some felt what had been achieved wasn't that important. "Self-esteem, that's one of the most overrated virtues in political life," said Alan Dershowitz of the Harvard Law School. "Sure, Jesse Jackson brought some self-esteem to many blacks in America. The Ayatollah brought self-esteem to many Iranians. And Adolph

Hitler brought self-esteem to many Germans. It's not hard to bring self-esteem when you just flex your muscles and go out there and say I don't care about anybody else—come and vote for me. So I don't think there's been all that much in terms of self-esteem," he continued.

The crowd on the vacant lot in Watts was jubilant. Stevie Wonder sang to them, and Jesse Jackson told them things would be better. "There's something in our hearts. There's a fire that won't go out," he said. As his motorcade drove away from Charcoal Alley, a group of kids playing basketball in Rogers Park paused to watch. One teenager held the ball over his head: "This is the only dream we got," he shouted.

If the final judgment about his campaign has to wait, if what he did cut both ways, if his contribution is uncertain, one thing does seem clear. "Everyone is learning from Jackson's candidacy," said Alan Dershowitz, and that may have been the greatest impact of all. The attitudes of some whites regarding blacks did harden, some black suspicions about whites were confirmed—but in between many other attitudes were tested, challenged—changed. "He removed the spectre that a black man could not run for president," said Charlotte, North Carolina, mayor Harvey Gantt. In Mobile, Alabama, Joe Reed reached the same conclusion: "Jackson was saying to white America: start thinking that a black man can run. . . . That's his contribution." Those who agree with that appraisal feel that the country was rejecting only one black man, not all black Americans. That while the country was not ready for *him,* it could be ready for another black aspirant. As his Alabama co-chairman Michael Figures put it, "I really believe that the country is closer to the day when a black person can run and be seriously considered for one of the major party nominations. I don't say that day is at hand. I just say it's closer than it would have been without Jesse Jackson."

Perhaps that assessment is far too rosy, hits only some of the target. Some believe his excesses, his shortcomings, actually harmed the cause of black empowerment, and that the consequences of backlash would not quickly disappear. The opposition, they argue, has been put on alert. But if bias did flourish, if many in white America did not try to understand or turned away in anger, for a moment at least even his detractors had been forced to look. That, said the historian John Hope Franklin, had never happened before:

> . . . this country got a good lesson. A lesson they've never had before. A lesson that I think few people could have taught. And that is that a black man has qualities—and qualifications—for the highest office in the land. . . . And the American people needed that. They needed that lesson. . . . I think we learned a lot about ourselves as we listened to this man. . . . What we might have learned as we went through the experience, that it was conceivable that a black man had the qualities to be President. We might have learned that.
>
> Or, *if we didn't learn that, we were forced to consider that.*

Clearly the confrontation did not change all minds. But few were untouched; no one could hide. Even those who despised him were affected. "If the campaign did nothing else—I don't care how much they hate him, how much they dislike him—white America can never look on all blacks any more as the same," said one of his earliest supporters.

So sometimes, if grudgingly, attitudes were changing, even though there was no radical transformation of the country and though the changes were often subtle, almost imperceptible. It was a beginning. "It's dangerous to drop a match in a certain kind of forest. It'll catch fire," said Tom Gilmour, the onetime sheriff. "That's been my experience when I was fighting forest fires back home. That the rain would come up and put it out. And it'd be left to stomp, then smoulder. And the wind would get back up again and dry up a little bit around it—and get it back up to burning again. I think Jesse set a political fire."

"I think what he has done is to pave the way for his kids and my kids and your kids," said Jackson State University professor Leslie McLemore. California assembly speaker Willie Brown put it in more practical terms: "I am convinced that what Jackson has done is make it possible for [Atlanta mayor] Andy Young, for a Basil Patterson [New York City political leader]. He's made it possible for a more regular Democratic politician with the same potential speaking ability, with the same celebrity-like status, and with the same attractiveness. And I think that 1988 will bring that about."

A pioneer of sorts. One even called him "A John the Baptist . . . out there in the wilderness." Harry Edwards used another comparison:

> . . . this is not Hollywood. It's not a situation where the good guys ride into town at 8:00 and by the time the ten o'clock news comes on everything has been settled, and good guys are riding off into the sunset to live happily ever after. . . . I think that in a very real sense Jesse Jackson is a significant rider in what would be analogous to the old Pony Express mail delivery system. That is approximately where black society is, where poor people are in this country, relative to mainstream politics. They're moving in the Space Age. We're moving along what is effectively a Pony Express system. Mr. Jackson is a very important rider; he is riding over some of the roughest terrain. But we should have no illusions about him riding all the way and delivering the mail. He is going to have to pass the mail along to someone else, and hopefully the terrain will not be as difficult. Hopefully they will have a faster horse.

At the back of a grimy hall in the worst of the Oakland slums, a young man about 20 years old, in a navy blue windbreaker, stood the entire thirty minutes Jackson spoke. He never said a word, never cheered or clapped. He just kept his right hand raised high over his head, his two fingers in a "V for Victory" salute.

In the dingy office several blocks from the Mississippi state capitol, Henry Kirksey's fist slammed down on the table top, and his eyes flashed. "It did change things. It changed people's understanding. That's the first damn step you got to take," he said. That, Tom Cavanaugh suspected, would be Jackson's lasting impact. Like Eugene McCarthy in 1968, Jackson would fall short of the nomination but perhaps accomplish more than that year's "winner," Hubert Humphrey. What Jackson's Tidewater, Virginia, campaign manager said had started "as a dream in fantasy land" had by now turned into a symbol. The street-hustler had become something of an icon, whether or not he had changed himself. "Now there are people who've got his picture up in their houses. Right alongside Martin Luther King, John Kennedy, and Robert Kennedy," Delacey Stith added. "He's already president," 6-year-old Tushina Washington told one of the authors in Baltimore. Those who needed to believe believed the most.

"He has unleashed a terror on the land and still you do not understand." James Baldwin shook his head and did not smile. He was 60 now but the fires had not been banked. On this midsummer evening in 1984, he spoke with the controlled fury of one who had learned long ago that the gulf between black and white in America is infinite—and unfathomable. "Some things have changed, you know. It is not quite as dangerous for a black boy and a white girl to be seen together as it was when I was young, not quite. Where they're gonna live is another question still. I am saying the attitudes of this Republic, which has told itself nothing but lies, nothing but lies as long as you leave it to itself, the real attitudes of this Republic have not changed."

Sitting in the book-lined study of the house he'd been renting in Massachusetts, James Baldwin doubted whether white America could ever understand what Jesse Jackson had tried to do; sipping a beer and occasionally puffing a cigarette, Baldwin spoke bluntly, angrily—and with little sorrow:

> We've always been pawns and tools. We never had anything resembling autonomy. We entered this country, to say nothing of the western world, on the auction block. People overlook what that means. And what that really means, if I entered to be sold, bought and sold and examined like a mule, that means I entered here with an apprehension of the western morality, which a slave master could not afford to endure. It means I've always historically known much more about you than you've ever been able to dare to imagine about me. I did not invent you. I did not write *Gone With the Wind.* You invented me and you live with that invention. I don't. I have to know what you really think about me. You act it out every hour of every day, what you really think about me. Every institution in this country is based on what you think about me. There are two things in the Jackson

> campaign which are terribly relevant. You are beginning to understand very reluctantly that your idea of yourself is not my idea of you. . . . You are beginning to understand that you may believe in Scarlett O'Hara but I didn't. Furthermore, you created her, so you're stuck with her. I'm not. Now here comes Jess. Young man out of the civil rights movement, out of the pain, out of the horror, and the Republic refuses, really, to recognize. How he comes we don't really know. But we do know this: that his presence presents the American Republic with questions and choices it has spent all its history until this hour trying to avoid.

James Baldwin paused to light another cigarette. He had been talking for nearly two hours about the Jackson campaign, and he had not yet finished. "The principle on which the country built itself was that my voice should never be heard. . . . Jesse comes from a long line of people, you know, a long line of people that the American Republic has deliberately ignored," Baldwin was saying. And though Baldwin felt that Jackson was doomed from the start, he also believed that the campaign had been triumphant in its own way. That running black had been both futile—and essential. And not just for Black America:

> It begins a challenge finally to the whole idea of white supremacy, the whole idea of racism in this country; it is very hard to deal with this. The whole country has been so manipulated for so long, as white and black, that it comes as a great shock to everybody that a candidate who happens to be legally black can elicit such a response. . . . Once we have heard this, no one will forget it. And nothing will ever again be what it was before. That is what the white world is terrified of. After all, not a single white American would have gone to Syria and delivered one of our soldiers who was in there, not to fight for my life, but for your interests. It's a very important matter; and if the people in Washington don't understand it, the people in Harlem do. And that is the terror, the real terror. And he has brought the people into the streets—not to break windows—but to make their presence known. And to change this country. . . . I

> think that what Jesse's brought to the surface is terror. Terror. Because a white identity is a false identity. And people don't like to be confronted with the lies they have lived with for so long. . . . Jesse is not revealing anything people don't know. He is forcing them to look at what they don't want to look at. . . . He may represent your only hope. Not mine. But yours. He's not of my country, never has been. Never will be. He knows something about you that you don't know about yourself. It is not a Negro problem, it is a white problem. And he articulates it. He makes it present for you and it disturbs you because you're gonna have to deal with you. Instead of pretending to deal with me.

Jacqueline Lavinia Jackson II stormed in from school one afternoon in late fall 1984 and demanded answers. She'd been told her father had won his race for president in "many different ways." She'd heard her father say, "We've won . . . we've won our self-respect, that's winning." So armed with news of the victory, 9-year-old Jackie, Jr., had gone off to invite her fourth-grader friends to stay at the White House with her in 1985. Now they were teasing her. Her father was not going to Washington, they were telling Jackie, Jr. He was too, she kept insisting.

The youngest Jackson had too conventional an idea of winning, her mother lamented later. "You see, we can't allow other people to interpret what winning is for us. But Jackie, Jr., represents a new day in an America without any history of what blacks have endured. Jackie, Jr., represents a whole new day. . . . She came to me and said, 'Mommy, you told me we won. Now there is an argument at school. They say we didn't win. I want you to tell me. Will we be in the White House in January?' I told her 'No.' She was so upset."

16.

JESSE

Thunder."

Jimmy Carter had been "Deacon," Gary Hart was "Redwood," but Jesse Jackson's code name was "Thunder." The Secret Service had dubbed him that, and from the first time he heard it he loved the sound of the word and all that came with it, loved to see the clean-cut agents in their dark suits mutter into the tiny microphones that dangled from their sleeves as they cupped their hands over their mouths so that no one but the secret brotherhood could hear the top-secret communiqués: "Thunder one to Chase. Bring that motorcade around back." Sometimes he would pretend not to hear, but sometimes he wouldn't even try to hide his delight, the magic word would crackle back and forth and his eyes would dance and he would smile that all this could be happening to him, the illegitimate child from the South Carolina textile town who not that long ago had been humiliated in his adopted hometown of Chicago; the night that Harold Washington won the city's Democratic primary, Jackson had jumped onstage and led the boisterous crowd in chants of "We Want it All" until embarrassed Washington men had yanked Jackson to the side and hustled him out of sight. Washington would need every vote Jesse Jackson could drum up to win the general election, but on primary night Washington's people worried that Jackson might upset things. Months later the episode still rankled. The sight of the government agents now helped. Washington, elected mayor, had his own bodyguards, but none of that could compare to this; the mayor's beefy, red-faced Chicago cops in their racetrack sports coats were oafish clowns compared to this elite, well-muscled corps that stood guard over Jackson and scanned every crowd for the would-be assassin he always expected, jut-jawed protection twenty-four hours a day, courtesy of the United States Treasury Department. "Why, those twelve white boys jumping out the car to look after one blood, I tell you, it was great entertainment," one black sociologist said later, knowing that each time the agents jumped, black America smiled: the white establishment, guaranteeing the personal well-being of the Reverend Jesse Louis Jackson, "Thunder." To Jackson, it wasn't just the image the word evoked: a deafening roar with lightning bolts, the heavens torn apart. It was also the way the word itself sounded: say it softly and it still seemed to boom out, to reverberate. He loved repeating it over and over to himself, loved to hear its echo, to savor its texture, its taste. To him, it was the taste of power.

Power. In the beginning there was none. Exposure to it—in its many forms—helped shape his early life. And he would spend much of his adult life in its pursuit. "Don't measure me by where I am," he would tell detractors, "measure me by where I started from," and by that yardstick he had come an enormous distance. Yet in another sense he had gone almost nowhere: Greenville, South Carolina, was his past—and his present. He left Greenville, but it was never far away.

He was born in Greenville on October 8, 1941, the illegitimate son of a 16-year-old high school junior and a married man almost three times her age who lived next door. The birth scandalized the neighborhood, and Helen Burns soon was driven out of the Springfield Baptist Church by a vote of its congregation. That was his first exposure to power, the power of condemnation that shamed his mother and grandmother and wounded the child: there was teasing from his schoolmates—"Jesse ain't got no Daddy, Jesse ain't got no Daddy"—and cold stares from adults. Jackson never forgot the taunts; thirty-five years later, the pain was still there. "When I was in my mother's belly, no father to give me a name . . . they called me a bastard and rejected me," he would tell audiences in the campaign.

When he was 8, he learned about white power. He was in a hurry one day at the corner grocery store and whistled at a white clerk for service. The grocer pulled out a loaded .45 and cocked it in the little boy's face. "Goddamn you, don't you ever whistle at a white man again," the grocer said. And there were other lessons. Young Jackson hawked peanuts and Coca-Cola during Saturday basketball games at the Furman University Fieldhouse. "Hey, nigger, over here," white spectators in Textile Hall would hoot, handing him a one dollar bill and then demanding that he give them change for a ten. "Grown men trying to shortchange a child," he would remember years later, the memory making him wince.

He would outfox the rednecks and keep his tiny profits not just because his mother needed the extra money to help buy groceries but also because the Great Selvy was performing on the court below. Frank Selvy, the Corbin Comet, would score more points in a single season than any other Furman player since, including a record 100 in a single game; Frank Selvy, slow and white, was one of Jesse Jackson's first heroes. The boy longed for the day when he could enroll in Selvy's school, and then the white folks who mixed Coke and bourbon in the bleacher seats would have to cheer for him. But the dream wasn't possible; even though Furman coach Bob King helped Jackson get a scholarship to the University of Illinois, Furman wouldn't accept a black student for another fifteen years.

Jackson would also not forget the trips downtown in Greenville, riding in the back of the bus. Why in back? he would protest, and his mother would shoo him along, pointing to the lettering overhead that instructed the "colored" to go to the rear. He remembered each step backward was a new wound. "I can still see that sign with my eyes today," he'd tell reporters later when they asked him what hurt the most back then.

As a schoolboy, he learned that power which could promote also left casualties; that what motivated some could thwart others. Power from the state decreed that he and his classmates could not set foot on the state capitol lawn. Or take a drink from public drinking fountains. Power from the local school board gave new books for white students and hand-me-downs for blacks; top pay to white teachers and lower salaries for blacks; new classrooms on the white side of town but shanty schools for blacks.

He saw the cruel power of the local police on Friday nights, when officers would sweep through the neighborhoods and arrest unemployed men as vagrants, put them in striped uniforms, then herd them back in manacles to clean the streets. He'd watch each week as the fathers and uncles and brothers of his friends were paraded in the humiliating stripes and chains past children who could only cry out "Please, sir, could I give my daddy a cup of water?" Years later, when he saw the striped prison clothes at the Holocaust Museum in Jerusalem, his thoughts would be wrenched back seven thousand miles and twenty years to those Greenville streets and his friends and their chipped water cup.

One personality dominated young Jackson's life. She provided him a haven from the hate and gave him reasons to persevere. From the start Matilda Burns, his grandmother, told Jackson he was "somebody," the Lord's child, inferior to no one. Again and again, as she made cobbler from potato skins or wove quilts from bits of cloth to help keep him and his half-brother warm, she hammered the notion of worth, even greatness, into him. When Jackson was 9, his mother married Charles Henry Jackson, who legally adopted him, and the taunts about his illegitimacy eased up. The family was close-knit. In his early childhood, Jackson's mother worked as a maid for upper-class whites in Greenville, and the family lived in a house with paper-thin walls, a wood-burning fire for heat, and no indoor plumbing, just mason jars—"portable units," he once joked. Moving into the Hillcrest Housing Project was a thrill, he would tell one campaign audience after another: "our own Kelvinator . . . our own house key . . . own mail box . . . utility bills . . . no more slop jars." Years later, he paused by a tree he and his stepfather had planted in his old front yard. "The tree made it," he said. "Anything's possible. I learned that here."

The family was religious and worshiped regularly. In the black church, the small boy felt safe; in numbers there was a security he encountered nowhere else. In the music there was a joy that brought him comfort. Here were the giants he needed: the larger-than-life figures in the Bible. "Long before we had black heroes, we had Biblical heroes," he said.

At Sterling High School, Charles McIver—not Jesse Jackson—was voted most likely to succeed. Someone else was elected class president; Jesse Jackson was elected business manager. By then, though, he knew that he was smart, that he could compete if he had a chance. "Growing up taught me to make As; when you do, people have to hang around you. With Ds, they don't," he said, and he made enough As to enter the National Honor Society in his senior year, one of seventeen on the football team to do so.

Football was his ideal forum. "He always was bigger than kids his age, towered over 'em. He got accustomed to people singling him out, giving him special attention," said his high school coach, Joseph Mathis.[71] Especially on the gridiron, at Sirrine Stadium where Sterling High played on Thursday nights (Greenville's white high school team got the more desirable Friday night slot). By the eighth grade, Jackson was riding the Sterling High bus with the rest of the team. As a junior, he took charge as quarterback. In one huddle, challenged to make a perfect pass by an older player, Jackson snapped back, "It'll be there—just make sure you are." As a senior, he starred. Nearly six feet three inches tall, almost two hundred pounds, Jackson switched to fullback for one game and scored three touchdowns. Classmates voted him Sterling High's best male athlete. If the rules were the same as on the football field or baseball diamond, if performance, not color, was judged, he figured he could excel in anything.

In 1959, Jackson left Greenville for Champaign-Urbana, where the University of Illinois had given him a football scholarship. The high school star dreamed of glory, but one hot afternoon in August the dream came to an end on an Illini practice field: only whites play quarterback here, an assistant coach told him. Jackson was positioned first at left half, then at end. Nothing he said or did could change the verdict. You people run better from the left side, the assistant said, leaving no room for argument. Before when he'd been slapped down by bigotry, Jackson had been resourceful enough to find a way around the obstacles. As a busboy in a Greenville hotel, for example, he learned to spit in the food of haughty white diners before he served them. But the no-black-quarterback rule was unbending and forced him to flee the huge university for the hardpack and scrub-grass of North Carolina Agricultural and Technical College in Greensboro, North Carolina. There he not only became quarterback but was elected student body president. He also helped organize protest marches at city lunch counters. In Greensboro, he became a campus hero; but twenty-five years later the scars from the University of Illinois experience still had not healed, and the memory of it would make his face tighten and his words turn hard.

Jackson graduated from A&T in 1962 with a degree in sociology and a decision to work in the civil rights movement. Already he had become for some the "somebody" his grandmother told him he could be. "We didn't see Jesse as being the type of guy we were," remembers his old college roommate, Robert Faulkner. Faulkner and others on the A&T Aggie football team used to help protect Jackson during those early Congress of Racial Equality (CORE) demonstrations Jackson helped lead. "Fighting just wasn't anything to us. We wanted to see him use his brains and out-talk them. And if it came to fighting, well, we could have excelled at that," said Faulkner with a smile.

Jackson enrolled in the Chicago Theological Seminary because, unlike law or politics, the ministry offered immediate, almost guaranteed returns: a Baptist minister, the recognized authority figure in the black community, could move easily between black and white worlds. As a minister, he would have access.

His seminary days, he said later, were "precious," but six months before graduating he dropped out, sickened and infuriated by what he had been seeing on television: police in Selma, Alabama, clubbing and mistreating blacks. He went to Alabama and began helping others organize. Martin Luther King, Jr., noticed the ambitious young black and recruited him to organize a group of students. Soon King brought Jackson onto his staff and dispatched him on numerous missions around the country, including the launching, in 1966, of Operation Breadbasket, a Southern Christian Leadership Conference Chicago-based project to improve economic conditions for urban blacks.

Jackson idolized King, but for him discipleship was an uncomfortable role. He despised taking orders. The cockiness developed in Greenville and cheered on in Sirrine Stadium rarely allowed him to doubt his own ability or judgment. He began to get into heated arguments with King. Finally, after one stormy session, an exasperated King turned on him: "Jesse, it may be necessary for you to carve your individual niche in society. But don't bother me. Don't bother me." And King, seething, had walked off.

King's assassination changed everything; after April 4, 1968, Jackson's relations with many black leaders quickly deteriorated. Before they had merely resented his freewheeling, egotistical style, his calling news conferences or staging marches without checking first with them. Now they were shocked to see him on national television and at the Chicago city council in a shirt reportedly stained with blood from the slain King, creating the impression that Jackson had cradled the dying civil rights leader in his arms. It wasn't true—the black leaders knew it wasn't, and so did Jackson—but Jackson did nothing to dispel the myth, and his critics were livid. Still, his talent was considerable, and King's successor, Dr. Ralph David Abernathy, tried to find Jackson a role. In the summer of 1968, Abernathy named him "mayor" of Resurrection City, the tent camp pitched by an estimated twenty thousand Poor People's Campaign protestors on the Washington Mall. For the first time, Jackson would tell a crowd "I Am—Somebody," and then ask them to repeat it after him. "I may be poor—I may be poor—but I Am—but I Am—Somebody. Somebody." With the refrain, a trademark was established.

Already he sensed that he could move a crowd better than the others; already he was more ambitious; the SCLC leadership, he felt, was timid, unimaginative, dispirited. On the other hand, Jackson had earned a reputation for being more interested in promoting himself than the organization. SCLC leaders also questioned how he was spending Operation Breadbasket money. In 1971, after Abernathy came to Chicago and virtually called Jackson a thief, Jackson quit Breadbasket and on a cold, Christmas morning announced that "a new child has been born." He called his new organization Operation PUSH, People United to Save Humanity. Later, in a less ambitious moment, the name was changed: People United to *Serve* Humanity.

With PUSH, Jackson was on his own, and he would use all the lessons he had learned in Greenville, in Greensboro and Chicago. "Take all the swift advantage of the hours," the superintendent of Greenville's schools had said during the Sterling High School commencement ceremonies, and Jackson understood Shakespeare's message. By then experience had taught him that opportunity came knocking only in storybooks. Wherever he'd lived, he'd learned that opportunities had to be chased, caught, knocked to the ground, subdued. He also sensed that the only way to outdistance his past was to seize the present. Grab it by the scruff of the neck. He would have to move quickly, improvise if need be, even shove others out of the way. No opportunity could be squandered—that too was a lesson he had learned. "Jesse is always *on;* he doesn't relax," Atlanta mayor Andrew Young once said. The urgency, said Young, that is what sets Jackson apart; that's what makes him different.

Of course I'm an opportunist, Jackson agreed. That's what Martin Luther King taught us. That was the lesson of his life: wring each moment for all it's worth. Then go on. That's how history is made. That too became part of Jackson's ministry. Reverend, he was told, you're not meek and gentle the way ministers are supposed to be. "Let me tell you a thing or two about Christian audacity," he would reply. "Jesus never was anybody's patsy—nobody pushed him around."

"History is better served by those on the make than by those who have it made," the Reverend William Sloane Coffin told Jackson once, and Jackson agreed. From Alabama, political strategist Joe Reed watched Jackson operate. "You know, we got a saying down here. While some folks is standing out on the front porch shaking hands, others are already out back counting the chickens." Jackson, Reed said, had been out there counting "a long time."

There wasn't enough money or staff, and there never would be. Words were the only weapons he could count on. He had only his wit, his instincts, and the language at his command. Early on he began to master some of the tricks he would need; as he later told a seminar of political broadcasters in 1985:

> If we speak too ungrammatically, we're called ignorant. If we speak grammatically, we're dull. So we say we're going to have "Demonstrations without hesitation. And jail, without bail." They hear that and they say boy, he's really rhyming. The reality is that if I take a minute and a half to say we're not going to demonstrate this afternoon, and we're not going to think about it any longer (at this point, his voice slows to a crawl, becomes dull, leaden) and we are willing to go to jail and willing to pay the price for bail and the bond, if need be—well, there ain't no telling whether that would get picked up! So "Demonstrations without hesitation—jail, without bail" becomes a way of trying to engage in the economy of words, knowing the discipline you subject speakers to. I've grown up in an era where I've some sense of what's required to communicate.

The early 1970s. Saturday mornings at Operation PUSH. In a huge, drafty old Jewish synagogue renamed Dr. King's Workshop, the powerfully built black man with the Afro and the leather vests with dazzling medallions around his neck would exorcise the devils and give his listeners a glimpse of hope; often he would stir in them the belief that yes, perhaps there is a chance—that maybe we are "somebody."

In the early years the crowds were small, but Jackson soon figured a way to make them grow. He would use the local media, especially the local television stations, to help build his fame. He distrusted them. He knew they weren't there because they cared about him or the cause but only because they knew he was good box office, controversial, outrageous, entertaining. And because it was Saturday, a slow news day.

So every Saturday the local stations would bundle off their mostly white camera crews and reporters to Jesse Jackson's southside emporium, where he was bound to accuse someone of something. The television people would carry on about how filthy and cold the place was and about how the show never seemed to start on time. "Jackson standard time," they joked. Mostly, though, they were nervous, surrounded by all those black faces, many of them young and proud and poor and blaming "whitey" for their misery.

One reporter who shared his colleagues' feelings arrived late one Saturday, after the service had started. Heads were bowed and the Reverend was earnestly in prayer as the reporter tried to walk forward. Suddenly, two dashiki-clad black men strong-armed him, blocked his path, and told him to leave. Part of Jackson's unofficial "security force," they would permit no intruders once the service had begun. And certainly not a white reporter yelping that he had to join his camera crew already positioned in front. Pointing at the crew, the reporter tried to brush past. Angered, the two guards pinned his arms to his sides and began to shove him backward toward the door.

At that point, although in mid-prayer, the Reverend noticed. "Help us, our Heavenly Father, we humbly beseech you," Jackson intoned, his eyes fixed on the scene at the back. Without breaking his cadence, he added: ". . . and release from bondage all those who dare enter this shrine."

The two bodyguards stopped, looked at Jackson, saw his hand signal, and instantly surrendered their prey. Minutes later, the Reverend called the reporter over to the edge of the stage. "Good to see you," he said, very matter-of-factly. "If you want to interview me, we can do it right now, here—or later, in the office. Take your pick."

He refined that "sense of what's required to communicate" all those Saturday mornings at PUSH in Chicago and on hundreds of stages throughout the next decade. Wherever he went, he was always rehearsing, always seeking the right voice. In Dayton, Ohio, in the late sixties and early seventies, a young talk-show host named Donahue was also polishing his act. Only a few cities carried the Donahue program then, but the minister from Greenville relished each appearance. "I'd rather be there than on those morning network shows," he'd say. "Up there in New York they stick you in between the plants and the violins," he'd complain. He also knew the network audiences, bolting down breakfast and racing to get out of the house, wouldn't really listen to him—but that in all those Midwest kitchens there were those eager for something more than soap operas and cartoons. With Donahue, the message could be fine-tuned, perfected: fewer people but more time, more feedback. This Dayton stuff is the bush leagues, one aide protested, but Jackson kept going on. And over the years, as the Donahue audience grew, Jackson rode the wave.

Sometimes the tricks he'd master for one arena would not work in another. In 1971, huffing and puffing that Chicago mayor Richard J. Daley could be defeated, Jackson permitted a write-in campaign for "Jackson for Mayor." But all the media tricks in the world wouldn't help him pull that off. When it was clear the effort was doomed, Jackson backpedaled furiously and tried to disassociate himself from the drive. But his critics would not let him forget. Gleefully, they chortled that he'd proven to be hot air, little more. "Jesse Jetstream," then *Chicago Daily News* columnist Mike Royko dubbed him. Many felt the episode left Jackson a political laughingstock, but one year later Jackson tried politics again. With Chicago attorney William Singer, he led a successful effort to prevent Daley and the regular Cook County Democratic organization from being seated at the Democratic National Convention; after a fierce, uphill fight, the convention in Miami voted to seat the Singer-Jackson group, not the mayor's.

Jackson, however, was hardly a political insider at that convention—in fact, he found out that party nominee George McGovern had selected Missouri senator Thomas Eagleton as his running mate while watching TV in a Miami hotel room. But Jackson did come away far more adept in media skills. He was becoming a master of the pithy phrase, the kind audiences could remember and editors could not trim. He was also becoming a veteran of the staged event.

May 29, 1980. The small room in the Fort Wayne, Indiana, hospital filled up quickly. In the rear, camera operators, technicians, and equipment competed for space; in front, the hospital staff and city officials crowded behind a table; in between, reporters wedged in so tightly they could scarcely write.

Carefully the young black surgeon explained how close National Urban League executive director Vernon Jordan had come to death in the early hours of May 29, 1980. Another fraction of an inch, said Dr. Jeffrey Towles, and the gunshot blast to the back would have killed him. As Towles was describing the 4½-hour operation, the room suddenly seemed to lurch forward as a tall man elbowed his way in from a side entrance and began inching his way to the front, his shoulders hunched and head down in a vain attempt to be inconspicuous. The proceedings stopped altogether as the latecomer took a position behind the medical team.

For a few moments he listened. Then, during a slight pause, he stepped forward to speak. The attempted assassination, Jesse Jackson said, demonstrated that there was "a hit list for black leadership." There were loud murmurs. Hit list? Who compiled it? Who was on it? Jackson gave no details, offered no proof. He knew he didn't have to—he knew the pithy phrase itself would make news, and he was right. "Hit list!" That night when the networks told America what had happened to Vernon Jordan, they also included Jackson's sensational statement. The "hit list" accusations almost dwarfed the shooting. Vernon Jordan had come to town and had nearly been killed, but that night Jordan wasn't going to be the only story in Fort Wayne, Indiana.

Five months later, the day after the 1980 presidential election, the plane had barely lifted off from Washington's National Airport when Jesse Jackson began criticizing NBC. That morning NBC's *Today Show* had invited Vernon Jordan into its studios to discuss the black vote. Hell, Jackson snorted, Jordan shouldn't have been in that studio—I should have. Vernon and I are friends, and I respect him, he argued, but after all I was the one President Carter asked to carry the administration banner to black America; I was the one who campaigned for him in eighty cities, not

Vernon. Jordan, he seemed to be saying, is not the spokesman for Black America—Jesse Jackson is. He talked as if he had carved out a niche for himself, and he would not share that position with—much less relinquish it to—someone, anyone else. He had forced himself onto centerstage, and he would not let anyone shove him off. Ninety minutes later, when the plane taxied to the ramp in Chicago, Jackson was still complaining.

October, 1984. For most of the campaign, the Secret Service agent had watched Jackson closely. Often he was the last person to talk to the candidate at night, the first to see him in the morning. During the campaign he had spent hundreds of hours with Jackson, had eaten with, flown alongside, shielded Jackson with his own body, joked with, even been stung by the candidate's anger. Like few others he knew both the public and the private man. The agent had seen and been appalled by Jackson's bullying manner—how he'd curtly snap orders and put down aides—but the agent also couldn't forget Jackson's kindness, how the candidate had gone out of his way to welcome and fuss over agents' families when they'd appear at campaign stops; or how Jackson had taken time Christmas day, 1983, to call the wives of agents accompanying him and apologize to them for taking their husbands away for the holiday. The agent had witnessed decency and pettiness; more than once he had heard Jackson deliver homilies from the pulpit—then pick up a telephone and use language the agent said made him cringe.

Long after the campaign was over, the agent was asked what he thought about the candidate. The agent was discreet; someday he might have to work with Jackson again, and he had no wish to say anything that might embarrass the Service. After a long silence, he finally answered. "The Reverend is a walking contradiction," he said. "The problem is—he's at war with himself." He was pulled in different directions. By the past—the present—and the future. Each competed and sometimes conflicted. The demands of the past, for example, were not necessarily the needs of the present. What he had to do in 1984—secure a black political base—might work against him, jeopardize his chances to emerge as a truly national figure, not as the black candidate. The obligations of the moment did not always dovetail with what might be best for him in the long run. He was trapped, pulled in different directions, and often he would strike out on one course, then another, providing fuel for his critics who complained that Jackson was all over the political map. There's no master plan, he's just winging it, flying by the seat of his pants, they'd say. "Moving between moments," as Bob Beckel told *Newsweek*.[72]

Often the criticism was valid. Sometimes Jackson was moving in different directions at the same time. In a speech he would demand that the party be united—and also hint of a walkout at the party's national convention. He was drawn to power—yet he often issued threats to the powerful. One set of instincts fought against the other. He both sought acceptance and shunned it. He would demand that the Democratic National Committee change its procedures to let more minorities participate, then balk at the beginnings of a compromise. He would rein in his whim to visit Nicaragua during the New Hampshire primary—then spin off on some offbeat course through Central America while the Mondale and Hart forces were hammering out a convention platform at home. The inconsistent demands on him would not subside. The Secret Service agent who knew him best was right—there was a war going on. Contradiction defined the man.

In part it was the conflict between the public figure and the private person. Onstage, Jackson was the visionary bound for the Promised Land. "Where are we going! There ain't no road there! . . . Nobody's been there before. How are you going? By faith! . . . Where are you going? Up the King's Highway," he would wail, his face streaked with sweat, and the congregations would weep and shout. Yet away from the crowds and the pulpit, he was a hard-bitten realist. "You lead with your strengths. That's why I go to churches. That's why I use parables. I ain't gonna waste my time with no goddamn bankers," he growled one day during the campaign. "What are they gonna do for me? You use what you got; you use what you know."

In the pulpit, onstage, in a studio, he would proclaim: "Strong leaders don't follow public opinion—they mold it." But when the cameras were gone, he would call CBS News anchorman Dan Rather or NBC's Tom Brokaw at home and ask them how a proposed trip he was thinking of making to Nicaragua would be played by the networks.

In the political arena and on street corners he could be flip, sarcastic, dazzling. "I'd rather have Roosevelt in a wheelchair—than Reagan on a horse," he would deadpan, always to applause. "You hear that Jesse Jackson has this big black vote, this big black vote," he told students at the University of Missouri, his voice then dropping an octave and booming, "what's he gonna do *with this big black thing?*" as the auditorium erupted in laughter. The public image was elaborately developed and carefully maintained—aides who failed to provide him with a freshly starched shirt knew he'd give them a terrible time—but in private he would sulk because the media saw only the persona he chose to give them. "Flamboyant? Slick?" he once said in disgust. "Look at this suit. What's flamboyant about this? I got no diamond ring on my finger. I ain't got no dye in my hair. . . . Mostly, I'm serious. I mostly think. I've not sat down with any big-time reporter without them staying up at night thinking of questions to embarrass me. They've not been very successful. I don't think of those answers because of my suit—I think of them because I do my homework," he said in a campaign plane over Florida.

He knew that his public expected, even needed, him to put on a performance that outshone the competition, and he'd work on the flourishes. Before leaving his plane in Pineville, Louisiana, he stood in a corner trying to get the timing right for a new broadside. "The president is now over in China, feeding Chinese pandas, not feeding American children." No, that didn't feel quite right, so he tried again. "Rather than feeding our children, they're feeding Communist pandas." For a full minute, Jackson kept looking for the right combination of words; by the time of his first speech that day, he had found it: "while acid rain falls on Smokey the Bear, Reagan is over there in China feeding the Communist bears," he said, grinning.

Yet good as the one-liners were, he knew they also could victimize him. After the Democratic contenders held their first debate in Hanover, New Hampshire, Jackson was annoyed when someone complimented him for appearing "serious." "The press was prepared for me to entertain them, by dominating with words, titillating their funnybone by attacking Mondale," he complained, insisting that the media always focused on the slangy phrases and rarely on the substance. He loved saying provocative things—"Poor folks 'steal.' Rich folks 'embezzle.' Poor folks on 'welfare.' Rich folks on 'subsidy.' Check comes from the same place. Playing word games, that's all"—but he also knew that the phrase-making could get him in trouble. "You reporters always pick out some frivolous, colorful adjective to describe me, as opposed to intense or earnest, reasoned or intelligent," he once snapped when he felt some reporters were treating him like a political burlesque. "My mind drives my mouth; my mouth doesn't drive my mind," he said firmly.

He could inspire—and manipulate, sometimes in the same moment. "If he saw some reporter who was about to blow up, made no difference if he was black or white, JJ'd pull them aside and give out some pieces of favored information, a piece of key information no one else had," said the campaign's coordinator, Gene Wheeler. In Jackson's view everybody, everything had its place; all things could be used: the congregations, the agents working the crowds, the bloodstained shirt he said he'd been wearing the day Dr. King was shot, Vernon Jordan's surgeon, Lt. Robert Goodman's captivity in Syria—each could be a backdrop, a setting: from Damascus to Harlem, from bayou parish to the embassy of South Africa, the world was his stage, and at any point he could give a performance, commanded only by himself. The black church, bulwark of black aspirations, mother lode of its leaders, also became a playing field. He would go often, but rarely, it seemed, to worship or to be alone. The message could be profound, the occasion might be solemn, but it was also grandstand, one more way station for the young man in a hurry. "Everybody fits somewhere," he'd say, intending no irony.

His detractors found other discrepancies as well. Jackson could tout himself as "the country preacher," could go to the United Nations and profess what he called "a kinship of suffering" with the Third World and its poor—but the same day he did that the *Washington Post* reported that his income for the previous year was over $100,000. And that for the preceding two years the self-styled leader of the poor had been paid in the six-figure range as well. His defense was pure Jackson: defiance and disdain. I could have pocketed far more, he said. Other organizations pay more to their leaders who do less. Money, he insisted, didn't interest him that much—he only wanted enough to provide for his family, that was all. "It's hard to care about the hungry when you're hungry yourself," he added.

But the contradictions that helped define him—that dogged, and sometimes tormented him—were more than contrasts between public utterance and private thought. Discrepancies like those happened to most people in the limelight. For Jackson, there was something more: a tug-of-war was going on inside, between the past and the present, between the present and the future.

Like racism in the campaign, the past for Jackson was a two-edged sword. It both haunted and helped him, bedeviled him and motivated him. Incidents like the signs on the Greenville buses, the drunken fans at Furman University, the tears when neighborhood kids called him a bastard, even the leftover turkey his mother would bring home after she'd cooked and cleaned in rich white homes—memories of all that stayed with him and goaded him. "We're tired of being laughed at, put down, and disregarded," he would say, speaking not just for others but also for himself, the little boy in Greenville. That past made him what he was. At the same time he felt he had been deprived, hobbled. That he had gone without what the others, those he now liked to consider his equals, had enjoyed. "Let me tell you something. My energy, my ability to think, if I'd had the options [former California governor Jerry] Brown had, I'd be senator now. Or governor. . . . White counterparts of my generation, Jerry Brown, Gary Hart, they have those options. I don't," he said one day glaring out the window of his chartered turbo-prop.

He was proud of what he had done—"I grew up in occupied territory . . . I have had to negotiate with a superpower all my life. . . . None of the other candidates has had to face the odds I have faced . . . I have come the farthest."—but at the same time it galled him that he had been forced to contend with so much; and sometimes the bitterness showed through. Even when he seemed to relax and poke fun at himself:

> . . . it has been said in some circles that Jesse Jackson and the Pope were in a boat, having prayer as two ministers. And a stiff wind blew and the waters became troubled. And the Pope's holy cap blew off. He reached for it and could not get it. Then he reached out with a long fishing pole and could not reach it. The waters became rougher, and Jesse Jackson got up—and walked across the water and got the cap. [laughter]
>
> He brought it back and gave the cap to the Pope, who accepted it with thanks and graciousness. And the press was in the next boat following us. Next day the headlines read—"Jesse Can't Swim. . . ." [laughter and applause]
>
> (Commonwealth Club, San Francisco, June 1, 1984)

The punch line always got a laugh. Jackson never got a fair shake in the media: that was the message. It was also more. Behind the joke was Jackson's seething anger that no matter what he said or did, he was always denied by the white power structure. This was Greenville talking again, this was the boy in the man, this was the lesson he never forgot: that he would fail not because of *his* shortcomings—but because of *theirs.* The argument took different forms: his handicap was his color; it was the South; it was the shortsightedness of others. That was the real meaning behind "Jesse Can't Swim." It was shorthand, a jagged reminder: it's them, not me. Because of that, he could say and do virtually anything and it wouldn't matter. If doomed from the start, he could hardly be held accountable. If condemned, he was also saved. With no real chance to "win," he could operate more freely than other candidates; with less at stake, less to risk, he could afford to speak out, to gamble, cut a few corners, be daring. But the "freedom" brought him little peace. The struggle within was too great.

Not only was there a contradiction between the past and the present—but also a contradiction between the present and the future. He was a creature of the here and now—"the right now crusade," he had dubbed his campaign—but behind the sloganeering, he cared passionately about his place in history. "In this campaign, we're running for two sets of people who can't vote. Our forebears, who couldn't see this day. And our children. We're voting for yesterday . . . and tomorrow."

Consumed with today's mission, he was perpetually in motion, speaking, acting, hurling charges, issuing demands, too busy to sit down and carefully plot out any long-range plan. He wanted historians to treat him kindly, but for him the future would be much like the past: a series of hit-and-run missions, another march, another speech; when one ended, another would begin. He was always moving. Afraid, it seemed, to be still.

"What do we do next? What's the plan?" staff members would ask him. And sometimes Jackson would tell them that he first had to "talk with God." Can he really believe that God talks to him? one staffer wondered when Jackson alluded to the divine conversations. Does he really believe that stuff? The staffer was never certain.

"Jesse is his own teacher. You can't tell him anything," California Assembly Speaker Willie Brown had lamented; others had similar complaints. Jackson listened to the grumbling and found ways to dismiss it. He persuaded himself that most criticism of him, of his mission, was jealousy, wrongheadedness, or merely unfair. "I'm not a perfect servant," he would say in his defense, insisting he was only a vessel, and that his defects were not that important. What counts is the message, not the messenger, he would say as if that rendered the criticism invalid. "We can be as crooked as a saxophone, but He can blow a perfect note through us," he'd say. When he heard ministers introduce him as "our Saviour . . . our Moses to lead us to the promised land," Jackson would chuckle. He knew he was no Messiah. But he also believed that he was more than his detractors would ever concede. Was it all just an ego trip? Did he care first and foremost about himself?—as his critics charged. That's how progress is made, Jackson believed. First, take care of number one—and in the process, others will benefit. That's how things get done, he rationalized: when those who refuse to accept the status quo, "those on the make," push up against accepted limits—and make things happen.

That too explained his approach to politics: keep up an attack, go for the jugular. "His talent and his technique are to find, or to create, confrontational situations, inject himself into them and then systematically increase the tension until, at a crucial moment, he agrees to defuse it in return for concessions materially greater than many supposed it possible for him to extract," observed syndicated columnist David Broder.[73] It was an approach that set him apart from consensus-building officeholders. Let them put together coalitions, he figured, his role was that of an outsider, the bastard child still running from Greenville. Through it all one goal was constant. "The bottom line is my self-respect; that is what they must come to terms with," he said at the end of the campaign. "Jesse's got to have his self-respect, his self-respect. That's what his people kept telling us over and over," Geraldine Ferraro told one of the authors late in 1985. "And it used to drive us nuts, really nuts because we could never be sure what that meant," she added. Issues, opponents, locations changed, but that cry for self-respect would be his absolute, his only absolute. Officeholders bartered for power. With no political base to protect, he could afford to reject compromise. They settled for the possible; he would try to go beyond. "Low expectations lead to low performance," he would complain. "I don't deal in a lot of details. Mostly, I preach." Let the consensus-builders be responsive to others; he would follow his own instincts, he said. Let other black leaders become absorbed into the white establishment; he would not be. They had goals beyond themselves. Ultimately, he was alone.

Heavy clouds hung over the South Carolina countryside one July, 1984, morning as he stared at the wet green hills. Do you think you will ever hold public office in this nation? he was asked.

"I don't know," he said simply. "I'm not preoccupied with it."

NOTES

Unless otherwise noted, quotations are taken from interviews the authors conducted (or took part in) over the last two years.

1. The section on Seldon Ardoin first appeared in "Somewhere over the Rainbow: A Jackson Campaign Album," by Nancy Skelton, *Los Angeles Times,* June 24, 1984.

2. "Sticky Questions for Jesse Jackson," by Lally Weymouth, *New York,* January 9, 1984, p. 40.

3. Frank Watkins memo, June 2, 1982, pp. 1–2.

4. ABC Poll, October, 1983, which showed that 51 percent of black respondents listed Jackson as the most important black leader in the country, far outdistancing runners-up Andrew Young and Martin Luther King, Sr.

5. *The Fire Next Time* (New York: Dial Press, 1963).

6. "New Powers, New Politics," *New York Times Magazine,* February 5, 1984, p. 24.

7. "Seeking Votes and Clout," by Walter Isaacson, *Time,* August 22, 1983, p. 21.

8. Non-Voter Study of '84–'85 by the Committee for the Study of the American Electorate.

9. "Four Years Later: Who in the U.S. Is Better Off?" by Peter Kilbourn, *New York Times,* October 9, 1984.

10. Cited by Robert Greenstein and Laura Weiss, in "Worse Off under Reagan," *New York Times,* October 30, 1984.

11. "America's Losers Lost Again," by Bob Kaiser, *Washington Post,* November 11, 1984.

12. *New Yorker,* May 28, 1984, p. 116.

13. "A Winning Jackson," by David Farrell, *Boston Globe,* December 16, 1984.

14. *I Know Why the Caged Bird Sings* (New York: Bantam, 1969), p. 115.

15. *Congressional Quarterly,* November 5, 1983, p. 2310.

16. *Philadelphia Inquirer,* May 21, 1984, in a piece by Knight-Ridder political reporter Charlie Green.

17. "If Jesse Jackson Runs," *New York Times,* October 14, 1983.

18. *New York Times* piece by Howell Raines, November 4, 1984.

19. Much of Jackson's version of his meeting with Assad came in a lengthy interview with Dan Rather.

20. Jackson referred to the pistol on separate occasions to Faw and Skelton, and the remark is also cited by Barbara Reynolds in her book *Jesse Jackson: The Man, the Movement, the Myth* (Chicago: Nelson Hall, 1975). The grocer in question has never been found.

21. "Eighteen Words, Seven Weeks Later," *Washington Post,* April 8, 1984.

22. "Off the Record and under Fire," by Carl M. Cannon, *Washington Journalism Review,* June, 1984, p. 23.

23. Ibid.

24. *Washington Post,* February 24, 1984.

25. "Blacks and Jews," by Jack Newfield, *Village Voice,* March 20, 1984.

26. *New York Times,* February 28, 1984.

27. "A Talk with Jackson," *Newsweek,* April 9, 1984, p. 35.

28. Jackson's comments were made November 11, 1974, at Operation PUSH headquarters at a gathering of black and Jewish leaders.

29. "Running with Jesse," by Lally Weymouth, *New York,* March 5, 1984, p. 39 (confirmed by Singer in conversation with Faw).

30. "Jesse and the Jews," by Charles Silberman, *New Republic,* December 29, 1979, p. 12.

31. This quote (which actually appeared first in the *New York Times Magazine,* April 9, 1967) was incorrectly given as appearing elsewhere in "Historical Impressions of Black-Jewish Relations Prior to World War II," by Oscar Williams, *Negro History Bulletin,* July, 1977, p. 729.

32. *Notes of a Native Son,* quoted by Rabbi Harold M. Schulweis in "The Voice of Esau," *Reconstructionist,* December 10, 1965, p. 9.

33. "Beyond Conflict: Black-Jewish Relations: Accent on the Positive," by Dr. Joyce Gelb, published by the American Jewish Congress (New York, 1980), p. 2.

34. Schulweis, "Voice of Esau," p. 8.

35. "Blacks and Jews: The Strained Alliance," *Annals of the American Academy of Politics and Social Sciences,* March, 1981, p. 56.

36. "Blacks and Jews: Friends or Foes," in *Keeping Posted,* 25/1, published by the Union of American Hebrew Congregations, 1979, p. 6.

37. "Black Anti-Semitism on the Rise," by Murray Friedman, *Commentary,* October, 1979, p. 33.

38. "Blacks and Jews Need a Real Dialogue," by Joel Dreyfuss, *Los Angeles Times,* April 27, 1984.

39. *New York Times,* August 24, 1979.

40. Pollster Lou Harris is quoted (along with a summary of his findings) in *Keeping Posted,* p. 23.

41. Barry Morrison, the Philadelphia director of the Anti-Defamation League, quoted in "Relationship of Blacks and Jews Has Cooled since Civil Rights Era," *Philadelphia Inquirer,* March 18, 1984.

42. Peter Straus made his remarks on the McNeil-Lehrer show, June 14, 1984.

43. *Washington Post,* March 2, 1984.

44. "The Capital of Everything," by Andy Logan, *New Yorker,* September 24,

1979, p. 138.

45. *Philadelphia Inquirer,* May 21, 1984.

46. "Farrakhan Stirs Black Hope, White Fear," by Lee May, *Los Angeles Times,* May 13, 1984.

47. "Deciphering Farrakhan," by Clarence Page, *Chicago,* August, 1984, p. 135.

48. *Newsweek,* April 23, 1984, p. 32, and phone conversation with Faw.

49. *Washington Post,* March 4, 1985.

50. *New York Times,* July 2, 1984.

51. "Jesse Jackson's Campaign: The Primaries and Caucuses," by Tom Cavanaugh and Lorn S. Foster, Joint Center for Political Studies Election '84 Report # 2 (Washington, D.C., 1984), p. 10.

52. *New Republic* editorial, "Rainbow's End," April 30, 1984, p. 8.

53. *Los Angeles Times,* July 2, 1984.

54. *New York Times,* April 9, 1984.

55. *New York Times* account by correspondent Joseph Lelyveld, November 20, 1985.

56. *New York Times,* June 27, 1984.

57. "For Jackson, the Convention Will Tell," *Los Angeles Times,* July 13, 1984.

58. *New York Times,* July 24, 1984.

59. Atlanta-based Voter Education Project report, November 2, 1984.

60. Figures for various states also come from various Voter Education Project reports of November 11, December 17, and December 30, 1984.

61. That Jackson had a "major impact" was the conclusion of the Committee for the Study of the American Electorate (CSAE), June 26, 1984, and was subsequently confirmed in conversations between Skelton and the center's director, Curtis B. Gans.

62. "Total of Black U.S. Mayors Up Sharply," by Robert Pear, *New York Times,* March 22, 1985.

63. *Los Angeles Times* article by Jack Nelson and David Treadwell that appeared in the *Cleveland Plain Dealer,* April 15, 1984.

64. *The Glory and the Dream* (Boston: Little, Brown, 1974), p. 947.

65. The Gallup Poll was commissioned in the summer of 1984 by the Joint Center for Political Studies; 1,365 whites were polled nationally.

66. "New Voter Sign-Ups May Favor the GOP," by Thomas Edsall, *Washington Post,* November 2, 1984. See also "New Voters Bring Surge in the Rolls," by John Herbers, *New York Times,* September 29, 1984.

67. "GOP Has Stand-Off in Registration," by Thomas Edsall, *Washington Post,* September 16, 1984; Richard Scammon's remarks to *New York Times,* April 1, 1985.

68. "Mondale Leaves Jackson Empty-Handed," by Charles Hardy, *San Francisco Examiner,* July 22, 1984. Daughtry grew fond of repeating the phrase for several months thereafter.

69. *Los Angeles Times,* July 18, 1984.

70. *New Yorker,* June 31, 1985.

71. "Running Came Naturally to Jackson," by Ken Denlinger, *Washington Post,* May 13, 1984.

72. *Newsweek,* special November–December, 1984, issue, p. 51.

73. *Los Angeles Times,* July 13, 1984.

INDEX